THE
HOGARTH LETTERS

THE
HOGARTH LETTERS

Introduction by
Hermione Lee

THE UNIVERSITY OF GEORGIA PRESS
ATHENS

Published in 1986 in the
United States of America
by the University of Georgia Press,
Athens, Georgia 30602

ISBN 0 8203 0827 7

Printed in Great Britain

CONTENTS

INTRODUCTION TO
THE HOGARTH LETTERS

"Lord what a summer!" Virginia Woolf said in a letter of September 2nd 1931. "... We spend hours in violent political argument." A couple of weeks later, she was writing to John Lehmann, the new assistant at the Hogarth Press, with lots of "wild ideas" for an exchange of letters about modern poetry: "Why should poetry be dead? etc. etc." Like these private letters, the public *Hogarth Letters* were from the first as much involved with the politics of the moment as with the future of English culture. "We are bound to our places in this universe," Rebecca West said in her letter, and Peter Quennell called the poet "the creature of his social and political setting", who "cannot escape the backwash".

The series of *Letters* was planned, by Leonard and Virginia and John Lehmann (as he recalled in *Thrown to the Woolfs*), to be "little booklets in paper covers of six or seven thousand words in length on all the topics of the day". They were published separately between 1931 and 1933 and in book form in 1933. No rules were set down for the contributors. Leonard Woolf wrote to E. M. Forster (March 13th 1931): "You may write the letter to anyone, dead or alive, real or imaginary, on any subject." The *Letters* were along the same lines as the other Hogarth Press series – *Day to Day Pamphlets, Lectures on Literature, Merttens Lectures on War and Peace, Hogarth Essays* – which were all specially commissioned as opportunities for well-known writers to air their thoughts, in a short space, about current issues. Harold Nicolson, reviewing two of the *Letters* in the *New Statesman*, suggested rather unkindly that they were an ingenious way of getting "the less industrious among our intellectuals" to commit thoughts to paper "which might otherwise have perished in the wastes of conversation." Conversation was the model: the device of private letters made public (which invoked the eighteenth century: Swift, Burke, Chesterfield) suggested a culture where private voices could share a common ground and could be profitably overheard.

The *Letters* did not, in the event, do outstandingly well*, but they were imitated. Virginia Woolf mentioned to John Lehmann (July 31st 1932) that the BBC wanted to do a series of *Letters to Unknown Listeners* ("but they're so inconceivably timid they won't ask any but old duffers"); John Lehmann commissioned Edward Upward, B. L. Coombes and Louis MacNeice (in *Folios of New Writing* for

---

*The contributors were offered 10% on the first 3,000 copies sold and advances ranging from £25 (Forster) to £10 (Walpole) or less. (They received 1d royalty on the omnibus volume.) The largest printings were 6,000 (Virginia Woolf), 5,000 (Cecil and Forster) and 4,000 (Lehmann), and the smallest 1,500 (Quennell.) But on February 11th 1936, all the contributors were told that there would be no more royalty statements, as the advances had not yet been earned (Forster still owed £4.10.2d on his £25, Walpole £2.18.6d on his £10) and sales were now down to about 6 a year. In America, Harcourt Brace had taken the first three *Letters*, but had sold only 125 copies by March 1932: "It seems impossible to do anything with pamphlets here," Donald Brace wrote to Leonard Woolf.

Autumn 1940) to reply to Virginia Woolf's essay "The Leaning Tower", and in 1948 a correspondence called "Why Do I Write?" was published between Elizabeth Bowen, V. S. Pritchett and Graham Greene. The advantage of the form was that it gave a sense of personality as well as a view of the times. John Lehmann, looking back, felt that the *Hogarth Letters* encapsulated their moment very precisely.

> The moods, the pleasures and preoccupations of the early thirties are so far away now that they seem beyond recapture; but as I turn again the pages of the little booklets of the *Hogarth Letters*, it appears to me that they preserve, like a row of jam jars on a larder shelf, the essence and flavour of the time.
>
> (*The Whispering Gallery*, 1955, p. 192)

In September 1931, when the *Letters* were first mooted, the "backwash" of political events was particularly dramatic. (A. J. P. Taylor, analyzing the political crisis of 1931 in *English History 1914-1945*, calls it "the watershed of English history between the wars".) In August, Ramsay MacDonald's Labour Government had broken up, in the wake of the General Strike and the American Crash, on the rocks of unemployment, falling prices and a run on the pound. The economic crisis had the bankers demanding a restoration of confidence; but nine members of MacDonald's cabinet couldn't stomach the recipe, which was to reduce unemployment

benefit savagely and to establish a Means Test, in
order to achieve a "balanced budget". (Mosley had
already resigned, in May 1930, over Labour's
unemployment policy, and formed his New Party in
February 1931). MacDonald, trying to prevent the
total collapse of Labour, and the Liberal-
Conservative coalition that would follow, formed a
National Government on August 24th, which was at
once seen, in left-wing circles, as a betrayal of the
Labour movement (and which did indeed, in the
September budget, make sweeping cuts in unemployment benefit). A. J. P. Taylor comments:

> Labour opinion grew more resolute. The crisis
> had resolved in a closed circle of bankers and min-
> isters.... MacDonald and those who supported
> him became not mistaken, but traitors.... The
> spirit of class war revived.
>
> (*English History 1914–1945*, p. 370)

John Lehmann recalls "the consternation and
gloom that settled on all our circle at the collapse of
the Labour Government in 1931". John Strachey's
very influential Marxist analysis of British politics,
The Coming Struggle for Power (1932), said that the
1931 crash had exposed MacDonald as "an ordinary capitalist politician" whose mind worked in
the same way as "the average occupant of, say, a
first class carriage in a suburban train, travelling up
to business."

Strachey's disparagement of MacDonald as the
embodiment of English capitalist complacency

points to a central theme in the *Hogarth Letters'*
critique of the culture. Though politically much
more extreme, Strachey's analysis is rather like
Francis Birrell's attack on the "hopeless self-
satisfaction" and barbarism of the English middle
classes, or Raymond Mortimer's condescension
towards the average English gentlewoman's aesthetic insularity, or John Hardwick's impatience
with the reactionary, parochial English church.
Such criticism had its application elsewhere on the
political scene in 1931. The League of Nations (so
named by Goldsworthy Lowes Dickinson, E. M.
Forster's Cambridge friend and mentor) was under
attack in 1930 and 1931 from a concerted "Home
and Empire" campaign in the right-wing press
(Beaverbrook's *Daily Express* and Rothermere's
Daily Mail.) What Robert Cecil, in his letter on the
League, called "the great 100% British campaign"
for independence from Europe (the idea was that
the Dominions would lower their tariffs on British
goods, thereby creating "Empire Free Trade") represented one current aspect of British insularity and
chauvinism. Another side of it was expressed by
Winston Churchill's hostility to disarmament and
to Indian nationalism. In opposition to this old
spirit of Empire, the League stood for anti-
imperialism, conciliation and internationalism, and
attracted many left-wing thinkers of the intellectual
middle class. Leonard Woolf described the League's
ideals eloquently in *Imperialism and Civilization*
(1928):

> The League stands for a synthesis instead of a
> conflict of civilizations, for tolerance and co-
> operation, for an international society of inter-
> related rather than warring parts, for the
> adjustment of relations and the settlement of in-
> ternational disputes by discussion, compromise,
> and adjudication.

This is the language of rational liberal optimism, of
Cambridge and Bloomsbury: it expresses belief in
the possibility of maintaining a free "civilization" in
the "jungle" of the modern political world. (The
terms are taken, again, from Leonard Woolf, in one
of the 1924 *Hogarth Essays* – precursors of the *Hogarth
Letters* – called "Fear and Politics: a Debate at the
Zoo".) But in 1931 such language, and such ideals,
were manifestly under threat. Japan's invasion of
Manchuria in September exposed the ineffectuality
of the League; behind that event was the growing
power of Nazism and Fascism – not amenable,
it was rapidly becoming apparent, to words like
"tolerance and co-operation".

Leonard Woolf was more deeply involved than
ever at this time in what he called in 1933 "the intelligent man's way to prevent war". As secretary of
the Advisory Committee on International
Questions, he was in close contact with the bitterly
divided Labour Party. In 1931 his influence as a
publicist for the moderate left increased, partly
through his quarrelsome connection with Kingsley
Martin, the new editor of the *New Statesman*, partly

through his co-editorship of the *Political Quarterly*. And he was using the Hogarth Press, as always, as an outlet for anti-imperialist, pro-disarmament pamphlets and books, among them Philip Noel-Baker's *Disarmament* (1926) and H. G. Wells's plan for international peace, *The Open Conspiracy* (1930). The two purely political *Letters* in this series – Lord Robert Cecil's account of the League of Nations and Louis Golding's personal response to anti-semitism – were very much in this polemical tradition.

Virginia, though, did not much like these particular contributions. In a letter of October 1932, she called "Cecil on disarmament", like Strong on Yeats, "d——d dull", and in April 1935 she described Louis Golding as "a little horror" with "a spotted soul". Her own first idea for the *Letters* was a much more literary one:

> I think your idea of a Letter most brilliant – To a Young Poet? because I'm seething with immature and ill considered and wild and annoying ideas about prose and poetry. So lend me your name – (and let me sketch a character of you by way of frontispiece) – and then I'll pour forth all I can think of about you young, and we old, and novels – how damned they are – and poetry, how dead. But I must take a look into the subject, and you must reply, "To an old novelist" – I must read Auden, whom I've not read, and Spender... The whole subject is crying out for letters – flocks, volleys, of them, from every side. Why not get

Spender and Auden and Day Lewis to join in?
(*Letters* IV, p. 381)

Spender and Auden and Day Lewis (the poets of
New Signatures, Michael Roberts's anthology, which
the Hogarth Press published in 1932) did not in the
end "join in". The *Hogarth Letters*, in spite of John
Lehmann's involvement (he called himself, writing
to his sister, the "Papa of the Series"), are not part
of the "Thirties" as represented by *New Writing* or
Left Review or the Group Theatre or *Tribune* or *New
Verse* or the Left Book Club. On the whole they are
middle-aged letters: as Harold Nicolson said, they
are "epistles in which the generation of 1910 con-
fronts the generation of 1932". And they don't share
the membership of a group so much as a tone of
voice. Rather than articulating a manifesto, they
express a feeling about culture which is individual-
ist, middle-class, Francophile, anti-war, anti-
Empire, respectful of the past and nervous of the
future, and which allows for the unembarrassed use
of words such as "taste" (Mortimer), "beauty"
(Virginia Woolf), "a moral world" (Walpole), "the
creative individual" (Hardwick), "modern civilized
man" (Golding), and "self-discovery" (Quennell).

This language of rational humanism, deployed
on behalf of intellectual tolerance and in opposition
to various forms of tyranny and reaction, from
Fascism to Podsnappery, was to be perfectly exem-
plified in Forster's essay of 1939, "What I Believe"
(published as one of the Hogarth Press *Sixpenny*

Pamphlets), with its modest, temperate appeals to "the holiness of the heart's affections" and its vision of an "aristocracy of the sensitive, the considerate and the plucky" signalling to each other like little lights in the darkness – a sort of flickering League of Souls. A similar tone is heard in William Plomer's novel *Sado*, published by the Hogarth Press at the same time as the Hogarth Letters, and quoted approvingly by John Lehmann in *The Whispering Gallery* on the same page as his description of the *Letters*. Plomer, like Forster, asks how the individual should behave at this time of darkness and crisis.

> One can be a reactionary, and seek security in the past. One can live in a hypothetical future of communism... One can stop thinking, drift with the crowd... Or lastly, one can strive to think, to keep one's balance, to treat past and future with equal respect ... questioning much, admitting only what rings true ... trying to base every thought and action on a sound understanding of what is constant in and necessary to human nature – a proper balance between head and heart ... and the recognition that it must always take all sorts to make a world.

These alternative prescriptions for the thinking liberal, markedly Forsterian in tone (especially "must take all sorts to make a world") are much on the minds of the Hogarth contributors, whether their subjects are arms, painting, poetry or religion, and whether they are writing about what is wrong

with England, or how English writers should deal
with the world around them, or what civilization
fundamentally consists in.

Their analyses owe a considerable debt to
Matthew Arnold. Francis Birrell invokes and imi-
tates *Culture and Anarchy*, and Rebecca West echoes
Arnold in her use of "sweetness, that human invention" to mean that which is "completely comprehended and controlled". The satires on England are
especially Arnoldian. Birrell, Mortimer and Hardwick might all have been reading "The Literary
Influence of Academies" (1864), where Arnold
compares the average Frenchman's "conscience in
intellectual matters" with the average Englishman's provinciality and conventional habits of
thought, allowing the English virtues to be "energy
and honesty" rather than "a quick and flexible
intelligence". Like Arnold, Hardwick (one-time
Chaplain of Ripon Hall, Oxford) sets Newman as
the solitary shining example against the muscular
Christianity, the business ethics and unthinking
patriotism of the English church.

Hardwick's attack on the legacy of the "Wilberforce efficiency-cult" – he criticizes the Church of
England's response to the Great War and its after-
effects, and accuses it of "running away from ideas"
into hyperactivity and fake patriotism – is a forceful
example of the preference for "creative individuals"
over "men of action" which runs through several of
the letters. (It is also rather hard on the "Life and
Liberty" movement of the 1920s, which was making

stalwart attempts to bring the church up-to-date by
such means as a democratically elected Church Assembly). Rosamond Lehmann proffers an im-
pressionistic choice between life as "purpose,
activity" and life as talk, dream, memory and
domestic pleasures. Rebecca West describes "men
of action" as "submen who will never renounce the
pleasures of a determined existence" and men of the
"analytic type" as "supermen who make an
attempt at freewill". The thinker, not the doer, is
the hero for these writers, and the trouble with
England is that doers outnumber thinkers.

The disadvantage of this critique is that it can
rather easily degenerate into a sort of spiteful snobbery about middle-class philistinism. Raymond
Mortimer's contribution (which the Hogarth Press
booksellers called "Mortimer's French Letter"), on
the great exhibition of French painting at Burlington House, is, as John Lehmann says, a "brilliant"
celebration of what that Exhibition offered to
Bloomsbury's "devotees of the French tradition":
"an intoxicating release from the stuffiness and pre-
tentiousness of the Royal Academy orthodoxy". But
Mortimer's advice to the bourgeois surburban lady
to look at the Poussins as eagerly as she would keep
an eye open for her "partner's discards at bridge",
or to do her homework on the Bouchers as if she
were hunting for samples of stuff for loose covers, is
irritatingly condescending. I prefer Francis Birrell's
savagely insulting "Letter from a Black Sheep",
which puts a Gallophile boot into the English bar-

barians from every conceivable angle, and is particularly sharp on the missed opportunities (arising
from an unimaginative insularity) in areas such as
the fashion trade, the tourist industry, and town
planning.

Birrell understands very well the drawbacks of
the nation's rulers being educated "to look at the
whole history of the world from the angle of the
[public] school chapel". The political dangers of
such insularity are spelt out in the letters by Cecil
and Golding. Cecil spent a good part of his life, as
President of the League of Nations Union, trying to
convince the British people that, for their own sake
and the sake of the world, they needed to think in
terms of Europeanism and not of Empire, of international co-operation and not of isolationism. Louis
Golding's rather over-written letter to Hitler makes
an equally crucial political point – a point which he
went on and on making: *Hitler through the Ages* (1939)
re-used the "Letter to Adolf Hitler", and *The Jewish
Problem* (1938) reiterated it. Anti-semitism, Golding
says, is not just of one place and one time, and if it
can be recognized as recurrent and ubiquitous it
can be better understood than if Hitler is treated as
an isolated monstrosity. His lesson had been
learned not only in Germany, but also in the playground of Manchester Grammar School (his name
for the city was "Doomington"), in English factories in the Midlands, and in the Anglo-Catholic
writing of Hilaire Belloc.

In these satirical and political *Letters*, the English

establishment is generally seen as being in retreat from the dangers and challenges of the modern world. It must be the writer's job, then, to find, as Virginia Woolf puts it, "the right relationship ... between the self that you know and the world outside", even with "a thousand voices prophesying despair". But what happens to the writer's privacy, sensuality, lyricism, dreams, magic – "beauty" – when the shocks and jolts of political reality, social conditions, scientific facts or colloquial speech are taken on board? The question couldn't be avoided in 1931. Auden's *Poems* of 1930 marked the beginning of a decade of writers "painfully" working out, as Julian Symonds says in *The Thirties*, a theory of "art's place in society". The *Hogarth Letters'* contribution to this painful debate is uneasy and uncertain, but extremely revealing of the dilemma, at that time, for writers who were not willing to commit themselves to any group or orthodoxy.

Some of the contributors, it has to be said, show few signs of unease. Leonard Strong's "Letter to W. B. Yeats" waffles on blithely about flames and magic and music and glory, without pausing to consider the politics of Yeats's poetry, and what bearing that might have on the 1930s. For Strong, Yeats's outstanding quality is that "in an age of change and mechanisation and vulgarism such as has never been known, you have kept your artistic life aloof from the age's infection". That the "infection" might have to have something to do with the "artistic life" is at least considered by Hugh

Walpole, who, in a letter which he described to
Leonard Woolf as "obstinate and challenging", en-
ergetically parodies a "typical" modern novelist for
his over-commitment to the abnormal and the
surreal. Unfortunately, though Walpole is concerned (as in his 1925 Rede Lecture on the modern
novel) about what seemed to him the sacrifice of a
"moral world" to mannerist sensationalism, he col-
lapses the argument into a nostalgic celebration of
Trollope's Barchester Novels, a nostalgia which
was to gain enormous ground during the war years.

The attraction to nostalgia is a powerful one.
Rosamond Lehmann, in her peculiarly indirect,
haunting "Letter to a Sister", seems to be holding
off an ominous future – the wind getting up, darkness, loss and loneliness – with visions of a safe,
rural, civilized English summer, doing up an old
house, a baby on the lawn, a mixture of "fruit and
wood and brick", memories of an over-protected
Edwardian childhood. Reality keeps edging in
through touches of modern language – "inferiority
complex", "a screen for chaotic images", "a bubble
in a microscope" – but the scene she paints could be
the material for the kind of novel which has not
exposed itself to the contemporary world.

Virginia Woolf recognizes the attractions of
nostalgia in her "Letter to a Young Poet". But
"nekrophily induces slumber": it's not good enough
to hanker after the great dead, like Walpole after
Trollope. Even so, her wary exploration of modern
poetry, which noticeably ignores Auden, is an

uncomfortable one. Her examples – from John
Lehmann ("To penetrate that room is my desire"),
Stephen Spender ("Never being, but always at the
edge of being") and Cecil Day Lewis ("There is a
dark room") are not the most impressive illustrations she could have chosen from the early Thirties.
Her criticism of the modern poet's attempt to
include "Mrs Gape" (one of her dubious prototypi-
cal charladies) seems as priggish as her notorious
distaste for Joyce. And her advice to young poets not
to publish till they are thirty is not persuasively
argued. That she felt herself to be out of her depth is
evident in her defensive reply, in her letter of July
31st 1932, to John Lehmann's criticism.

I admit your next point – that is that my quotations aren't good illustrations: but as usual, I
couldn't find the ones I wanted when I was
writing; and was too lazy to look. Anyhow my impression is that I could convince you by quotations: I do feel that the young poet is rather
crudely jerked between realism and beauty, to
put it roughly. I think he is all to be praised for
attempting to swallow Mrs Gape; but he ought to
assimilate her. What it seems to me is that he
doesnt sufficiently believe in her: doesnt dig
himself in deep enough; wakes up in the middle;
his imagination goes off the boil; he doesnt reach
the unconscious automated state – hence the
spasmodic, jerky, self conscious effect of his realistic language. But I may be transferring to him

some of the ill effects of my own struggles the
other way round – writes poetry in prose. Tom
Eliot I think succeeds; but then he is much more
violent; and I think by being violent, limits
himself so that he only attacks a minute province
of his imagination; whereas you younger and
happier spirits should, partly owing to him, have
a greater range and be able to devise a less steep
precipitous technique. But this is mere guesswork
of course. . . . But the fact is I'm not at all satisfied
with the *Letter*, and would like to tear up, or entirely re-write.   (Letters V, p. 83)

In spite of this uncertainty, both the reply to
Lehmann and the original *Letter* are of great interest, for two reasons. One is that the *Letter*, in its
unease with the realism of modern poetry, reflects
her anxiety about her own work-in-progress, which
would eventually become *The Years*, the novel in
which she wrestled most painfully with the relationship between art and propaganda. The other is the
question she raises about solipsism. Is the modern
poet inevitably thrown back on himself – "a self that
sits alone in the room at night with the blinds
drawn"? How can he "stand at the window" and
take on the world outside?

As far as the novel was concerned, Virginia Woolf
had been arguing in her essays since 1919 – and dis-
playing in her own work – that modern times
required new forms from fiction, which could
somehow maintain the threatened connection

between the private creative self and the cata-
strophically "other" public world. But modern
poetry still seemed to her more resistant to "foreign
bodies"; it was still (to use her own reductive terms)
half nightingales and half charladics. Peter Quennell's response, in his "Letter to Mrs Woolf", was to
describe the poetry of the Thirties as necessarily
transitional, still struggling to take on board "the
prodigious melodrama of modern Europe", moving
from traditional forms and rhythms through difficulty and harshness to a new kind of beauty. "The
Leaning Tower", Virginia Woolf's 1940s essay on
England's public school Communist poets, shows
that she was not convinced either by Lehmann or
Quennell.

The choice of "realism or beauty" could be
posited in other terms: Marxist or bourgeois (as by
Christopher Caudwell or John Strachey), secular or
religious, committed or escapist. But the essence of
the argument always came back to the negotiation
between individuals and the civilisation which they
at once inherit and create. Here, the most remarkable of the *Hogarth Letters* are those by E. M. Forster
and Rebecca West: the latter's, Virginia Woolf
caustically noted on November 15th 1932, was "9
months and 10 days late". It was held up, West
explained, by a year of "family responsibilities and
sudden shocks" and by her writing a Life of St
Augustine, and was thus not delivered in time for
inclusion in the 1933 volume.

Rebecca West's "Letter to a Grandfather" is a

history of England, a philosophical meditation on
the opposition between free will and determinism, a
theology for its time, and a mystical celebration of
"a hereditary faculty of vision". (As such, it probably tried to do too much: she always found it difficult to condense.) Her Anglo-Norman family, the
Beauchamps, which the letter takes from the twelfth
to the twentieth century ("a peculiarly detestable
phase of existence") intermittently throws up "visionaries" with that full life of the spirit which is
"lived only by certain human beings, and by certain
parts of human beings". The visionaries fill the
void, which is the "world of appearances where we
spend our everyday lives" with a greater reality –
"that is, our intimation of the forces which lie
behind these appearances". But this spiritual gift is
of value only as it is disciplined by the "world of
appearances". For all its mysticism (and Rebecca
West firmly believed in supernatural experiences)
the letter preaches a difficult and necessary realism.
The essence of a *rational* vision is not to be ashamed
of the truth "as one's position in life shows it to
one". So her family figures – the builder of the grim
Norman abbey, the "sweet" Renaissance art
patron, the seventeenth-century theological poet,
the philosopher of the Enlightenment, the Victorian
mathematician – are cited for the extent to which
their "vision" made sense of the world they lived in.
Her sweeping, robust attack on Romanticism as
self-conscious, "languid and febrile", is meant as a
warning to twentieth-century writers: when science

gives us too much knowledge, and faith is in retreat, solipsism is more than ever to be feared. Her own epiphany, the negro at the Paris fair – grotesque, mechanical, at once urban and primitive – makes a startling conclusion to the argument. False consolations – Catholicism or Communism – are severely dismissed. The task for the creative imagination at this "cruel" time is to accept "the tragic spirit", not to retreat from it. The narrator has seen, as Rebecca West said in a letter to Virginia Woolf, (Nov 26th 1931), "this age's form of what would have in other ages been a vision of the Madonna or Christ".

Rebecca West's vision is of a civilization which thinly overlays and arises out of barbarism. Though her gesturing negro is a long way in time and mood from E. M. Forster's gentle, amenable child of nature, Prince Lee Boo, the moral drawn from both "savages" is connected. And for all its characteristic elegance, wistfulness and urbanity, Forster's indictment of English "civilization" is more lethal, and less forgiving, than Rebecca West's.

Forster retells, with brilliant irony, George Keate's story of the *Antelope*'s journey to the Pelew Islands in 1783 and the "exchange" of Lee Boo, son of the native king, who was taken to England and died there, for able seaman Madan Blanchard, who chose to stay behind at "the ends of the earth". Lee Boo's history was well known in the later eighteenth and early nineteenth century. The East India Company was being investigated for its exploitative dealings, so the *Antelope's* unsuccessful attempt to "annex" these Pacific islands was of general interest. And the figure of the Noble Savage was a popular one. Keate's narrative emphasized throughout the ironic contrasts between the virtuous savages and the corrupt crew:

> The people of Pelew, tutored in the School of Nature, acted from her impulse alone, they were open and undisguised; unconscious of deceit themselves, they neither feared nor looked for it in others. Our countrymen, born and brought up in a civilised nation, were fashioned by education to suspicion and distrust, and awake to all their busy suggestions. Such is the fatal knowledge the world teaches mankind!

Keate's book went into several editions; there were versions for children ("The Interesting and Affecting History of Lee Boo") and poems by William Lisle Bowles, Joseph Cottle (Coleridge's publisher) and Coleridge himself ("To a Young Lady, with a Poem on the French Revolution [1794]") who linked his pity for the Child of Nature with his exultation at the course of the Revolution:

When slumbring Freedom rous'd by high Disdain
With giant fury burst her triple chain.

There was a precedent, then, for using Lee Boo's story as a metaphor for the destruction of "nature" (freedom, equality, truth) by "civilization" (greed, repression, imperialism). Forster plays this hand lightly, but by slipping in words like "hostage",

"annex" and "murder", and by sending his
message to Madan and the reply to it backwards
and forwards through the "progress" of history (a
fine device, which exploits the letter form more skil-
fully than any of the other contributors) he makes it
quite clear what he thinks of Western civilization,
whose privileges and advantages are so closely connected with the "heart of darkness".

Forster, unlike Swift, whom he ruefully invokes,
is not a nihilist: he has faint hopes for those
members of the civilization who manage to "break
step". But what did become of Madan Blanchard?
The postscript refers us teasingly to a later account
of the Pelew Islanders written by a clergyman eager
for their conversion – which Forster had thought of
incorporating into the *Letter* but decided "would
weaken the effect" – where we find that as soon as
the *Antelope* left, Blanchard "left off wearing clothes,
and was tattooed like the other inhabitants ... and
I am sorry to say that the natives ... spake very in-
differently of his conduct while among them."

Like other escapees and misfits in Forster's
writing, Blanchard was no hero. He was, though,
one of those "who've got hold of something which
we know is there, but have never dared to grasp in
our hands." To the extent that these *Letters* stand
apart and "break step", they have an exhilarating
and encouraging quality. What was to come in the
later 1930s – and after – was worse than could be imagined: the *Letters* about disarmament and antisemitism, in particular, seem in retrospect like

candles blowing out in the wind, rather than little steadfast lights. But even if this volume displays the ultimate ineffectiveness of British liberalism, it's also an attractive repository of the inquiring, flexible, sceptical, unconforming intelligence necessary to any analysis of a "civilization". "Thus I cannot help thinking," says Virginia Woolf, "that though you may be right in talking of the difficulty of the time, you are wrong to despair."

                              Hermione Lee, York, 1985

A LETTER TO MADAN BLANCHARD

E. M. FORSTER

NOTE

My correspondent is not imaginary. See *An Account of the Pelew Islands, situated in the western part of the Pacific Ocean. Composed from the journals and communications of Captain Henry Wilson and some of his officers, who in August* 1783 *were there shipwrecked in The Antelope, a packet belonging to the Hon. East India Company;* by George Keate, Esq., F.R.S. and S.A. Dublin, Luke White, 1788.

See also India Office, *Marine Records*, 570*a* and 570*c*, where his name is spelt Blanshard.

See furthermore Rupack Street, Rotherhithe, London, S.E.

April, 1931.

MY DEAR MADAN,

Captain Wilson keeps telling me about you, and I feel I should like to write you a line. I shall send it by air mail to Paris, but from Paris to Genoa in a pre-war express. At Genoa the confusion will begin. Owing to the infancy of Mussolini the steam packet will not start on time, and will frequently put in for repairs. So slow is the progress that the Suez Canal may close before it can be opened, and my letter be constrained to cross Egypt by the overland route. Suez is full of white sails. One of them, tacking southward, will make India at last, another bring tidings of Napoleonic wars on a following breeze. Smaller boats, duskier crews. Brighter dawns? Quieter nights anyhow. The world is unwinding. What of Macao, where no news follows at all? What of the final tranship-ment? The last little vessel scarcely moves as she touches the Pelews, the waves scarcely break, just one tiny ripple survives to float my

envelope into your hand.   As the tide turns, I
reach you. You open my letter a hundred and
fifty years before it is written, and you read the
words My dear Madan.

Before I forget, there are messages. Don't
lose the compass you asked for. Maintain the
pinnace and her tackle in proper repair. Help
the natives to work any iron they recover from
the wreck, and look after the arms and ammunition for them. £23 8s. 3d. wages are still due
to you—do you want them?   Above all
Captain Wilson asks me to " request Blanchard
he will never go naked, like the natives, as by
preserving the form of dress his countrymen
have appeared in, he will always support a
superiority of character; that he may be better
enabled to follow this advice, he was furnished
with all the clothes we could spare, and directed,
when these were worn out, to make himself
trowsers with a mat." He hopes that all this
has been done, and that you have not forgotten
your Sundays. You may follow Pelew customs
in other ways. He sees no objection to two
wives, since Abba Thulle offered them, indeed
a refusal might well cause offence, but Sunday
stands apart. Knot a string to remind yourself

of it, or count coral insects, or something.
Prince Lee Boo saw the importance of Sunday
as soon as he landed in England, and has indeed
gone so far as to be buried in Rotherhithe
Church. How about baptizing your Cockilla
and Cockathey?—though this is my suggestion,
not the Captain's. He says that I am not to
plague you with niceties, especially as you can't
read, and indeed wants me to draw a picture
of a church and a pair of trousers, and leave
it at that. But I'm writing, because there's
just a chance that, on the turn of the tide, the
answer to my question may float back to me.

I want to know why you stopped behind
when the others went.

At the present moment I'm stuffed in between
books, and old ladies with worried faces are
making notes in long arm-chairs, so I feel it
natural enough you should stop. The ends of
the earth, the depths of the sea, the darkness
of time, you have chosen all three. But when
you chose them you were stuffed in somewhere
or other yourself, latitude 16' 25" N., longitude
126° E., date November 12th 1783, so what
were your grounds for deciding? Did it start
as a joke? Your mates never took you seriously,

and Wilson talks of your dry sense of humour.
You helped them to the very last to build the
sloop, you even came aboard as she was
moving to show where a sail had been stowed,
then you took leave without the least regret,
" as if they were only sailing from London to
Gravesend, and were to return by the next
tide." They couldn't believe their eyes when
you went and sat down with the savages and
the canoes, it seemed like a dream. Even
Prince Lee Boo was amazed. He pointed to
you as the canoes fell astern, and then he
pointed to himself and said, " I go with his
people, he stop with mine. But I go with wise
English, he stop with the savage Pelew. I go
to visit King George and God, he only visit
King Abba Thulle my father. Oh mystery!
How curious! " Captain Wilson then invited
him to dine, after which he started being sick.

   That ramshackle craft got safely to China,
looking more like a packing-case than a sloop,
with every sort of rag flapping, and the black
and white magic stuff still showing round the
stern. The John Company officials at Canton
were not too pleased with the vision. They had
sent out the *Antelope*, you see, one of their best

vessels, and this was what came back, and they
questioned Wilson pretty straightly over what
had happened. I suspect—owing to my knowledge of history—that the *Antelope* had been
despatched to annex the Pelew Islands for
Great Britain, instead of which the Pelews have
annexed the *Antelope,* and she now forms part
of the coral reef at Oroora. Wilson had to
explain this away as well as he could, also the
disappearance of the stores, the death of
Quarter Master Godfrey Minks (drowned
through swimming ashore with two suits of
clothes on), the mortality among the Chinese
crew (occurring no one remembered when) and
the absence of two dogs and yourself. On the
other hand, he could point to Prince Lee Boo,
and this certainly calmed the officials. Lee Boo
was a hostage, though the word was never
used, he ensured the good behaviour of his
father. The Company's plan was to educate
him in England, and send him back to rule the
islands for us; he was to take with him horses,
dogs, cows, pigs, goats, seeds, clothes, rum,
and all that makes life bearable; he was to oust
Qui Bill from the succession, conquer the
Artingalls with musket-fire, and reign over

corpses and coconuts in a gold-laced suit. The
small-pox had something to say to all that, and
there will be no more talk of annexation yet
awhile. You may rest in peace, my dear
Madan, if rest is what you want, and your king
Abba Thulle has saved his kingdom at the
moment he lost his son. Such an amiable
youth, and so intelligent. First he was puzzled
by houses, then he called everything a house; at
Portsmouth he was " put into a little house
which was run away with by horses, most
agreeable, the trees and fields went the other
way," and so reached London, which was
"all fine country, fine house upon house up to
sky," and skipped about half the night in a
four-poster bed, peeping between the curtains,
and crying, " in England a house for everything. How wise! " He must have been
charming. But I am more intrigued by you,
about whom I know nothing except that you
preferred the ends of the earth, the depths of the
sea. Answer this letter if you can—there are
various methods—and let me know why you
went native, and how you are.

I enclose the Prince's picture as it may amuse
you—you will hardly recognise who it is. I

Prince LEE BOO Second Son of ABBATHULLE

meant to break his death to you gradually, but
the news is already out, besides, I don't see why
you should mind. You saw him going on
board man-naked, with masses of wild fruit in
his arms. Well, in a week they taught him to
wear clothes like these, in a fortnight he
wouldn't take even a waistcoat off except in
the dark, and a year later you might have seen
him in Mrs. Wilson's dining-room at Rotherhithe, offering her, with exquisite grace, three
small cherries in a spoon. He had offered them
in his hand at first, whereat the old lady had
smiled slightly—you too may not know, but
cherries are never handed in the hand. Observing her smile, he resorted to a spoon,
and " a blush actually forced itself through
his dusky complexion." Nothing was too
refined for him, or too moral; he embraced
civilisation with the grace of a courtier and the
restraint of a curate. He admired all Englishmen. He adored all Englishwomen ; he called
the old ones " mother "—the young ones—we
shall never know. I wish he hadn't died—he
must have been a dear. He seems to have loved
his country. He was always talking about it,
and collecting rubbish to sow there when he

got back. His chief treasure was two little barrels of blue glass on stands, which an official gave him in Canton. His chief pleasure: driving in St. James' Park, close to where I am writing to you now. The Wilsons would not take him about much, for fear of infection. He went to see Lunardi go up in a balloon, but failed to mistake the balloon for a house, so was bored. Most days he was at school—an Academy for young gentlemen close by, and many a merry tale did he bring back, but never an unkind prank. The Wilsons were devoted to him—he and young Harry used to practise javelin-throwing for hours in the attic—and there is no doubt that he came to his end among friends. You can tell this or not tell it to Abba Thulle as you like. Probably you had better not tell it, for the noblest of savages is apt to be deranged by the death of a son, and whatever else this letter does I do not want it to do you harm.

Though the good CAPTAIN and his house-
    hold strove
Each other to excel in deeds of love,
Will this, when told thy father (noble chief!),

Stop the strong current of resistless grief?
Has not imagination, in alarms,
Portray'd his son return'd with arts and
    arms,
To bless his kingdom with a lasting race
Of warriors all, and all in love with peace?
Shall he, regardless of each social tie,
Calmly resign LEE BOO without a sigh?
And will unmoved thy generous uncles stand
To hear thou dieds't regretted in our land?
Ah no! . . .

This is from an anonymous poem which someone sent Wilson after the funeral. I, too, feel
" Ah no! " If the generous uncles realise that
we have, with the best intentions, committed
murder, they will not be unmoved, and when
they see you alone among them, and you're just
his age—well perhaps they'll make you
their king instead, but I wouldn't risk it. I
would watch Abba Thulle tying a knot in a
string at every full moon until his son comes
back with the wise English, and I would say
nothing.

What about your own relatives? I don't even
know whether you're English or French. I

find you signed on to the *Antelope* at Falmouth, but that means anything, and the books in the library here make their usual imbecile noises when I mention your name. Here are *Metamorphoses, mœurs et instincts des insectes*, by Emile Blanchard. Would this attract you as a connection? Or Samuel Laman Blanchard's *Collected Poems*. May I send them you? Or a letter from Pierre Blanchard, *Sur les questions qui divisent l'Eglise gallicane*. Or Edward Blanchard's *Descriptive Guide to the Great Western Railway*. Or Frank Nelson Blanchard's *A revision of the king snakes: genus Lampropeltis*. This is what is termed research. The Madans offer even wider scope to the earnest student, but I shall not pursue it beyond *Thelyphthora, a Treatise on Female Ruin*. This helpful work was composed by one Martin Madan, only three years before the *Antelope* struck, and him, if anyone, I assign to you as uncle. I haven't any news about your mates either—they scattered and got other jobs —Nick Tyacke, little Will Cobbledick, and all. Young Mr. Devis stopped in India, to paint portraits there, the rest of the party proceeding to England as aforesaid, via St. Helena. The two arrow wounds he got on your expedition still hurt him in the jaw. Do you remember when Mr. Devis drew Abba Thulle's wives, and they were so frightened—Ludee in particular, that very pretty one? Are your Cockilla and Cockathey very pretty too? I suggested to Wilson that they might be, which would explain your vagaries, and he answered yes, they very well might be, but no one knew, since they had not arrived from the interior by the time the sloop sailed. He also said that you were known to have formed " no special attachments on the island "—it seems rather to have been a general feeling, something connected with the Artingall wars. It was in a canoe among savages and Englishmen mixed, coming back from the second war, that you said " I mean to live here for ever." Wilson was irritated, for he had noticed nothing remarkable about you; you were like any other seaman at £2 a month, good tempered, inoffensive, quiet, enjoyed fighting—the usual thing: he took it for insolence when you stuck to it, and perhaps still isn't quite sure. " Did you ever want to stop on there yourself, sir? " I asked him. He sighed, " Ah well, ah well," and looked at his wrist. The bone with which Abba Thulle invested him

still encircles his wrist, he won't have it removed,
and polishes it every evening to keep his luck, as
he was told. "This denotes that I am a Rupack,
or noble, of the first rank," he continued,
smiling, " and it was conferred on me by the
natives in front of one of their public assembly
halls or ' Pyes.' Dr. Keate says the bone belongs to a whale, but in my judgment it is a mer-
man's, for they are not uncommon in the China
seas." I questioned him more on the Pyes, and
he said, " Ah well, the Pyes, most remarkable,
most." I like to hear him sigh " Ah well." It
runs under so much of his talk. He will never
forget the three months he spent on the island,
or the Apples of Paradise they brought him the
morning he sailed, or the canoes escorting him
over the reef while they cried, " Come again to
us, good Englishman, come! " The English will
not come again—at least I hope not. Your
island has swung away from ours into what we
choose to call darkness, and into what I can't
help calling life.

Look at Lee Boo! Think how it ended, in
spite of all the care they took. Mr. Sharpe
(your late surgeon) never let him out of his
sight, and as soon as the first trace of infection

appeared they sent for Doctor Carmichael
Smith too. Doctor Smith examined him, and
told the Wilsons at once that he must die. A
few days later he knew it himself. He was walking across the room, saw himself in the glass,
and was disgusted—shook his head, and said
that his father and mother, thousands of miles
away, were grieving. To Mr. Sharpe he said:
" Good friend, when you go back to Pelew tell
Abba Thulle that Lee Boo take much drink to
make small-pox go away, but he die; Captain
Wilson, Mother Wilson, very kind—all English
very good men—much sorry he could not speak
to the King the number of fine things the
English had got—he do all they tell him, but he
die." The little barrels of blue glass were to be
given to the king. As long as Doctor Smith was
with him, he complained of his symptoms in
case he could be cured, but at other times he
thought only of his friends. To add to their
misery, old Mrs. Wilson lay ill in the next room,
and he kept calling out to her " Lee Boo do
well, mother," to comfort her, or tried to visit
her, and had to be stopped. Hot baths,
blistered back and legs—the boy endured it all,
sensible, unselfish, ultra-civilised to the last.

What he really thought, no one knew or has dared to guess. He managed to pass away without distressing the Christians or disappointing the philosophers, and he has a tablet in Rotherhithe churchyard consequently. John Company paid for it, and for the funeral, too, though the Wilsons would gladly have settled it all themselves. All Rotherhithe attended— the two little painted figures up on the alms houses couldn't ever have looked down on so vast a concourse—officials from London, all the young people from the Academy, although it was their Christmas holiday. The stone was put up after a year, which gives enough time for all flesh to decay.

To the Memory
of Prince LEE BOO,
A native of the PELEW, or PALOS Islands:
and Son to ABBA THULLE, Rupack or King
of the Island COOROORAA;
who departed this Life on the 27th of December,
1784
aged 20 years;
This Stone is inscribed
by the Honourable United EAST INDIA COMPANY,

as a testimony of Esteem for the humane and
kind Treatment afforded by HIS FATHER to the
Crew of their Ship the ANTELOPE,
Captain WILSON, which was
wrecked off that Island in
the Night of the 9th of August, 1783.

Stop, Reader, stop!—let NATURE claim a Tear
—A Prince of *Mine*, LEE BOO, lies bury'd here.

I almost shed a tear, but not quite; he was
rather too harmless a blackamoor—such a
puppet, he always did as he was bid, and people
like that don't seem quite real. The people who
touch my imagination are obstinate suddenly—
they do break step, and I always hope they'll
get by without the sergeant punishing them.
It was so like poor Lee Boo that he loved above
all things to see the Guards drilling in the Park.
They are drilling there still, so are the ladies in
the long chairs in this library, so are the books
in the shelves. If it isn't one set of rules it's
another, even for heroism. I ought to feel free
myself, as I've health, strength, and am middle-
aged, yet I can't keep my hat on in a church,
for instance, even if no one's looking, and if I'm
fighting never manage to hit below the belt.

While not getting fussed over this, I can't but remember the people who managed better, and it's in order to meet them in the flesh that I study history. Here and there, as I rake between the importancies, I come across them—the people who carried whimsicality into action, the salt of my earth. Not the professional whimsies—their drill's drearier than anyone's—but the solid fellows who suddenly jib. The queer thing is we all admire them—even when we're hard-bitten disciplinarians like old Wilson. They've got hold of something which we know is there, but have never dared to grasp in our hands. A sort of stinging nettle. I went down to the tomb the other day, and thought " No, he isn't quite good enough, he was stung when he wasn't looking, which happens to anyone." I took down a lot of notes about Rotherhithe church, the neighbourhood, Shad Thames, etc., thinking they would interest you, but if they interested you, you'd have come back to them, so I tore the notes up and wandered about feeling rather tired and out of place, then I got across the river to Stepney, and through in at Aldgate and out at Newgate, back to this part, where I mostly am.

Well, that concludes my news, and now it's your turn. I will enclose you one more poem, and then wish you good luck:

> O'er the mighty Pacific whose soft swelling
> wave
> A thousand bright regions eternally lave,
> 'Mid rocks red with coral and shellfish
> abounding,
> The note of the parrot and pigeon resound-
> ing:
> Crowned with groves of banana and taper
> bamboo
> Rise the gay sunny shores of the Isles of
> *Pelew*.

This is how a Miss Heisch, afterwards a Mrs. Hookey, imagines your present home. I laughed the first time I read her poem, but the second time I found myself sighing " Ah well! " Write to me if you possibly can—I suppose on the bark of some tree. Lower it one evening as the tide turns, and watch it drift out through the coral reefs. The monsoons will hurry it westward, and the spray begin whispering " Progress " against it. Swifter boats, paler crews, and an intelligent interest among

savants as it is raised aboard in a dredge off,
let us say, Réunion. " C'est bien une lettre? "
Pourquoi pas? It is addressed? Apparently!
Then forward it onward to England. The
waves are rising, the world's winding up, but
King George is still on his throne, so's God.
Boom! Before the last echo of 1815 dies away,
1914 strikes, and here we are. Your letter now
takes to the air. Heavily surcharged, liable to
customs duty, enterable under income tax,
subject to quarantine, notifiable, censorable,
confiscatable, it crashes through the library
window, and explodes in my hand. None of the
old ladies notice it—they are still researching.
I wait until the envelope of smoke has vanished,
I find my right spectacles, and I decipher a
hundred and fifty years after it was written, the
single word: " aaa."

What can " aaa " mean? Perhaps you have
forgotten your English. I will send for a
Pelew dictionary. While it is coming I have
one more thing to say to you.

Once I used to come across an Irish clergyman—an unusual fellow, I never liked him
much, he died before your time. He invented
a group of islands to relieve his feelings on, and

oddly enough placed some of them south-east of Formosa—that's to say, more or less where you actually are. One of these islands contained very small men, another very large ones, a third was inhabited by horses, and the fourth flew. The clergyman was too bad tempered to take much notice of what he was doing: I mean whether the men were big or little they were intended to make men of his own size look small, and so with his horses: he didn't care for horses but he hated people, and used horses for saying so. Well, in one of the islands he imagined men living for ever. It sounded like Paradise, but of course there was a catch—I will not tell you what, but it is a terrifying one, and nothing he has ever said to me has upset me more. If he is right on the subject of eternal youth in the Southern seas, don't answer this letter, in fact you won't want to. But if I am right, send the answer that tells everything, the answer I have imagined for you, " aaa " (Pelew for Yes).

Yours ever,

E. M. FORSTER.

NOTE

My letter was never delivered. An explanation for this can be found in *A Supplement to the Account of the Pelew Islands; compiled from the journals of the Panther and Endeavour, two vessels sent by the Honourable East India Company to those Islands in the year* 1790; by the Reverend John Pearce Hockin, of Exeter College, Oxford, M.A. London, printed for Captain Henry Wilson by W. Bulmer and Co., Cleveland Row. 1803.

A
LETTER TO AN M.P.
ON DISARMAMENT

VISCOUNT CECIL

My Dear Brownjohn,

On February 2nd 1931, there will meet at
Geneva the greatest international Conference that
has ever been assembled. It will consist of representatives of some sixty sovereign states, including
Russia and the United States, and its purpose will
be to draw up a general Treaty for the reduction
and limitation of World Armaments. *It must succeed!*
That is the keynote of the whole of my reply to
your letter.

You say that you are wondering how far foreign
affairs really interest the British elector, and you
tell me that you are a typical Member of Parliament. If you will allow me to say so, I believe
that you are; and the more credit to you. Like
almost all your colleagues in that honourable House
you are a loyal supporter of your Party, that is, you
desire its success at the General Election. To
achieve this object, of which your own return to
Westminster is an essential part, you are prepared
to take any measures " within the rules of the game."

There is a tendency among superior people to
run down party politics and to treat enthusiasm
for a party as a form of moral delinquency. That is
all nonsense. There could be no effective Government in a democratic country without a system of
organised parties, though you would, I believe,
confess with me that Party is a nuisance if it becomes
an end in itself. It is a means to an end, which is
the welfare of the nation; and there are emergencies
when " none is for the party and all are for the
State." But within those limits your vigorous sup-

port of a party programme in the constituency and
in the country is as natural as it is necessary. You
act in this way because you honestly believe that
a Government formed by your leaders to carry out
the policy of your party would be the best adminis-
tration in the interests of this country and of the
Empire.

Perhaps you attach more importance than I do to
party differences on domestic questions. I do not
doubt their urgency. No Member of Parliament
could possibly afford not to expound definite
solutions for such internal problems as unemployment, the resuscitation of industry, tariffs and
taxation.

But I am sure you would agree that Disraeli was
right when he said in 1872:

"The relations of England with the rest of the
world, which are 'foreign affairs,' are the matters
which most influence the Briton's lot. Upon them
depends the increase or reduction of taxation.
Upon them depends the enjoyment or embarrassment of his industry."

Since more than three-quarters of our annual
taxation at the present time is devoted to payment
for past wars and preparations for wars in the
future, and since commerce and industry are still
staggering under the weight of the World War,
Disraeli's words do not seem exaggerated. When
Lord Grey says, "If we do not end war, war will
end us," he is giving utterance to a thought far
more profound than any political slogan or catch-

word. It may be true of the generality of nations that another great war would, with the newly-devised methods of mass destruction, do them irreparable damage and dislocate the whole of their economic and political organisms. But it is even more true of the British Empire.

It can never be true of any country that the maintenance of peace with foreign powers is a matter of indifference to the ordinary citizen: and wherever we see the great issues of foreign policy subordinated to the exigencies of domestic policies, or left to a handful of statesmen and diplomats without the control of popular interest, we may be sure that a country is in an unhealthy and dangerous condition. That is particularly the case of this island whose population, as the census has just recorded, is, with the possible exception of Belgium, the most dense of any country in the world. We can only produce from our own land, even if we developed it more intensively than we do, a fraction of the necessities of our life. Not only is that notoriously true of our food supply, but it applies equally to our industry. Vast cities have grown up around factories which depend for their very existence upon a continuous flow of raw materials from all parts of the globe, and upon the assurance of a market for their manufactures in Europe and elsewhere. Our imports are even greater than our exports. In a word, our industry, the basis of so much of our prosperity in the past, with all the towns and villages that hang upon it, can only maintain its life by a continual process of buying and selling with other countries.

Upon which there blows up from time to time the old controversy about Free Trade and Protection and Empire Preference, which I must leave you to fight out with your fellow-Members. All I would ask you to observe is that, whatever fiscal policy may be expedient for Great Britain at any given time, we are dependent more than any other country for our very subsistence upon free communications with every part of every continent of the world; upon a condition of international confidence and security without which foreign trade is paralysed, and upon the ability of other countries to buy our wares. We are more than the shopkeepers of Europe, as Napoleon called us: we have one foot in the old world, one foot in the new.

That perhaps is not the most cogent reason for regarding the preservation of peace as of paramount importance to Great Britain. For no nation is deterred from war, if war seems the only way of vindicating the Right, by a cold calculation of economic disadvantages or the loss of money. Certainly our own people can be depended upon, when a sufficiently clear and cogent issue presents itself, to make almost any sacrifice. Considerations of commercial advantage did not restrain us from going to war in 1914, and by themselves would probably not restrain us if similar circumstances arose.

There is another reason why peace is the greatest interest of the British Empire, and that is that it is not a simple political unit like other States. It consists of a commonwealth of nations, each with its own problems, each tending more and more towards complete self-government and independence, with the Crown as the only constitutional and political link between them. The time will come—I myself believe that it is at hand—when the process of re-integration must begin, and, the idea of a Mother Country and her dependencies being abandoned, the organs of common consultation and action be devised for the alliance of British nations. But at any rate no one will question the fact that the commonwealth is going through a particularly difficult phase of evolution. With Canada, Ireland, South Africa, Australia and New Zealand, not to speak of India, busily asserting their free nationhood and even emphasising their independence by the making of treaties and by appointing separate diplomatic representatives to foreign capitals, a serious European war might impose an intolerable strain upon the unity of the British Empire. We have neither right nor reason to assume that those distant Dominions would, with any of the alacrity of 1914, join in a European conflict of the old kind in which this country found itself entangled. They would, I believe, be true to their duties under the Covenant of the League, if it were a plain case of the League as a whole being arrayed against a wanton aggression. But if, for any reason, the League machinery failed, it is by no means certain that in every case of conflict the whole of the Empire would follow the lead of the United Kingdom. It is, therefore, of the utmost importance to the welfare and peaceful development of the Empire that the League should be sufficiently

strong, united, and effective to stifle any outbreak
of war in Europe. That is why Mr. Baldwin is right
when he says: " Our hope is in the League of
Nations."

Let me interrupt here my main line of thought to
ask you if you have not remarked among your constituents a growing interest in international and
especially European affairs, a certain inquisitive
spirit concerning your own position in these matters?
England has always been a part of Europe economi-
cally and politically. But the fact was vividly
brought home to numbers of our fellow-countrymen
by the Great War. The decision to stand by Belgium
was a national decision if ever there was one; and
that first expeditionary force has, metaphorically
speaking, never finished its expedition.

We rightly decided to intervene in an essentially
European controversy, and we cannot, even if we
would, leave our task half done. After helping to
win a great victory we have not forgotten and we
must not forget the principles and the purpose for
which we fought. They have become the principles
and the purpose of all peoples who want justice and
liberty; and difficulty after difficulty surges up
against them. That—in a confused sort of way—is
what is at the back of the mind of the thoughtful
Englishman. And that is why the British Press,
almost in spite of itself, cannot keep off the international problem. Note the fate of that ill-starred
attempt which was made, a few months since, by a
group of popular newspapers, to start a great 100
per cent. British Campaign. It was a flash in the pan.

I know nothing of the motives of this " stunt," but I suppose that the proprietor or editors concerned imagined that the British public twelve years after the war was sick and tired of the worries and tangles of Europe. A complete policy of " splendid isolation " being too much for the most gullible reader to swallow, a policy of economic self-sufficiency for the Empire was brought forth with a great appearance of novelty.

On the face of it there was much to be said for it. But as soon as the general was reduced to the particular and theories brought into contact with realities, it was found that some of the Dominions had already grown and others were growing into independent economic units which had no intention whatever of abandoning their right to fix their own tariffs and to protect their own industries. Driven to take the less inspiring form of a plan to unite the home country and the Crown Colonies in an economic unit, the doctrine of the new imperialism was in danger of " fading out " until a fresh method was tried. The League of Nations was suddenly and sensationally discovered to be utterly opposed to the true interests of the British Empire. Ineffectual, dilatory but tortuous, the League was shearing the mane of the British Lion like Delilah the locks of Samson. And why was Britain to be so weakened and robbed of her liberty? It was all so that she might be tied to the chariot wheels of France, against whom the old national prejudice was aroused in the most reckless and extravagant manner.

The British public is not so easily misled. A

counter-attack was launched which, among other
things, brought the signatures of the Women's International League's petition for general disarmament
up from 300,000 to over a million in about a month.
Yet more significant, almost the whole of the reput-
able newspapers and reviews rallied to the support
of the League of Nations. Even those who had
bothered very little about the League saw that its
disappearance would be an international disaster.
Shortly afterwards, a national demonstration in
favour of an all-round reduction of armaments was
held in London with simultaneous meetings, to
which the speeches were relayed, in a hundred other
towns. The Prime Minister and his two predecessors
in that office spoke for the first time from the same
platform. And none were more surprised than the
organisers of the demonstration at the vast numbers
who sought admission, and the volume of editorial
support which it received from the London and
provincial newspapers as a whole.

This is only one out of many instances which I
could give of the place which foreign affairs are
coming to play in the minds of ordinary people in
England. I would almost say in their subconscious
minds. For the conviction that war is a mad and
evil thing; that peace can only be secured by a
continuous effort; that the maintenance of highly-
developed armies, navies and air forces is inconsistent
with peace; that something must be done to diminish-
ish them—all that, I believe, is beginning to be
axiomatic for the majority of our people. I am sure
that it is taken for granted by a much greater num-

ber of men and women than talk about it or join
societies or go to meetings. This chain of thought is
connected in the minds of many with the vivid
experiences of the war; and the deeper the Englishman's feelings the less he talks about them.

And here the " party machine " is more often
than not obsolete in its methods. While the mind of
the nation as a whole has been moving towards a
greater realisation of the importance to itself of
international peace and gives evidence of arriving
slowly but surely at certain conclusions concerning
the way to maintain it, the whole apparatus of a
party—central office, speakers, local party associations, candidates, agents—is chiefly concerned with
the game of catching out the other parties. The stock-
in-trade of controversy tends to be confined to the
old terms—food, drink, money, class, industry,
agriculture—and to have as its object far less the
achievement of measures than the advancement or
defeat of men. I am not sure whether this is not
partly the cause of the apathy of which all parties
complain and the deplorably low percentage of
votes cast, particularly in by-elections. There is, I
believe, a growing proportion of the electorate which
is not primarily interested in current party issues,
because they think them stale and narrow. And I
have yet to learn of the candidate for Parliament in
recent times who did not gain by showing that he
had a good grasp of the international situation; that
he cared for peace, and that he had clear and con-
structive ideas about the best ways of preserving it.
Duff Cooper's victory at Westminster is a case in point.

You will see that my digression into the realm of what ordinary people are thinking about, and what newspapers find it necessary to write about, has brought me to the same point that I had reached by the original sequence of thought which I tried to trace at the beginning of this letter, namely, that the maintenance and reinforcement of the League of Nations is of paramount importance to Englishmen. It is to the League that praise and criticism, enthusiasm and discontent, hope and impatience, perpetually return.

I will not labour the point further. If we may take it as agreed that permanent peace in Europe is one of the first concerns of the British Empire, and that it takes a strong and trusted international authority to keep the peace, it is worth examining what are the principal dangers to the League's authority. I think none could deny that, in the world at large, the pace of the peace movement has slackened, and that the League has been passing through difficult times. An acute economic crisis, partly the cause and partly the effect of the feverish nationalist revivals of the last few years, has bred in some quarters a feeling of defeatism in regard to the League's possibilities, if not a bad-tempered impatience at its failure to produce miracles. But I have no doubt in my own mind that the main cause of this *crise d'autorité* of the League, as the French would call it, is the armaments situation. I will not harass you with statistics; you will have no difficulty in learning from *White Papers, Answers in Parliament,* the *League's Armaments Year Book,* and other publications on the subject, the present extent and cost of the armies, navies and air forces of the principal Powers. Roughly, the world spent in 1930—twelve years after the war; in spite of the League and the World Court having built up a good reputation for conciliation and arbitration; in spite of more and more systematised co-operation between Governments in social, industrial, sanitary and other practical spheres; in spite of the Kellogg Pact—over nine hundred and fifty million pounds upon preparations for warfare. How can you expect the plain man to have undimmed faith in Pacts and Covenants to renounce war under these circumstances? He will be little disposed to listen to long stories about this and that technical difficulty which has delayed disarmament. He will reject the contention that these vast sums of money spent on improving the speed and efficiency of bombing aeroplanes, perfecting naval gun-fire, mechanising armies and preparing for chemical warfare, are merely the modest requirements of " national safety " and are quite consistent with those elevating speeches at Geneva about international co-operation which are repeated in his newspapers, his wireless, and his talking film. He will begin to doubt whether it is not all a ghastly farce. *That* is what paralyses the moral authority and prestige of the League; and it is the first fact in the armament situation which stares us in the face.

The second fact—and I confess that I did not myself at first feel the full force of it—is that German resentment at the failure of the Allies to implement

their promises to join in a general reduction of armaments, threatens to get out of hand. It has become
one of the most disturbing factors in the life of
Europe. It has, indeed, its disreputable aspects.
There are many Germans and many German newspapers who are quite flagrantly working for the
failure of the World Disarmament Conference which
is to meet in February 1932, because they believe
that this will leave Germany freer to re-arm. They
will get no sympathy from you or from me. They are
doing a very bad service to their own country. For
two can play at that game of force; and the pre-
ponderance of military power (I speak not of right
or wrong) is still very plainly on the side of those
whom a re-armed Germany would have to count
as implacable enemies. That is not the attitude of
Dr. Brüning and Herr Curtius. They are, I am
convinced, sound friends and advocates of general
disarmament. But neither they nor any other
German Government could possibly, in the existing
state of feeling, put their signatures to any Disarmament Treaty or Convention which reaffirmed the
inequality of states in armaments as between the
" vanquished " and the " victorious " Powers.

Here again I need not trouble you with quotations.
Mr. MacDonald recently read to the House of
Commons the exact text of the promise made by
M. Clemenceau to the Germans on behalf of the
Allies during the Peace Conference; the opening
words of Part V of the Treaty of Versailles; Article
8 of the Covenant of the League of Nations. The
main issue is plain. We obliged the Germans and

their allies to accept the virtual annihilation of their
military strength; the disbandment of their con-
script armies; the destruction of their air forces, and
the sacrifice of quantities of military material and
ships, on the definite understanding that it was to be
part of a reduction of armaments by all nations,
" which it will be one of the first duties of the League
of Nations to promote." We incorporated that
undertaking in the military clauses of the Treaties
to which the United States is a party just as much as
we are. We embodied in the Covenant of the League
a definite obligation to join in a general reduction of
armaments. We reasserted that obligation in the
Final Act of Locarno. We have repeated it in
numerous international statements and resolutions.
And we have not yet carried out our promises.

When I say " we," I do not, of course, mean Great
Britain alone; I am referring to the former Allied
and Associated Powers as a whole. We British have
at any rate shown that we have an uneasy conscience
in the matter. We have made an honest attempt to
kill competition in naval armaments; we have, or
think we have, economised where we could in other
directions, though it is disquieting to note that the
figure of our expenditure on armaments is now nearly
four times as great as that which drove Randolph
Churchill to resignation in 1887. But no disarma
ment is feasible unless it is universal, and no one
nation unaided can achieve it. Both French and
British spokesmen have in the last few months
demonstrated with impressive arrays of figures that
they have reduced as much as they reasonably can

in the last ten years. Experts haggle interminably
over these statistics and contrive to draw the most
varying morals from them. But the fact remains
that expenditure upon armaments among these
Powers is far greater than it was before the war; and
taking technical improvements into account, not to
speak of their financial assets, their fighting strength
is manifestly overwhelming compared with that of
Germany.

Faced then with these ugly facts—the vast amounts
of national resources spent upon armaments; the
crushing burden of taxation so caused; the under-
mining of public confidence in the League of Nations
which results from all this, and the inevitable reaction in Central Europe against what is becoming
a gross breach of faith—must we not conclude that
nothing is more vital to peace than to bring about as
swiftly as possible a binding agreement to decrease
and limit these national armies, navies and air
forces not yet reduced by the Treaties? Should not
the fate of the World Conference, convened for this
purpose, command our undivided attention? This
is not a matter which concerns Cabinets and Foreign
Ministers alone; it involves the conscience of a
nation. It calls for the formation and expression of
an overwhelming body of public opinion. And in a
democratic country such as ours, you and the other
Members of Parliament are those whose plain duty
it is (so it seems to me) to guide that opinion and to
make it articulate.

If, as I sincerely hope, you share this view, you
will naturally want to be able to set forth and defend

a concrete plan to advance disarmament, both before your constituents and in Parliament. May I,
then, put certain practical considerations before
you?

I have dwelt upon the German position. Of
Russia let me say only this; that I am sure you will
not be gulled into believing that members of the
League of Nations cannot, for fear only of Russia,
reduce those ships, aeroplanes, fortresses and military formations which they have quite notoriously
created for possible use against one another. Not
that Russian armaments can be altogether dis-
regarded. They may not be the efficient cause of the
warlike preparations of western powers. But as
long as they are unlimited the neighbours of Russia
will make that an excuse not to reduce their armaments, and if they remain fully armed their neighbours will claim to do the same, and so on till the
western ocean is reached. But Russia is to attend
the Conference next year and will, I believe, accept
any genuine scheme of disarmament agreed to by
others. I believe she will also carry it out. But if
not, precautions must and will be taken, as I shall
point out later on, to protect other nations in that
or any similar case.

France requires special study; for disarmament
means nothing unless it means a considerable and
visible reduction of the armies and air forces of the
great military group of Powers—that is, France and
the countries associated with her. What matters to
France and Belgium, and to a hardly lesser degree
to the countries of Eastern Europe, newly formed or

enlarged by the Peace Settlement, is security from
invasion. It has come to be assumed as a matter
of course by most English newspapers that France
is cynically and immovably attached to the notion
of exercising a military hegemony over Europe.
I believe myself that it would be utterly unfair to
accuse the average Frenchman of any such design.
What he wants is safety; safety for his dearly-loved
land which has twice in a lifetime been deeply
invaded and ravaged from the East. His politicians
and his military experts may be going the wrong way
about getting true safety for France. But the object
is a right and natural one. The only possible alternative to preparing to defend your country *contra
mundum*—if you are in that state of mind—is to know
for certain that, if you are invaded or attacked by a
Power which flouts arbitration, the rest of the world
will be on your side. There would never have been
any League of Nations had not this fundamental
notion of mutual assistance against aggression been
incorporated in its Covenant. Could any organised
society of nations keep together without such practical consequences and symbols of solidarity as are
contained in the Tenth, Eleventh, Fifteenth and
Sixteenth Articles of the Covenant? After all, they
only lay down in very moderate terms that military
aggression is an international crime and a victim of
it is entitled to the aid and protection of other members of the League. Is not that the very essence of an
international community? And have not we in
England, by slurring over these obligations, mini-
mising them, even suggesting in some of our papers

that we intend to get out of them, played right into the hands of the militarist in France and other Continental countries who is already too little disposed to trust to the League for his nation's security? I cannot think that some of our most rightly respected newspapers are altogether without blame for the state of mind which they deplore on the other side of the Channel. We must show that we mean to stick to our obligations of international solidarity, whatever our speculations—optimistic speculations in my case—about America's attitude to League action against an aggressor. I can see no objection to our reaffirming our adherence to those articles of the Covenant and of Locarno at the opportune moment. But there is another side to the picture to which you will no doubt wish to devote attention both in and out of Parliament.

It is that these promises of mutual assistance do not stand alone: they are only part of the whole conception of the new international order. The other essential parts of that whole are the establishment of arbitration as the recognised means of settling international differences; and disarmament. And it may be necessary to say plainly that, unless a nation gives evidence of a real readiness to implement these unconditional Versailles promises of reduction and the treaty obligations which embody them, the British Parliament and people may ask themselves how far they are bound by their part of the bargain.

I make no apology for dwelling thus upon the political aspects of the disarmament problem. It is

essentially a great political issue—far less a matter
of strategic calculations and technical statistics.
Experts we must have, but, as they say in America,
" they must be on tap and not on top." That is
why I should like to see Parliament take this matter
of Disarmament into its own hands and try to carry
it to a finish.

You will already be acquainted with the Draft
Convention which, after many delays and com-
promises, was adopted by the Preparatory Commission for the World Disarmament Conference.
The official German attitude is still that this document should not determine the Conference's delibera-
tions. But as the majority of Governments intend
that it shall be the basis of discussion, I think it
hardly conceivable that the whole work of preparation will be wasted. The Convention, in spite of
obvious defects, is to my mind an instrument of
great importance. For the first time it puts before
all nations a definite framework into which can be
fitted reductions and limitations of their different
kinds of armaments. Let me, without entering too
much into detail, outline its main provisions.

The Convention provides first for the limitation
and, so far as is possible, the reduction of all types of
armaments. It begins by the Land Forces. Their
number is to be reduced and limited. It is
not proposed to abolish conscription. The whole
of the Continental Governments were against that.
Even Germany and the other " vanquished "
Powers who were deprived of conscription by the

Peace Treaties would like to go back to it. This is partly because it is far the easiest system of recruiting and the least expensive, and partly because it is thought to be right that every citizen capable of bearing arms should undertake his share of military service. But the Convention lays down that military service is to be limited; that is to say that in each country the aggregate number of days' service with the colours in each year given by all soldiers and officers is to be fixed. This covers both the first training of recruits and the refresher courses of reservists, so that all—both in the regular army and in reserve—will be limited. A good deal has been said about the supposed failure of the Draft Convention to limit trained reserves. But a moment's thought will show that the only way trained reserves can be limited is by limiting the number of men trained. Once trained, they then and there become trained reserves. The only true criticism that can be made on this point is that there is no direct provision in the Convention for limiting the number of the Annual Contingent taken by conscription. To have done that would have been a direct challenge to the principle of equality of sacrifice, and it seemed better simply to limit the total number of serving soldiers and leave to each country the adoption of the machinery necessary to produce the result agreed upon.

But it is not only numbers that must be limited. Quality also is of the utmost importance. Fundamentally, the object is to diminish and ultimately remove the facilities of each country to attack its neighbours. The more competent the soldier, the more likely he is to be used for aggression. It is, therefore, proposed to limit specifically the officers on whom so much of the strategic value of a fighting force depends, and also the numbers of professional or long-service soldiers. Even in conscriptionist countries there is a tendency to have more and more of a " stiffening " of such troops. The French army includes more than 100,000 of them.

Further, the period of service of the conscriptionist forces is to be limited. This is very important. If all armies could be brought down to a militia basis—involving a first training for six months or less—the danger of military aggression would be much reduced. Moreover, efforts in this direction have a good prospect of success, since it is the length of training that is unpopular everywhere.

It may be claimed that the provisions in the Convention for limiting personnel of armies make it possible, if agreement can be reached, to reduce to the utmost the numbers and efficiency of the men in the land armies. And similar provisions are to be applied to sailors and airmen. Personnel, then, seems adequately dealt with, except that there remains the inequality between victors and vanquished, since the first have and the second have not the right to a system of conscription.

When it comes to material, greater difficulties arise. Everyone agrees that material in a modern army is becoming increasingly important. The old panoply of war, with its columns and lines of battle, its cavalry and its charges, its lances and bayonets,

is as extinct as armour and archery. For them we
have substituted rifles and machine-guns, bombs and
gas projectors, tanks and aeroplanes, big cannon and
howitzers. It may well be that in a future war, if it
should take place, battles will be fought by relatively
small numbers, using machinery of greater and
greater death-dealing capacity, and victory will rest
not with the largest, but with the most successfully
mechanised army. From a disarmament point of
view this presents two features, one bad and one
good. The bad feature is the difficulty of directly
controlling material. Men cannot be trained
adequately except in public, and whatever is done
in public is immediately known all over the modern
world. But rifles and even the spare parts of many
of the larger machines can and indeed must be made
and stored in closed factories and arsenals. If, then,
their numbers are to be internationally checked
there must be a complete system of international
inspection on the same lines as that established in
Germany after the war. That involved a foreign
mission resident in Berlin with all sorts of rights of
visit and search. To establish a world-wide system
of that kind would be impracticable and almost
certainly ineffective. On the other hand, the cost
of modern weapons and war machines is great and
growing. That is where you and your fellow-
Members of Parliament come in. In every civilised
country there are arrangements for checking by
publicity state expenditure. It is easy for experts to
know within very little what each country is spending
on the equipment of its armed forces. If the sums

involved were small, concealment might be achieved
by manipulating the public accounts. But that
would mean unscrupulous falsehood on the part of
the officials concerned and the absence of domestic
criticism by the opposition which is fortunately rare
in present conditions. And since the amount of
money required for the armaments of to-day is
enormous, these difficulties of concealment become
so great as to be insuperable.

It was for these reasons that the framers of the
Convention decided to rely on restricting the cost of
land material as its sole limitation. That is what is
called Budgetary Limitation. Its practicability was
called in question and a committee of budgetary
experts drawn from all the chief countries in Europe
was appointed to investigate the point. They
unanimously reported that the plan was quite
feasible and that it had the additional advantage of
limiting improvements and new inventions which
could not be done by mere limitation of numbers of
machines. The German pocket-battleship is a case
in point. By spending more than twice as much as
the cost of any other ship of equal size the Germans
have produced a vessel of very much greater fighting
power. Without in any way transgressing the limits
they accepted at Paris, they have in fact rendered
those limits largely nugatory.

It is probably true, nevertheless, that the Convention goes too far in relying solely on budgetary
limitation for land material. There seems no reason
why big guns, which cannot easily be hidden, and
perhaps tanks, should not be specifically limited.

Though even in those cases a budgetary limitation as well is desirable.

When it comes to sea and air, the Convention does limit specifically the numbers and size of ships and their guns, and the number and power of aircraft.

In aircraft the opposite mistake was made, and the Commission which drew up the Convention refused to limit their cost. That was clearly wrong. Aircraft, continually changing in character and increasing in cost, are particularly in need of budgetary limitation, unless indeed we can secure their abolition.

There are several subsidiary provisions of the Convention which need not be discussed. But three points should be mentioned. In the first place, full information as to armaments is to be given. This in the Convention is not extended to material in stock. But that is clearly a mistake. The strength of an army in the field depends on how far it can be equipped and armed. In particular the value of reserves of men is measured by the degree to which they can be armed. Clearly, therefore, secrecy as to stocks must be abolished, and indeed the Covenant itself provides for complete interchange of military information. Next, though the system of inspection elaborated in the Peace Treaties cannot be applied to every nation in the world, some supervision of the execution of the Disarmament Treaty by an international authority is essential. It is therefore proposed to constitute a Permanent Disarmament Commission at Geneva, whose duty it will be continuously to study the armaments of the world and see how far each nation is acting up to its promises. The chief material it will have to work upon will be the published accounts and estimates of the different countries. But it will be authorised to receive and consider any other information brought before it. In addition to this supervisory function it will be expected to watch the operation of the Treaty and point out defects to be considered at its periodical revisions. The Commission will consist of impartial persons of high character and position, appointed in concert with the government of the country to which they belong but irremovable during their term of office, which should be fairly long, except in case of disability or resignation. This is the system on which the Mandates Commission is constituted and it has proved efficient in operation.

I spoke of revision just now and that is an essential part of the scheme. However successful next year's conference turns out to be, it is not to be supposed that it will reach a final result. At best it can only make a good start in the direction of Disarmament. Moreover, circumstances may arise which will make the proposals adopted unjust or inapplicable. Suppose, for instance, as I have earlier suggested, that one of the High Contracting Powers fails to carry out its obligations, obviously its neighbours cannot be bound by theirs. Or again, if a country so develops its civil air-service as to constitute a threat to other states, some means of meeting the menace must be provided. Accordingly, it is proposed that the Treaty shall only in principle last for a definite period, say five years, and before that time

there shall be a fresh Conference to consider what
more can be done. Further, if unforeseen events
occur which make any High Contracting Party unwilling to continue to be bound by its obligations, it
may give notice to the Permanent Disarmament
Commission, and subject to certain precautions it
may be temporarily relieved of those obligations.
In that case, too, a new Conference may have to be
held.

All this is mere machinery—very necessary, but
not in itself bringing about a reduction or even a
limitation of armaments. The main work of the
Conference will be to fill into the skeleton, contained
in the Convention, figures or other positive provisions
as to the actual strength of world armaments. That
will be a complicated and difficult problem. In
every country the belief is firmly held that all other
countries ought to reduce their armaments, but that
for itself it has already cut them down to the very
bone. Thus very distinguished leaders of British
opinion believe that our Navy is already dangerously
small, our Army has been so much reduced as to be
scarcely able to fulfil its imperial duties, while the
weakness of our Air-force fills them with anxiety. In
France, similar language is held. The French Government has recently put out a paper explaining how
largely they have cut down their fighting force, and
their Ministers quote or misquote with approval
British statements to the effect that reduction is out
of the question. Professions to the like effect have
been made in other countries. Indeed, Italy stands
almost alone in saying that she is prepared to cut

down her armaments to any extent provided other countries will do the same.

Meanwhile, Germany and the other disarmed countries clamour for the fulfilment by the " victorious " countries of the disarmament promises which they made to the " vanquished " at Paris. It must be admitted that the Germans have a strong case. As I have already pointed out, in the Covenant, in the Disarmament Clauses of the Peace Treaties, in the correspondence between the Allied and Associated Powers and Germany which preceded and formed the basis of the signature of the Treaty of Versailles, it was distinctly stated that German disarmament was to be the prelude to universal disarmament. The same promise was given to the other defeated countries and it has been repeated in various forms by a number of international pronouncements and undertakings. It is possible to argue—what, indeed, cannot be argued?—that the obligations to disarm of the victorious countries are qualified and conditional, that they only apply subject to the requirements of security, and that in any case they do not mean that the armaments of all countries are to be on an equal scale. But when all due allowance has been made for considerations of this kind, no honest man can doubt that there rests on the victorious countries an honourable duty of the plainest kind to limit and reduce, not unilaterally but by international agreement, their armaments so as to be purely defensive in character, and to accept as the model of such reduction the principles of disarmament imposed by the Peace Treaties on the defeated Powers.

How can these various national views be reconciled? The problem at first sight seems almost insoluble. And yet it must be solved. Public opinion the world over demands it, and it is the only hope for the maintenance of peace and the preservation of Western civilisation. How can it be done? In the first place, we must establish the truth that if the present distribution of armament amongst the Powers not disarmed by Treaty is reasonably satisfactory and proportionate, reduction all round will not make any of them worse off as between themselves. Next, the doctrine that security can be obtained by competitive armaments must be exploded. It is manifestly untrue. All it means is that the country which has for the time being the greatest resources can make itself safe. But the moment there is anything like equality of resources this ceases to be true. France can make herself safe from attack by Switzerland. But Belgium could not by armaments alone render an attack by Holland foredoomed to failure. The French, and indeed most Continental countries, are quite ready to admit this. They concede—at least, the reasonable French do—that security by unilateral armament must ever be precarious. Many of them will even admit that the present artificial superiority over Germany cannot be perpetuated. Quite apart from the Treaty obligations or the rights that flow from membership of the League, no serious observer can doubt that sooner or later the sixty or seventy million Germans will insist on an armed strength proportionate to their numbers and resources.

But the French contend that reduction of armaments alone is no solution of the difficulty. History
shows that wars can be conducted with small forces
as well as big. Waterloo was fought by armies which
would have been considered almost negligible in
size measured by the standards of the late war, and
the same is true of many if not most of the decisive
battles of the world. Therefore they contend that in
order to obtain world order and security a system
must be established by which the general community
of nations will protect each of its constituents against
lawless aggression, just as each national society
secures the individuals who make it up against
assault and battery. They point out, as I have
stated, that this principle is conceded in Article 16
of the Covenant of the League of Nations, and they
ask that the ambiguities and imperfections which, as
they think, at present surround its terms, should be
removed. Once that is done they will be quite ready
to reduce their armaments.

The French contention is put forward with the
national force and " logic." To a large extent it
seems to me sound and true. But there is a good deal
to be said on the other side. In the first place,
security depends not solely or indeed chiefly on
material considerations. It is not true that the
extent to which law and order prevails in a country
depends mainly on the severity of its laws or the
numbers of its police. In the old days the laws
against agrarian crime in Ireland were more severe
and the police better armed than in England, yet
in that respect England was far freer from crime

than Ireland, because the public opinion of the two
countries differed diametrically on this point. In
other words, the supremacy of the law is a moral or
psychological far more than a material achievement.
The same is true internationally. Wars would not
exist but for the tradition which makes them a
legitimate method of enforcing the rights or interests
of any sovereign state. Get rid of that tradition and
international security is achieved. That is indeed
one of the chief arguments for international reduction
of armaments. It is a positive demonstration that the
countries of the world are abandoning the old anar-
chical theory that international rights depend on
international might. Even apart from disarmament,
much can be done and has been done to displace
the war traditions. The Covenant of the League,
the Treaties of Locarno, the Kellogg Pact, the proposed Treaty for Financial Assistance and other
minor international documents are founded on the
principle that aggressive war ought not to be used as
an instrument of national policy. Coincidentally with
this positive reprobation of war has gone the setting
up of alternative pacific methods of settling international disputes by the creation of the Permanent
Court of International Justice at The Hague, by the
extension of its jurisdiction to all international disputes of a legal character in the acceptance of the
Optional Clause, and more recently by the signature
of the General Act of Arbitration by which all international disputes of whatever kind are to be decided
by the Court of Justice or some other pacific tribunal.
   Therefore, in the first place we must reply to the

French that, in relying on armed strength for their security, they are ignoring the very essence of the problem. International disarmament will not decrease but, on the contrary, will greatly increase their security. If, however, they reply that their people are not sufficiently enlightened to appreciate and rely on this truth, then for my part I should be quite ready to discuss with them what transitional measures may be necessary to reassure them, provided they are ready to accept a real and effective instalment of Disarmament.

If I am asked what that means, I would reply by a reference to the Resolution adopted by the Federation of League of Nations Societies at Budapest this year. The annual meeting of this Federation is becoming increasingly important. It consists of representatives of the League of Nations Societies of all the principal countries in the world. Naturally, these bodies differ in importance. But in America, Japan, the United Kingdom and to a lesser degree France and some other countries, they are a real political force. This year they adopted without dissent a resolution on Disarmament drawn up by a Committee over which I had the honour to preside, and which was attended by four French representatives of weight and influence. It is too long to quote, but it will be found in the Appendix.

In substance it lays down that:

1. There is an absolute treaty obligation to reduce and limit armaments;

2. The present degree of international security is such that a first step amounting to a reduction

equivalent to 25 per cent. of the total cost of armaments might be taken;

3. If and when security is increased, further steps might be taken;

4. The principle of equality in armaments for all nations should be recognised;

5. First steps towards that equality should now be taken.

6. Among those steps might be the prohibition for all nations of those types of armaments forbidden by the Peace Treaties to the defeated countries, e.g. military air-craft, tanks, submarines, large land guns, warships over 10,000 tons.

One word about the last paragraph, and I have done. These armaments were forbidden to Germany on the ground that they were essentially aggressive in their nature. That is true, and if so, they ought to be equally forbidden to all the countries who have renounced war as an instrument of national policy, that is, practically all the civilised countries of the world. Some of these weapons represent a reaction to methods of barbarism of a terrible character, such as bomb-dropping on undefended cities. If national military aviation could be abolished it would mean an immense advance towards disarmament, and it might render possible the establishment of some kind of international air force sufficient to deal with the preoccupations of the French and other countries. Above all, it would be a guarantee to Germany that the other powers do recognise the justice of her claim to eventual equality in armaments. Without giving her some satisfaction on this point, and to France some satisfaction as to security, I am convinced that no settlement is possible.

Such, then, as I see it, is the present state, and such the immediate future of the Disarmament question, which evidently dominates the international horizon. I believe that you will agree with me that no Party, no political group, no Member of Parliament, can afford to disregard either the problem itself or the swelling volume of public opinion which demands a solution of it.

Peace was only half won at Versailles. The habit of war still sits entrenched amid this monstrous accumulation of the implements of destruction, and saps the mutual confidence of nations. It may well be that before very long the politician will be judged less by the dexterity with which he tilts against other politicians, than by the part which he has played in this noble and critical adventure of " winning the Peace."

Yours sincerely,

CECIL.

INTERNATIONAL FEDERATION OF LEAGUE OF NATIONS SOCIETIES

PLENARY CONGRESS

Budapest, May 1931

DISARMAMENT

Plenary Congress,

Recalling the resolutions adopted at its previous Congresses,

Considering that the Council of the League of Nations has definitely convened the first Disarmament Conference for February 2nd, 1932,

Endorses the recommendation of the French delegate, M. Aristide Briand, according to which:

"Between now and the opening of the Conference a great propaganda effort must be undertaken to enlighten the mind of the public on this important question."

Urges Societies to launch at once and to maintain without intermission until the opening of the Conference a methodical campaign with the public and their Governments; and

Adopts as the basis of it the following principles:

I

THE NECESSITY OF THE CONFERENCE CULMINATING IN A POSITIVE RESULT, VIZ. AN INTERNATIONAL CONVENTION

In this connection should be recalled:

1. the definite, unconditional pledge given by Members of the League of Nations in Article 8 of the Covenant to reduce armaments within certain limits and thereafter not to exceed these without the concurrence of the Council;

2. the formal promise given to the States disarmed under the Treaties that the exceptional regime applied to them is only a stepping stone to a general system of universal limitation and reduction;

3. the opinions expressed by statemen, economists, jurists, publicists regarding the mad race in armaments;

4. the pronouncements of contemporary historians upon the
extent to which this race was responsible for the last war;

5. the disastrous effect that a failure of the Conference would have
on the peace of the world.

II

NECESSITY FOR A SUBSTANTIAL REDUCTION IN ARMAMENTS

Article 8 of the Covenant provides that the limits fixed for armaments in each country shall be the " lowest consistent with national
safety and the enforcement by common action of international
obligations."

1. This safety is increased by the mere existence of the League of
Nations, which, in ten years, has gained experience, affirmed its
authority and perfected its organisation.

2. Since 1924 it has been recognised by the Assembly of the League
of Nations that progress in arbitration has generally implied progress
in security. Moreover, since 1928 the majority of the States have
adhered to the Optional Clause of the Statute of the Permanent
Court of International Justice; an increasing number have adhered,
or announce their intention of adhering, to the General Act of
Arbitration; special agreements of conciliation and arbitration have
been multiplied.

3. At Locarno, where special guarantees were given to certain
States, it was expressly declared that the entry in vigour of the
treaties and conventions there concluded would strengthen the
peace and security of Europe and would effectively hasten on the
Disarmament envisaged in Article 8 of the Covenant.

4. The outlawry of war was realised by the Paris Pact (Briand-
Kellogg).

5. A convention for financial assistance has been signed.

The situation is such as to justify even now a considerable reduction of armaments and the Federation esteems that, apart from the
reduction of personnel and material which should be effected, provided suitable proportions are laid down for the different States
under the conditions mentioned in Section IV hereunder, the Conference should achieve an all-round reduction of 25 per cent. on the
total amount budgeted for armaments.

III

DEVELOPMENT OF THE FACTORS FOR MORE COMPLETE DISARMAMENT

In order to facilitate still further reductions in armaments, means should be sought to strengthen the mutual guarantees of security and loyal observance of the treaties, as, for instance,

1. the universalisation of the League of Nations;

2. the adherence of all States to the General Act of Arbitration, the complement of the Paris (Briand-Kellogg) Pact;

3. the inclusion in the Covenant of the League of Nations of the definite prohibition to resort to war, subject to the general sanctions of the Covenant;

4. the reinforcement of the action of the Council in preventing war and in defining aggression;

5. failing this general measure, the extension of the system of special guarantees by special agreements for guarantee and security;

6. the international organisation of aviation under the auspices of the League of Nations in order to ensure to the Council the best means of communication and of supervision;

7. the prohibition of all preparation for chemical and bacteriological warfare;

8. an advance in moral disarmament through the abandonment of bellicose or aggressive propaganda and the consideration by the League of Nations of measures appropriate to that end.

IV

ADVANCE TOWARDS INTERNATIONAL EQUALITY

The International Federation of League of Nations Societies is convinced that it is indispensable that the League of Nations should officially recognise the principle of equality in disarmament between the " vanquished " and the " victorious " powers and that the 1932 Conference must begin to effect such equality.

This equality must not be attained by increasing armaments already reduced under the treaties but by the proportionate reduction of those of other States.

In any case, the Federation considers that the principle of limitation and reduction of armaments should be the same for all States and, consequently, that:

1. each State should be bound to limit the amount budgeted for its navy, army and air force;

2. the prohibition of certain material, naval, land or air, enjoined in the treaties should apply to all States signatory to the Convention;

3. the observance of the obligations thus contracted by the States should be ensured by a Permanent Disarmament Commission established at the seat of the League of Nations and exercising its control equally over all nations.

A LETTER
TO A SISTER

ROSAMOND LEHMANN

DEAR—,

We got back home this very day from our summer holiday. Here am I, sitting up late after a long journey to write and tell you so. Don't be alarmed— I'm not going to tell you where we went and what we saw. Holidays, if you enjoy them, have no history. All the same, Chartres, Poitiers—but no, I couldn't even if I wanted to, even if you wanted to hear.

Home again.... Settling in again for a country winter.... These facts seemed to hold no undertone of emotion. They were as sober and sedate as the voice and motion of the train that puffed us by slow stages into our branch line station. I thought about—domestic arrangements; at least I suppose I did: thoughts that are such second nature to you and me by now, that the difficulty is to stop thinking them. "If only I could afford" ... we say, "If I weren't out of practice" ... "If I weren't sure Ellen would give notice" ... "I could leave the children." ... In brief, we are not really young any more.

Do you remember that sharp glittering black and white satin lady coming to tea with our mother ages ago, smoking (horrors!) a cigarette, and urging upon her the need for Self-Expression, Self-Development—and our mother murmuring "these vampires" as she looked at us? The word was new to us, but it sounded rude and derogatory; and, though she smiled, we felt wounded, self-conscious, unwanted and indignant. Do you realise that we are where

our mother was when she said that? Self-
Development is now old hat; but the lady, so
abreast, so free, so inferiority-complex-producing—
she's the same, we've both poured out tea for her;
and we too repeat ourselves as we sit behind the
teapot and deprecate our bonds. I wonder by the
way if it's a delusion that the children aren't *quite* the
same? Would one find them nowadays playing, for
instance, Lady O'Blang and Little Christopher (do
you remember?) or Bad Bertha and Good Little
Mary? Society isn't what it was, surely it has lost its
glamour in the nursery; the thrill of virtue and
wickedness is less, rewards and punishments are out
of fashion? Children are tougher now, I do believe. I
can imagine Vampires being a favourite game.

But to go back: the symbolic little train squealed
to a standstill and dropped us off, and the station
taxi painstakingly deposited us at our front door.
Then, as I need hardly tell you, there were trunks to
unpack, stores to order in, people to see, one or two
alterations and repairs to inspect.... Of course I
am perfectly well aware that I have never really
grasped the elements of it all—that I am nothing, in
fact, but a day-dreaming fraud and muddler.
Perhaps you have found this out long ago? Perhaps
you know that in me exists a great and unbridgeable
gulf between the fact and the performance; between
being mistress of a house and controlling its internal
economy; between clothes and the making and
mending of them; between loving my garden and
digging and planting in it. Do *you* feel the same in

your heart of hearts? When we exchange recipes and say how high the books are, do you feel a secret twinge of guilt? Or don't you? If not, I shall regret this confession for the rest of my life! But this is the hour for truth.

When, as I was saying, by some process mysterious to, although in appearance emanating from, myself, the machinery had once more been set in motion—when, that is to say, my superficialities had been tacitly supplemented by the thoroughness, my darkness politely submerged beneath the noonday common sense of others; when in each vital spot of the house the wheel had started to go round again with a mild little hum and motion—(the motion of peace to the householder, the sound of silence)—then I had nothing more to do. So I walked round the garden. And there was nothing left in the beds but a clump or two of Michaelmas daisies and a few decaying dahlias and, besides these, a patch of those crushed-raspberry, button chrysanthemums, prim and stiff-standing among their crisp grey leaves: unreal plants these, parading a simple Victorian charm, a flavour as fascinatingly period as patchwork, or wax and shell decorations, or the early poems of the Sitwells.

Still all was flat, colourless. I couldn't remember what had been before, in summer—or see what was to be. Then, after supper, I came into my bedroom and it was dark; and with the thought: "Already!" I had a sudden flick of surprise and confusion—the first stir since my return, of an inward mood; realis-

ing, with more emotion than such inevitable, such
platitudinous facts warrant, that the days were
drawing in, that the season had changed, Autumn
was here.

Then all at once, standing in the dark, I had—
how can I describe it, communicate it to you at all? I
had a curious experience. Not a mystical one, not a
vision. (Do you remember that frothing hot-
gospelling temperance-man with the strawberry
nose whom we listened to once, years ago, in Cambridge market-square? Infinitely impervious to his
eloquence, those marketing faces gazed while he
told them how he himself had found salvation when
going upstairs late one night—drunk, he manfully
admitted—and seeing "a great light in the
bathroom." It seemed such a simple yet tactful way
of turning a person's attention to the importance of
water—so different from God's usual bludgeoning
methods.)

But don't be flippant, don't disbelieve. I didn't
see a great light. Yet I was pierced all of a sudden by
some penetrating evocation. It wasn't an image or a
sound or a scent, though it seemed to hold something of all these, some blend of sensory impressions
that I couldn't fathom. It was more like an echo of
some complicated state of mind, some old poignant
mixture of emotions. It had come and gone in a
second, I suppose, and I was left alone. Yes, I felt
alone, and I was conscious of the mist, the wind
blowing out the curtain, autumn pressing up
against the window. I felt freed—and a little dazed,

as if I had been pressing my shoulder against a
jammed door, and had unexpectedly burst it open.
All summer was before me again, alive, and I
flashed over it rapidly, with a crystalline sharpness
and lucidity.

This year, it had been a bustling sort of season. I
thought of moving into our house, the packing-cases
and hammers, the mops and scrubbing brushes, the
heavenly mixing of paints and distempers, the day-
long absorption in bundles of entrancing patterns,
the anxious matchings and desperate decisions—all
the pleasure and fatigue involved in the acquiring of
possessions.

I thought of all our guests—of the TALK there
had been . . . discussions on the lawn, arguments at
the breakfast-table, debates at midnight, dissen-
sions in the bath. What enthusiasm for painting,
what views on writing, what sidelong, discreet but
yearning glances at enigmatic music; what inability
to stick to the point—and what dreadfully ribald
jokes, what shouts of laughter!

I thought of the blissful fortnight of hot weather—
of picnics, and deck-chairs in the shade, of packing
into the car to go down to bathe before dinner, to
plunge from the trodden grass bank into the warm
lit evening water, of the infinitesimal flicks of gold-
dusty midge-swarms; the glimmer, the clinging
touch, like a soft threat on the limbs, of the ribbon-
weeds; the swallows and willow-herb, and the
reflections.

I thought of the garden's particular surprises: the

big queer-coloured poppies that sprang up un-
awares, to our astonishment, and rioted over tended
seeds and careful cuttings in flaunting independence; the orange lilies growing wild in the long
grass, the white owls that nested in the walnut tree,
lovely in the dusk and swooping, crying all night
with noises as weird, as raucous, as dire, as indifferent to human pity as the noises issuing from the
throats of beaters in autumn woods.

I thought of the extraordinary charm of my baby,
naked in the sun, plumping and browning on his rug;
of summer frocks, of dishes of raspberries and mul-
berries, of picking a bowlful of peaches from the wall
one hot evening. The deep bowl is made of fruit-
wood, silver-brown with age; and old brick and fruit
seemed blended one into the other, so warm, so
yellow and rose, so ripe were both. It was very satisfactory, that mixture of fruit and wood and brick.

I thought of that last night before we left home for
our holiday—sitting late in the breathless indigo
garden, staring at tree-shapes, hearing nightjars
and the restless barking of dogs, while the coloured
play of lightning went on and on, now here, now
there, in different quarters of the sky, as if in Oxford,
then in Wantage, then in Henley, they were letting
of rockets. I remember thinking that night that I
was sitting still and letting a root sink down into my
new surroundings for the first time. I had been so
busy over trifles; I had imposed myself on the
welcome house and neglected to pay my respects to
it; and I felt conscious of being watched from behind

by an ancient and ruminative eye—an eye that had seen a lot in its two hundred years of time and couldn't be bamboozled by external activities and agitations. I felt graceless, I remember—superficial and rebuked. I thought of the generations succeeding one another within these walls, of births and weddings and funerals—heavens know what dramas of life and death. I thought of the initials cut in the wall by the front door above the date 1750, and wondered whose they were, and suddenly saw living fingers carving them, a flesh-and-blood figure, dressed in 1750 fashion, leaning there in the sun, brown warm hand at work, while lightly, daydreaming, whistling under his breath, he scratched out on the stone the symbol of his identity—set down as idle "I am."

He had been here ... as I was now; and then vanished for ever ... as I shall be soon.

These intimations of mortality which visit me rather frequently, are they a last— the very last—growing-pain? Before long a crack will show—will it?—in the anguished self-importance of one's ego. We shall be reasonable beings, and wake up in the middle of the night and say: "It is even so. It doesn't matter any more."

Shall we?

Well, I am not, I shall never be what I would like to be, that's certain: something absolutely solid, something active and exact, of the nature of a biologist, a physicist, an economist or a surgeon. Nor doubtless shall I ever realise my grandest daydream: to find by chance in some old trunk or lumber-room an ancient manuscript volume written in an arch hand; and, reading, find the matter packed close, rich with every conceivable kind of treasure of self-revelation—thoughts, griefs, fears—names flashing out—an inimitable turn of humorous phrase—and think: this is ... surely this must be ... and then know it *was*—Shakespeare's private Journal! (But your ambition was sublimer: to be the Christ of animals; to die for them, so that none should ever suffer any more.) I am nothing but a screen for chaotic images—images assembling, blurring, dissolving—with here and there an attempt at synchronisation—husky indifferent records of other people's voices, fragmentary echoes of laughter and weeping.

A bustling summer it had been, a domestic contented summer, full of change and variety, but empty of experience.... Doesn't it sound pleasant? It was. Oh, it was so *safe*! ... Yes, that's it, that's the point. Now that I am alone again how strange that seems—to be so safe, to be always accompanied. Why, it's years now since I've been alone. Tomorrow it won't be so. To-morrow my safety will have surged round me again; I shall almost have forgotten what it's like to look back from an uninhabited island, as I do tonight, over a world of seas to the sunny and populous mainland.

Do you see now what it was, that complicated pang I spoke of? It was a ghost rising up, crying *Remember!* as it swooned out and vanished; it was a rocket going up in the dark, lighting the waste land I'd left; it was a warning.... *Not so very long now till all this is over and you're old and living alone again....* The reality of that strikes me to the marrow; but how can I express it?

Living alone: as in girlhood, before one was broken in upon.... Do you remember that waiting?—that being caged up away from the rest of humankind, the dome of many-coloured glass pressing close all round one? How stifling the air was! One peered through the rich distorting crystal at bewildering vistas tinged with lurid dyes. Awful accidents there were: one hadn't enough space; one had to move warily, delicately, and one couldn't. The violence of some clumsy, unpremeditated, unaccountable movement sent one sprawling, left one badly damaged among a rain of splinters; and still there was no release. One stared out at the passing procession, hating, fearing, adoring it—crying: "Nobody knows what I'm like. Nobody's going to stop and listen. In all the crowd no one will wait for me and walk in step...." As I look back it seems a voluptuous pain. We don't get it any more. I shouldn't mind a taste of it—would you?

Well—Time that let us out, will draw down the shutter once again. Behind the brittle panel we shall sit, quietly now, and look out upon the world. We shall see all, our children and all, through a glass—not too darkly, I hope—just through uncoloured glass. It won't be so bad really as long as we can take our places at about the same time and sit side by side.

The wind's getting up again. I wish you were here. I don't like being alone. Do you remember:

> *Now first as I shut the door,*
>   *I was alone*
> *In the new house; and the wind*
>   *Began to moan.*

And *old at once was the house; And I was old* ... and then:

> *All was foretold me, naught*
>   *Could I foresee;*
> *But I learned how the wind would sound*
> *After these things should be.*

Really that says it all, doesn't it? Now I come to think of it, I dare say the whole thing was the fault of the wind again—running to hide in the curtain as I came in, catching me out again, as it always did. (In some Diary or Letters I read recently, an invalid speaks of a touch of wind round the heart, and I thought: "I know. I've had it as long as I can remember, and it's a painful complaint.")

From far away and long ago rises the wind ... and time spins topsy-turvy in its wake. I remember what we sprang from—and how it will all end. I look back to the beginning and it's all dark and the wind's blowing ... snatching away the frail hold.... Gone, gone! ... whirling down infinite giddy labyrinths of self-loss and disintegration. I see in the darkness the flicker of the nursery fire, the glint on the brass rail. I see someone move, bend

down—dark back, dark stooping head and
shoulders. It is our father. I hear him singing to us.
All along out along down along lea. Magic syllables. . . .
What else can I hear? . . . The hot and morbid
burden of a merry-go-round, the hoot of the last
steamer, the regatta band playing from up the river,
mournfully gay, romantic. These are midsummer
sounds. I hear the train come in towards the middle
of eternal winter nights, and shunt and whistle and
go off again; blessed comforting train, punctually
bringing the longed-for tidings: that ordinary accustomed things are still there, light will come back, the
Last Trump will not sound to-night.

What do you remember?

I look forward and I see—ah, now I've forgotten
what I see. It will be dark, I suppose, and the wind
will blow. But a moment ago—

You know what it's like, coming round from an
anæsthetic. . . . Wrenched suddenly from some
other element or dimension where a second before
you had your being, existing harmoniously as a fish
in water—suspended still in an uneasy vacuum—
you cry: "Wait a minute! I'll tell you. I was—where
was I—" and then to your surprise the nurse is
saying loudly, encouragingly—"It's all right,
dear"—and then just as you are about to catch at
and grasp the astonishing experience in all its enormous significance and value, it's gone— . . . Well,
that's what's happened to me. It's gone. A moment
ago I could have prophesied, I could have said a lot.
But now it's gone. I've come round.

Oh, but what *was* it all about? "Nothing," says
the nurse, brisk, soothing. It was a dream, I
suppose, a fantasy, a wild-goose chase. And I
thought—I thought it was *about life*. I took up my
pen in haste to give you, you only, a confidential tip;
and behold, it explodes like a bubble in a microsco-
pic and ephemeral flurry ... returns no answer, but
disappears *with a curious perfume and most melodious
twang*.

One is left wanting to whimper. The strain was so
intense, one felt so near.... Impotence flows like an
ache, a sickening weakness over brain and limbs.

I must compose myself and think of some comforting maxims.

I don't know whether it's mere chance, or if it's
because in old days people were born with the
secret—and now have lost it—but I can recall no
historical instance of inquiry into the subject of *life*.
What is truth?—What is love?—but never, till now,
What is life? It is not my voice but the voice of Virginia Woolf that I hear asking the question. She
asks, but she gives not an answer; and doubtless her
American fan mail reveals many a painstaking and
troubled mind. "*You ask, What is life? but give no reply.
Is this because you are yourself in doubt? Or can I take it that
your next work will furnish a clue? I am not a frivolous
novel-reader, but a serious student of life, so please tell me.*"
Or possibly, distrustful of something airy, discon-
certing, faintly mocking in the tone, they give her
the correct answer: It is real, it is earnest.

Naturally you reply at once: "Quite the contrary..." but, you know, critically examined, that doesn't quite do either.

"Life is purpose, activity. It is reaching the North Pole, finding the Pharaoh in his tomb, the sunken trireme; it is flying alone to Australia." I think: "You haven't even begun to know, you never will. Never will you man the lifeboat, shoot the tiger as he springs, ride the winner of the Grand National."

What do you think about it? Things happen to you more frequently than they do to me. You are an enterprising, courageous character: one who can cope. You have leaped into a flooded river to save the cat. You have been bolted with, and thrown out hunting. (*Le cheval est un animal fougueux.* I never could trust one.) You have been in a motor smash. You have set yourself on fire in the middle of the night. In fact, I see now you've had a very eventful life. Whereas my record is simply pitiful. One fall out of the apple-tree, one fall into the fish-pond; a few bee-stings (no wasps)—this about completes my list of accidents. As for my one adventure—I mean that one called A Twenty-Mile Tramp in a Blizzard, or My Most Exciting Christmas (I think you've heard me mention it before?)—well, even that is getting very dim. Did I truly rise up from unconsciousness one Xmas eve, after having been flung from a snowbound van in the far far North, and fortified with whisky float over snowhills and skim down sheer frozen valleys, infinitely powerful and exhilarated, and see the moon riding as full as full in dark blue deeps of air at half-past three in the afternoon? I know I thought at the time: "This is life indeed." I'm getting sleepy. Good night. I must go to bed.

PS. I take up my pen again to scribble one more line. A few moments ago, leaning out of the window to breathe the autumn scented dusk, I had another curious experience. Again I felt myself *silently addressed*: but this time the voice was not backward-pointing, nostalgic, it seemed to be as if coming from the future, as if from the cave, the subterranean place wherein hides a portion—perhaps the major part—of my own identity, still unconsolidated, amorphous, mostly sleeping or drowsing. An authentic voice, rather anxious, but above all *intensely expectant* I was being told ... something foreknown—that there will be no sitting down together, exchanging memories and illusions self-indulgently; that I am still in the dream time; that one day I shall leave it, or be thrust out of it; that I might get lost. For a moment I felt extraordinarily lonely. I wonder, where will *you* be? Still within call, I hope.

THE
FRENCH PICTURES
A LETTER TO HARRIET

RAYMOND MORTIMER

with the compliments of

The University of Georgia Press

Athens, Georgia 30602   (404) 542-2830

Title:	The Hogarth Letters
Author:	Introduction by Hermione Lee
Publication date:	March 4, 1986
Price:	$20.00 (cloth)

We would appreciate receiving

two copies of your review.

Better Business Bureau
of Metropolitan NY
INC.

---

257 Park Ave
533-6200

6 Gordon Place,
W.C.1.

DEAREST HARRIET,

I loved my week in the country. You were
evidently designed to be a hostess, from the days
when you used to invite me to your house (a
tent-shaped willow-tree) and give me ginger-
nuts and pour out tea, which was water from
the garden-tap with bull's-eyes in it that obsti-
nately refused to melt. Thank you and Tom for
everything, including the weather, which you
must have ordered with all the other good things
from Fortnum's, and remember that Dick is to
come to a play with me next holidays. He
promised.

I didn't read my novel in the train, though it
was by Miss Dorothy Sayers. I thought instead
about your last shouted words, as the train
coughed its way out of the station: " Then we'll
see you after Christmas when we come up for the
Exhibition." And all the way up to Paddington
I was wondering—you've never minded what I
said since we quarrelled on the respective merits
of my Swiss nurse and your English Nanny—I
was wondering what pleasure on earth you expected to get from walking round thirteen gloomy
rooms hung with French pictures. There will be

thousands of people making the same weary
promenade, and museums are not made less
depressing by being crowded. Will you get any
satisfaction save that of having done what it is
thought right and desirable to do, of being able to
make a little conversation on the subject with
Dr. O'Flaherty's wife next time you see her ?
Won't you just struggle back very much exhausted,
and go on with your ordinary life as if you had
been to the Eton and Harrow Match or Eleven
o'clock Service ?

Now I'd like you to get a kick out of the Show,
such a kick that you'd leave Burlington House a
changed person, or rather with changed eyes, like
a motorist suddenly converted by dropping into
your village church one morning (if you can
imagine anyone being converted by Matins and
Mr. Cumberbatch's preaching) and at once setting fire to his motor and becoming a saint. I'd
like you, I mean, to walk out of the Exhibition
and wander along the streets for hours, forgetting
all your engagements, simply drunk with the
pleasure of using your eyes, gloating over the
flopping of the flags in Bond Street, and the green
ivory knives in the old silver shops, and the
stream-line motors, and the pillars of St. Martin's
Church, smirched by the soot on the lee side, and
the wrinkles on the beggars, and the haze which

makes Whitehall from the St. James's Park lake
look like the pleasure domes of Xanadu. And in
the evening at the theatre you'd be astonished by
the shape of the 'cellos and fiddles as if you had
never seen one before, and you'd refuse to take a
taxi back to Dover Street, in spite of the rain, for
the pleasure of seeing the sky-signs reflected in the
wet streets and in the glass of the shop-windows.
And back at home the next afternoon even your
beloved garden would look different and a
thousand times more exciting, perspective playing
the oddest tricks with the shape of your clipped
hedges, the bare boughs of the elms beyond the
tennis-court making a formal pattern, and—is it
possible—the yawning space where one yew has
died in the avenue you planted, showing itself as
a heaven-sent balance to the giant poplar. For a
moment, in fact, the new pleasure would prove
stronger than your gardening pride.

Actually of course, when you leave the French
Exhibition, you will collapse into a chair at
Stewart's, ask for " a fresh pot of China Tea," and,
being a peculiarly honest woman, thank Heaven
that *that's* over. You enjoy music (you sing
Schubert admirably and you know it), and I've
never known you taken in by a second-rate book.
You were highly indignant when they ran a line
of pylons across the moor (I'm not so sure that I

agree with you about that, but certainly you were
very sincere in finding them detestable). And you
arrange to admiration the colours in your her-
baceous borders. Finally, there is nothing ugly in
your house. Yet you don't use your eyes, I maintain. And if there is nothing ugly in your house,
it is because there is nothing (except the baths)
made since 1830. "Harriet has such marvellous
taste," your friends say, but your taste, where sight
is concerned, is merely negative. You would have
the sense not to have an Orpen in your room, but
still less would you have a Matisse. You don't see
much to choose between a Gainsborough and a
Romney, except that the clothes are a little
different, and at the French Exhibition you will
like Pater as much as Watteau. Don't they both
paint the same prettily dressed people in the same
charming parks ?

Use your eyes, Harriet, use your eyes.

But, I wondered, looking at the spire as the train
drew into Salisbury, and thinking of Constable,
but how can I persuade her to ? One learns to
use one's eyes, one can't be taught. For the understanding of French painting it is useful to know
about François 1er and Port Royal and Madame de
Pompadour and the Romantic Movement and the
Goncourts. And all this you do know. But when
you go to Burlington House, I would like you for

an hour to forget all your history. You might
catch hold of what I want you to get, if you could
look at the pictures as if they were outside time.
Imagine, I mean, that all these painters are alive,
each working independently to make the object
he desires. Otherwise you'll find yourself looking
for influences instead of looking at pictures; you
will recognise a period or school, and miss the
individual; you will use your intelligence upon
the things described, and you will not use your
senses upon the paint that describes them.

Don't be frightened: I'm not going to give you
a lecture on æsthetics. Other people have done
that far better than I could. (If you haven't read
Clive Bell and Roger Fry, do so at once.) I'll only
say this: the subject of a picture is often interesting
and sometimes important. But what really
matters is the object, the picture itself. And that
is why I want you, at any rate the first time you
go to the Exhibition, to forget everything you ever
heard about French history or French painters,
and to look at the paintings as a child might—
"Aren't those pretty colours ? ", " What a funny
shape! ". The first feeling I want you to have is
surprise. If you could get that, the rest might so
easily follow.

You know how completely habit blinds us. If
we do a thing very often, we cease to be conscious

of doing it. You are so familiar yourself with the
profile of the moor on the horizon, that you don't
now notice it, save when some strange light touches
it, or when a stranger starts to gush. In the same
way you are blinded by familiarity to the appearance of forks and kodaks and apples and egg cups.
A painter never is. He goes on being surprised.
He is a man who can see objects divorced for the
moment from their purpose, origin, and meaning.
He sees like a man blind from birth who suddenly
recovers his sight. It would be the most thrilling
experience to spend one day seeing the world as
Claude or Renoir saw it. If you are really to
enjoy pictures, you too must somehow shake your
blinkers off.

When you visit the French Exhibition, I'd like
you to go straight to the Nineteenth Century
Rooms. If the pictures here don't surprise you,
you are lost indeed. They are not only good, very
good, some of them I think as good as any pictures
ever painted, but they are probably less familiar
to you than the older masters. (Our Christmas
card manufacturers have not yet started using
Manets and Cézannes.) Moreover, in nineteenth
century France, painters were more excited than
ever before by the mere look of things. They gazed
wide-eyed at commonplace buildings, at newspapers, at tall hats, just as I want you to gaze at

pictures. Catch their astonishment, as you might
catch the measles, and then you will be able to
see, but really to see, the Watteaus and Chardins
and Bouchers.

Now let's pretend, Harriet, as we used to when
we played Red Indians, let's pretend that you've
caught the infection, got back the use of your
eyes. Like the child in Hans Andersen, you see
the Emperor without his new clothes, you see his
body, what a surprising, complicated shape it is.
The next point is to discover which shapes you
enjoy. And once your eyes are open, I don't
think you should find this very difficult. You like
your Hepplewhite chairs, and you've banished the
rose-wood furniture that your mother bought
when she married—fifty years ago, wasn't it?—
at Maple's. Pictures are not so very different
from chairs: you prefer your Hepplewhite, not
because it does its job any better—the Maple
chairs are just as solid and just as comfortable
—but because it is more beautiful. The lines
are more graceful. You recognise in fact that it
is better designed. In the same way when you
look at chintzes for new curtains or loose covers,
there are a lot of stuffs which are equally
durable, and you finally decide on one because
you think that in line and colour it is the best
design.

Have you ever looked at pictures as if they were samples of stuff ? I don't suppose you have, but that is just what I want you to do. For every picture is a pattern, every good picture, I mean, and the beauty of a picture depends more than you have ever dreamed upon its merit as a pattern. Of course in a picture it is far less obvious and immensely more complicated than in a chintz. But if you look at the large Bouchers in the Wallace Collection, for instance, or at any of the more decorative seventeenth and eighteenth century pictures in the Exhibition, you will be able clearly to detect the pattern. The French inherited from renaissance Italy a certain tradition of design which they developed but did not abandon till about the end of the eighteenth century. This was not a recipe for making good pictures—there ain't no such thing—but it usually prevented them from making very ugly things, either pictures or buildings or stuffs. Certain simple rules were observed, the pattern balanced. It was left to the bad painters of the nineteenth century to make pictures with no more shape than casual snapshots, pictures in which the lines and colours represented places or persons and had no harmony of their own.

This matter of design or composition is difficult to write about but it is of enormous importance in

French painting, in all painting for that matter. You have read Racine and Baudelaire, some Voltaire and a little Renan. I take the most divergent individuals, but how thoughtfully planned is the writing of them all, how elegantly constructed. It's the same with French pictures. You'll understand best what I mean by looking at the Poussins. And when I say " looking " I mean it. The first secret of enjoying pictures is to have a good long stare. In face of one which you like or which you believe to be good, you must try to do your bit as enthusiastically as the painter did his. All art is a collaboration between the artist and his audience, he is sending you messages, so that you must keep your eyes open, as you do for your partner's discards at bridge, and use your imagination to reconstruct what is going on in his mind. It is fatal to be passive, and to take it for granted that a picture is what it is. Ask yourself why the painter made it like that; why he placed the principal figure so far to the left of the centre, what the large round pot is doing in the right-hand corner, why the floating scarf is just the colour that it is. The figure bending down in the background certainly doesn't contribute anything to the " story " of Actæon—ask yourself why it is there, and soon you'll see it is essential to the pattern. Sometimes you'll be stumped, but once you start asking such questions, you'll find pictures twenty times more interesting.

And with no pictures is the answer so easy as with Poussin's. He was the most deliberate of all the Old Masters, he left nothing to chance. He bent one figure forward, another back, stretched a satyr's leg exactly parallel with a recumbent column, balanced an arched back with a semicircular drapery, and froze a kneeling nymph into a right-angled triangle. At first sight you might easily think his pictures dull. The female figures are rarely the type we now find attractive, their postures are anything but spontaneous, and it is often difficult to see his sumptuous colours. (The pictures in the Louvre are for the most part covered, like *boeuf à la mode*, with dark brown jelly.) But once you see what the artist was up to, he is as exciting as Palladio or Bach. Of course geometry is not enough. Learning all Boileau by heart would not enable a man to write one couplet of " Phèdre." Poussin is a grand master to study because the framework of his pictures is always so powerful and clear. But it is the working out which matters, a conglomeration of touches which words are quite incapable of defining.

Incidentally that is what makes writing about pictures so futile. What painting says, can be said only in paint. Writing about Poussin is like play-

ing the piano about Milton. But I'm enjoying
writing to you, so I'd better not dwell upon that.

I've suggested that you should look at the
Impressionists to catch their sense of what a surprising place the world is. I've suggested that you
should look at the Bouchers, and still more at the
Poussins, to get yourself interested in the way a
picture is composed. (It's the greatest folly to
try to look at very many pictures at one go. I
advise you never to spend more than an hour at a
time in a museum.) Now I want you to look at
the Chardins and Courbets, so that you may
recognise what the French call " la belle matière,"
the quality or texture of paint. This is the most
difficult of all pictorial virtues to describe in
words, its appeal is entirely sensuous. To get hold
of what I mean, you must forget what the picture
represents, you must almost rub your nose against
the paint as if it were a beautiful fur or something
good to eat. Have you ever noticed the beauty of
a Brie cheese, with its brown and white rind ?
I think this is more like really rich paint than
anything else in our ordinary life. The red
mottlings on the dry russet of a Cox's Orange
Pippin have again something of the same beauty.
But it is difficult to find an analogy in other
materials, because what one likes in any material
is largely its peculiarity, the thing about it, I

mean, which makes it different from other
materials, the sponginess of the sponge, the velveti-
ness of velvet. Horsehair, shantung, American
cloth, crocodile-skin, each of them has its own
peculiar character. So has the material of which
a picture is made, oil paint. But whether its
character is pleasant or unpleasant depends upon
the way it is applied. The varying thickness of
the paint, the lines made by the brush hairs, the
multiplicity of colour hidden in what at a distance
seems a uniform smear—all this contributes to the
quality and texture. Compare a Chardin Still
Life (seen from very close) with a Dutch one, or a
Courbet with a Raeburn—you can't miss the
difference. Another instance. You may know
Sargent's " Carnation, Lily, Lily Rose " in the
Tate. (Wasn't it Whistler who re-christened it
" Darnation Silly, Silly Pose " ?)   It is an
astonishing piece of conjuring. From a distance
of a few yards, it seems a most detailed piece of
realistic painting. Look into it, and the petals that
seem so carefully outlined are just smudges of
colour. The same is true of many Impressionist
pictures. But—and this is my point—in Renoir
or Sisley the smudges are pleasant in themselves,
apart from the effect which they coalesce to make
at a distance. In the Sargent the smudges are
thoroughly unpleasant. I particularly want you to

catch on to this, for texture is not only intensely enjoyable but a great test. You can tell a Watteau or a Guardi from an imitation by one of their followers instantly by just this quality. Similarly this explains why the best coloured reproductions of oil paintings are so unlike their originals. To get them right you'd need to make a cast of the picture's surface, like a relief map. Moreover this love of paint for paint's sake has become increasingly important in each century. Fresco does not give the same opportunity for richness of texture as oil, and similarly oil as used by the Primitives is less rewarding than it is in later pictures. Titian and Rembrandt in their old age managed miracles of texture, and Rubens at his best is sumptuous. But nowhere will you find greater richness than in the French painters, Chardin, Corot, Courbet, Renoir, Cézanne.

At this point, Harriet, you will say "And what about Ingres?": at least, I hope you will. Probably the most unpopular of all great painters is Rubens, in fact you can tell whether a person really cares for painting by asking him his feelings about Rubens. It's all because he liked the women he painted to be fat. I've no doubt he also liked the women he loved to be fat. It's a great mistake, I fancy, and a modern invention for a painter to concentrate on models which he

does not find humanly attractive. Somebody said
you ought to paint a door-knob as if it were a girl.
A lot of our most respectable contemporaries paint
girls as if they were door-knobs. (I have not noticed
this Puritanism in the Old Masters.) Anyhow,
since the sixteenth century the fashion in figures
has changed, and as a result the Man in the Street
hates Rubens. But once forget about figures, and
you must love Rubens, the dash of his designs,
the sunset splendour of his colour, his witchcraft
in the use of paint. Monsieur Ingres is a very
different kettle. He really is difficult to enjoy.
" Dreary colours," you say, " and a surface like a
chromotype." In fact you think his texture
horrible. (I feel encouraged. You have evidently
been looking at the Chardins and Courbets as I
asked you to.) It very often is horrible. He draws
like an angel, like Picasso, like Raphael, but that
is not the point. I'd like to suggest that there can
be a beauty in smooth paint as well as in rough,
though I agree that it is a lot harder to get the
hang of it. Ingres has it in his best work, Botticelli
had it, so I think did Petrus Christus. I'll agree
that his theories were a horrid handicap to Ingres.
But with one hand tied behind his back he did
better than almost anyone with both hands free.
He is an odd instance of a reactionary genius.
Freedom of handling had been growing in the

eighteenth century: Fragonard, following Rubens, developed something very like Impressionism. Ingres, like Metternich, tried to stop the flood, and, like Mrs. Partington, he failed. Later the Pre-Raphaelites in England tried, with infinitely less talent, to do the same thing. The history of nineteenth-century painting is the history of ever growing freedom.

There are still people who believe that freedom of handling is a sign of incompetence. "Why don't they finish their pictures?" is a question you will probably hear some dear old lady asking in front of the Impressionists. And her companion will no doubt answer, "Because they can't." And then they will both trot back to admire the Clouets, which they feel, not altogether wrongly, are more like dear Sir John Millais's works. In point of fact the Impressionists painted as they did because they were intensely anxious to represent the visible world. And it is only by the Impressionist technique that the appearance of things can be at all truthfully rendered. Monet's picture of the Gare St. Lazare is far more like the appearance of a railway station than Frith's "Paddington." The Impressionists, you see, were careful not to state all the facts, because they knew that when we look at a person or a street, we do not perceive all the facts. It is only when we focus on a small part of the person or the street that we can see that part in detail. No one has ever seen a figure as Madox Brown or Burne Jones painted it. Frith's " Derby Day " represents not what he could see at one moment, but a recapitulation of the various things he saw at a number of different moments. The Impressionists, on the other hand, painted what their eyes with no alteration of focus could perceive. If representation be the main object of the painter, they win all along the line. The odd thing is that it is just the people (for instance the two old ladies) who think pictures ought above all things to be " like," who also have most attacked the Impressionists. It was indeed to make their pictures " like," that they carried freedom of handling further than it had ever been carried, except by Turner. The best Impressionists, however, were good painters, not because of their skill in representation, but because they had the artist's instinct for rhythm and order. Even so they were often dangerously over-interested in putting down on canvas exactly what they saw. Like Turner, they toppled over into anarchy. A recall to order became necessary. The man who made it was Cézanne.

It's rather bad manners to say " I told you so." But for those of us who can remember the First Post-Impressionist Exhibition, the French Show

has a special spiteful charm. Do you remember
the Van Gogh reproductions I had in my rooms
at Oxford in 1913 ? You were almost the only
person who wasn't rude about them. The
Primrose League Dames do not regard Lenin with
greater horror than the Royal Academicians have
regarded Cézanne. And now instead of hanging
him, they have got to hang his pictures. Most of
them, it is true, have a hearty and rational dislike
of the Old Masters, and I take leave to doubt
whether the President can tell the difference
between a Giorgione and a Guido Reni. But they
have made vast sums by letting their premises for
the Dutch and Persian and Italian Exhibitions,
and this time I presume they will make even more,
as instead of getting a fat rent they are running
the show themselves and getting a share in the
profits. It's a scandal that they are given one of
the most expensive sites in London rent-free, but
at least they have to pay for it out of their self-
respect. They now have to sponsor Cézanne. I
can imagine no greater humiliation.

You won't find it difficult to appreciate Cézanne.
His design is as solid as Poussin's, his texture is as
rich as any a painter ever achieved. He had little
success in his life, because he lived at a time when
even the best painters were supremely interested in
representation. His aim was to apply the freedom

in the use of paint which the Impressionists had
developed to compositions arranged in the tradition of the Old Masters. He achieved his aim, and
has now taken his place among the chief glories of
European painting. His influence has been
prodigious, like Masaccio's: except for one or two
septuagenarians, I doubt if there is a good painter
alive who has not been affected by him. And one
reason why I am so keen for you to start liking
pictures is that painting to-day is the healthiest of
the arts. It is important not to draw all one's
pleasure from the past: to do so is to begin that
retreat from reality which ends in madness. Now
there is no poet alive, I think, who can reasonably
be placed with the very great, with Pope or
Wordsworth or Baudelaire. Nor have we a
novelist of Balzac's stature, or Tolstoy's or
Proust's. And in music also there seems to be a
mass of talent but precious little genius. Architecture at last is stirring from sleep, but the best of
our architects are still in that protestant mood
which distrusts pleasure. But painting is alive,
certain of itself, and full of gusto. You can't give
artists marks as if they were prize cattle or candidates for the Indian Civil. But unless all the hours
I have spent looking at pictures have been wasted,
Picasso is a really big man—you could put his
work in any room in any museum in the world

without dwarfing it. And Matisse is a greater
colourist than any Venetian. And Braque in his
way is just as good as Chardin was in his. And in
England we have never before had such a good
decorative painter as Duncan Grant. So if at the
French Show you catch on to what painting is
about, you will find the modern world a much
more respectable place.

I'd like therefore to talk about the peculiarity
which makes contemporary painting difficult for
some people to enjoy. It's a peculiarity which you
can see beginning in the nineteenth-century
pictures. You'll notice that the painters began
then to be less explicit. Even those Impressionists
who were so fascinated by the look of the world,
and who developed such an unequalled technique
for representing it, were forced in their pursuit of
realism, to imply rather than to state. Light does
not usually reveal the whole of an object. It makes
part of it very clear, and shrouds the rest. And
these Frenchmen, with their passion for light, did
the same thing. And in doing so, they incidentally
hit upon a psychological truth: they discovered
that other people beside themselves had imagination and liked to use it. The worst bore in the
world is the man who in telling you a story spares
you nothing, gives every detail equal importance.
(I am still suffering from the Sahib you asked to

dinner who took twenty minutes and four glasses of port to tell me one anecdote about pig-sticking.) The painters, then, started to throw out hints, which it was our business, our pleasure, to pick up. (The writers of the time were experimenting in the same method, for the intelligent public was beginning to find long-windedness boring.) Painting ceased to be explicit. Daumier quite early in the century, Constantin Guys and later Toulouse-Lautrec, drew incisively, but drew only what it was necessary to draw. They deliberately left a lot to the imagination.

This telegraphic method has now been pushed pretty well to its limits: the best modern painters, and writers too, incline to leave so much to the imagination that their work is incomprehensible to most people. Still it is extraordinary how the man in the street is getting his eye trained. Half the posters now in the street would have seemed unintelligible, I fancy, twenty years ago. The best athletes, we are told, are those that make the fewest unnecessary movements. Similarly there is added force in the concision of a phrase, the economy of a single line, whether written or drawn.

Side by side with this distrust of the explicit has come an increased concentration on pattern or design, a desire above all things for rhythm and order. And in pursuit of this painters have grown

more and more ruthless in their treatment of
natural appearances. Distortion has always been
a part of the painter's traditional method; Ingres,
for instance, was howled at for his distortions just
as modern painters and sculptors are. And when
our Academicians assume that distortion is an
offence, they are only advertising their own
ignorance. They have evidently either never
looked at or never appreciated Chartres or
Ravenna, Oriental painting, or Greek sculpture
before Phidias. This brings me back to the
wretched question of representation. (How I hate
the word.) How important is it ? Making up
your mind on the point will not help you to
enjoy pictures, Harriet, and anyhow, you'll
probably change your mind the next day. All
that matters is that you should not refuse to enjoy
a picture because it fails to represent accurately
anything in nature; or, for that matter, because it
represents it too accurately. I'll only say two
things. Firstly carpets and cubist pictures which
represent nothing, can undoubtedly be beautiful.
Secondly, most great painters, even those most
free in their use of distortion, have been acutely
interested in representation. If you conclude that
representation is not essential to visual art, but is
usually important in it, you won't, I think, be
dangerously wrong.

It is very easy to say that the subject of a picture is of no importance. But I doubt if it is very true. Of course a painting by Chardin of a bottle and a loaf is finer than a painting of the Muses by Le Brun; of course a flayed ox by Rembrandt is better than an unflayed woman by Madame Vigée-Lebrun.

> *D'un pinceau délicat l'artifice agréable*
> *Du plus affreux objet fait un objet aimable.*

Of course some of the worst pictures ever painted are as it were anecdotes in paint. (And like so many anecdotes, they are intensely boring. There is nothing interesting that I can see in Cardinals drinking the Cook's health, or in a doctor sitting by a child's bedside.) But if the painter has a very different aim from the historian and the novelist, he really is rather like the poet. Schoolmasters and clergymen may like Shakespeare for the moral platitudes in which his characters too frequently indulge. But the point of Shakespeare is not in the truths he states but in the way he states them, the imagery and the diction. All good pictures are painted as it were in verse. I think you get a better notion of what painters are up to by thinking of the poets than by reading all the lives of all the painters. A picture has its origin in facts, in a stone bridge, a girl drinking absinthe, or a model standing in an uncomfortable position in a room with a north light. But painting is not mere description any more than nature-poetry is geology or botany. To take another analogy, a painter " sets " natural appearances, rather as a composer sets a text, he creates a new object which retains a relationship to the object which caught his attention. All good pictures are painted as it were to a melody.

And once you have got interested in the way pictures are made, you'll find, oddly enough, an increased fascination in what they represent. A picture of a wood is not interesting because it is like a wood, but because of the way the painter has seen the wood, and the way he has made a picture out of his vision. Every good painter, though he may think himself a realist, represents the world of his individual imagination. It is easy and frequent to write bad poetry or paint bad pictures on the subject of marble palaces on a sea-shore in the sunset. But Baudelaire infects us with his own nostalgia when he finds in a woman's hair

> *un éblouissant rêve*
> *De voiles, de rameurs, de flammes et de mâts:*
> *Un port retentissant où mon âme peut boire*
> *A grands flots le parfum, le son et la couleur;*

Où les vaisseaux, glissant dans l'or et dans la moire,
Ouvrent leurs vastes bras pour embrasser la gloire
D'un ciel pur où fremit l'éternelle chaleur.

And Claude produced the equivalent in paint when he invented his " *vastes portiques que les soleils marins teignaient de mille feux.*" The subject is important not in itself, but because it excites the artist. A plate of apples could throw Cézanne into the ecstasy which Claude found in trees, rigging, columns and the sky; and he would make of it a Still Life which in its rightness and solidity seems to be more enduring than bronze. All great painting in fact stimulates through our sensations an exaltation of mind. The range of method is enormous, and the exaltation may be tinged with melancholy, desire, or even amusement. But the artist is equally a man of imagination, whether he turns his vision on the actual or the fabulous world. The silvery groups of solid peasants shown us by Le Nain, the jockeys of Degas, Seurat's woman powdering her face, Géricault's lunatics, Manet's barmaids, Chardin's housewives and the dignitaries of Ingres belong to the same world as Poussin's satyrs, and Watteau's gallants. It is a world as various as that we inhabit, but where everything is significant, rhythmical, inevitable and right.

Indeed once you are familiar with pictures, you will often see the world with something approaching a painter's eye. Plain walls will take on a new interest, because you will find in them reflections of Corot: Courbet and Pissarro will have taught you the colour and influence of snow: sand will become translucent, as in Seurat, and the tree-trunks will echo the grave melodies of Cézanne. You will in fact find in the actual world images of the painters' ideal world.

So don't imagine that I want you to go to Burlington House with this letter in one hand, and the catalogue in the other, giving this painter nine for texture, and that one zero for composition. And above all, Harriet, don't be frightened by prigs like me. If you take to a picture because the girl in it has a pretty neck or an amusing hat, you are perfectly right. The painter no doubt liked the neck or the hat, and you have caught his signal. There are a hundred reasons for enjoying pictures, and they are all of them good. How can there ever be too much enjoyment—that's why I want you to open your eyes. Don't complain because Boucher is not like Cézanne, or because Ingres is not like Corot. Keep an open mind as well as an open eye. Then you may find, at the age of thirty-five, isn't it, a whole new world of pleasure unfolding itself before your enraptured gaze.

But perhaps not, Harriet. Perhaps you had
better not look too closely. Politicians and
admirals, speaking at Academy Banquets, often
talk about art as a harmless and indeed com-
mendable recreation from the important affairs
of life, something to kill time with when it is too
wet to play golf, a sort of refined Lady Companion
with unimpeachable references and a talent for
parlour games. Art is not like that. It is much
more like a tiger. And if your eyes were once
opened to these pictures, you would find in them
not an escape from reality, but an escape into
reality, and then you would be in deadly danger.
There is no telling what you might do. Your hus-
band, your son, all your well ordered life, might
dwindle into phantoms, and I see you leaving
them all behind, not cruelly but just forgetful,
taking passage on the first ship that turns up,
bound for Martinique or Newcastle, you don't care
which, living by your senses and in your mind,
living in the moment and for the moment upon
the " terrestrial nourishments." Perhaps you had
better keep away from the French pictures,
Harriet, and then for certain I shall be able to
come again and admire the magnolia, listen to
the lawn-mower, eat drop-scones with Devon-
shire cream, bathe in the pool with Dick, chatter
to you about the past, and enjoy once more the

perfect hospitality for which I have tried to thank you with what must be the longest Collins that ever man wrote.

Love, lots of it, from

Your affectionate

R.

P.S.—I stupidly left behind a dressing-gown and a novel called *Men and Wives*. Please be an angel, send me the former, and read the latter, as a reward.

A LETTER
FROM A BLACK
SHEEP

FRANCIS BIRRELL

LES TILLEULS,
NEAUPHLE-LE-CHÂTEAU, S. ET O.
December, 1931.

DEAR COUSIN JOHN,

The very moment I am back, even before going down to look at my beloved winter cabbages (I am so sorry you have had to " put down " two of your greenhouses—Jane's cottage hospital will miss your muscatels), I am writing to wish you a happy new year and to thank you both for being so kind to me during my short visit. Quite apart from the particular unpleasantness, I know how intensely you have always disliked me, and I don't think anyone but English people could have behaved so sweetly under such difficult circumstances. And I'm very sorry I jeered at your firm's carpets in front of the workmen. I quite understand that when one is at the head of a large and unsuccessful family business it must be trying to receive advice in public from a black sheep, who has never in the whole course of his life earned as much money as you have frequently lost in six months. And I was doubtless very irritating about those cheap Dufy curtains that I had just bought. But you, in turn, were unfair I thought when you jeered at me for living out of England. Left to myself, I should have tottered on in Middlemarch to the last, and you know quite well that I only went abroad

because that was the cruel condition on which
Aunt Mary, incited of course by that horrid
Major McChutney of the County Constabulary,
consented to continue my allowance. Aunt Mary
is the kindest of women and if left to herself quite
broadminded.

I'm sure you didn't mean to mock at my mis-
fortunes: still, during those long arguments conducted by you with such patience, and by me, I
fear, so raucously, I was pained by the frequency
with which the word " unpatriotic " fell from
your lips. That hurt, John. In my old prosperous
days, I may not have appreciated all the joys of
Middlemarch. But a lot has happened to me
since.

> I travelled among unknown men
> In lands beyond the sea.
> Nor, England! did I know till then
> The love I bore to thee.

(I know you never cared about poetry, but, you
may take it from me, it's what the English do
best.)

The scenery of the Ile de France is the most
civilised I know. But now I love the Midlands far
better. I have read and re-read the first chapter
of *Felix Holt* till I know it by heart, and I dream all
night of the stupid little hills and commonplace
copses, where Adam Bede walked with Hetty. It was

a real grief to me that it poured so pitilessly during the whole of my visit to Middlemarch. I longed to go round the dear old places once more, and no country looks so well during a fine winter as England.

Still, as you did banish me from your circle, like an unpleasant truth, you mustn't blame me if I've now developed a critical sense, as an armour for my self-respect. Grousing is the exile's privilege, and if I must be frank, though perhaps there is no necessity for it, I thought you were the stuffiest set of provincial fools I'd ever met in my life, frightfully sweet and all that, but unimaginative beyond words. I know your contempt for the French with their limited horizons and unambitious standards of life. And there's a good deal in it, I admit. But compared with you, we're comparatively up-to-date, even at Neauphle. Your society is inconceivably antiquated. You're all tied up in snobbery, my dear John, tied up in it till you can hardly breathe. You spend your life aping a social system, which no longer has any real existence. That awful word " Gentleman " kept cropping up every moment. Everybody in Middlemarch fusses incessantly as to whether he is more of a gentleman than his neighbour. I don't wonder your business is going down hill. The only man with any go in him is Cramp, and you won't make him a partner, merely because he's not a gentleman, which simply means he wasn't in our absurd house at Rugby. Since when have there been so many gentlemen at Middlemarch ? and while on the point, why do *you* call yourself a gentleman ? Grandpapa certainly wasn't a gentleman, and he, as we all know, was a great man. He built up the business and I still live precariously on the sweat of his brow. Unfortunately even he was a bit of a snob, who took in his latter days to going to the Established Church because he was sending our parents to Rugby; and at once the business began to slow up. When one comes to think of it, were there *any* gentlemen in Middlemarch in the great days when Grandpapa and others like him were doing their hardest work ? Ladislaw had taken Dorothea away and nobody ever replaced old Mr. Brooke. Then everyone seemed to lead sensible Equalitarian lives, just as if they were French people.

The whole trouble began when Nonconformists took to going to the public schools, appearing on public platforms with bishops and generally becoming respectable. I admit that they began doing so the moment the occasion presented itself. The saturation of nonconformity by the public schools has been deadly. For the mingling of the territorial aristocracy with the commercial middle-class has produced a hybrid which lacks the better qualities of each, the English gentle-

man in fact. And we do not sufficiently remember
how recent the public schools as we know them
are. Neither of us are likely to forget that Arnold
went to Rugby in 1828, but most of the schools
were either started or reborn in the fifties and
sixties and I should say that the whole deadly
routine only got thoroughly well going in the
seventies. For sixty years then the public schools
have provided the English governing class and
we can see what's happened in the state of your
business. I understand that even the secondary
schools are now trying to start a sort of imitation
Cadet Corps, to breed a team spirit and all the
familiar rubbish. You're all frightened about
losing your gentility, like any old maid, and have
never learned how to think. Such unadventurous-
ness would have been impossible in Grandpapa's
day and where are his likes now ? The worst of it is
you have made the atmosphere so damned
depressing for everybody else. If you want to get
to the top, or do anything at all considerable, you
have to be an absolute Napoleon like Morris.

Not that I think Grandpapa was perfect: he
was a hopeless old Philistine, and had he been a
bit more civilised, he wouldn't have allowed to
grow up round his works that hideous slum, which
has now had to be pulled down and rebuilt with
such disastrous consequences to the rates. Still,
as he stumped up so handsomely for the Adult

School, his own conscience was clear. Aunt Christine told me of his great contempt for Matthew Arnold. He found her one day when she was a girl with a copy of *Culture and Anarchy* in her hand. " Matthew Arnold," remarked Grandpapa with much finality, " is a conceited ass." I don't deny there was something in the description, but as a complete statement, it strikes me as rather *trop simpliste*. I believe you never saw Aunt Christine and I dare say in your position it was impossible. She was the black sheep of the older generation and that naturally brought us together. A very wise and witty old lady she was. Still, I quite see that the whole affair was a horrible business at the time, especially when the boy turned out so abominably well. But then Christine was a " born mother " which neither of our poor mammas were, and that no doubt was the cause of the whole sordid tragedy. That and your grotesque institution the King's Proctor, who is paid £2,000 a year by the tax-payer to organise an elaborate system of espionage and keep unhappy people together. It is tire-some to be, like the Norman kings, illustrious only through our bastards. Incidentally Aunt Christine's *rejeton* was the only male of the family not to go to Rugby. Valentine is an absolutely splendid fellow, as free and easy and simple as may be, though he's now far the biggest man in Iraq and

I am told, though I can hardly believe it, calls
Stalin by his Christian name. I know I didn't tell
you (I was shy about mentioning his name) that
he spent a few nights with me here, when he was
passing through France. He is exactly my idea
of a more intelligent grandpapa. I simply can't
make out how he can spend all his time in Mesopo-
tamia working like a black at his engineering, and
yet know all about Proust and Joyce, and modern
painting and modern science, and all the things
you've never heard of. It was a liberal education
in itself, to go about Paris with him. He is my
ideal of an Englishman. I shall write and recommend him to take on Cramp. He could pay him
more than you do, and Cramp would have an
outlet for his imagination and talents.

Incidentally, Valentine was perfectly furious
about the way in which we have muffed our
opportunity to construct Russia. He quite admits,
of course, that the Bolsheviks are susceptible and
tiresome. But he is sure that we could have got
round them and that eighty years ago the Brasseys
and the Petos would have done so. He is a real
expert on the subject and I think I remember
some articles attacking him as a traitor in one of
the London papers just as he was on the point of
putting through a great fat contract for some
people he knows in Birmingham You *do* deserve
anything you get. Not but what you and Jane

were perfectly sensible on this point and threw, I remember, the whole blame on to Winston and Jix. I rather doubt its being only that which is wrong ; but if it is, it only shows what fools you all are for letting such lunatics govern you. You all say terrible things about French politicians and the bulk of them certainly are a narrow-minded, ill-educated lot, with no ideas beyond the parish pump. But I can hardly imagine any leading French statesmen playing Old Harry with the self-evident interests of his country to the degree to which your Conservative politicians do. They are all either cads or prigs.

Englishmen like Valentine must have been quite common during the eighteenth and nineteenth centuries. Our hopeless self-satisfaction had not yet set in with the public school system. As far as I can make out, in the old days, whenever anything had to be done an Englishman was called upon to do it. And I don't mean only big heavy things like railways, engineering, etc. But even smaller, more elegant things, which you would not associate at first sight with the British genius. Quite obviously we simply ran France throughout the eighteenth century and landed them in the Revolution at the end of it, one of our more sensational though less happy efforts.

I don't think economic historians adequately allow for the money and distinction brought to

England by the genius and prestige of, say, a William Kent or a Capability Brown. Why, a Frenchman could hardly lay out a vegetable garden without getting an Englishman in to help. Horse racing is almost the only activity in which we keep up our *chic*, and once when I visited the stables and saw the English jockeys at Chantilly, I breathed in a sweet scent out of our English past. One is still proud to be an Englishman at Chantilly. French racing-men still talk English, as they used to do in the eighteenth century. Then, what a tremendous figure Poole was in the nineteenth century, perhaps the most famous tailor the world has ever known. To be dressed by Poole was the greatest ambition of every young German, French or Russian snob. He made the Englishman the *arbiter elegantiarum* throughout Europe. And now we see all our young *gommeux* running over to Paris to buy their clothes, and other people in England unconsciously doing the same thing. What would the world say if a French woman took to going to Berlin for her frocks ? Scotch tweeds are, of course, incomparable, and I suppose our English tailor still is the best cutter, but why do we play second fiddle so badly in the hosiery business ? Why should all the prettiest jumpers and ties be made in France ? It's no good pretending they aren't, because they are ; and what's more I can tell you the reason.

Because French people employ artists and " high-brows " in their shops. Also despite their pre-posterous nationalism, the French have never hesitated to employ a foreigner if it suited them. They realise it's better, in the long run, to employ one Russian to design one tie that ten thousand people want, than two Frenchmen to design two ties, which nobody will ever look at. Not that I suggest for instance you can't find in England as good designers as anywhere else. The French are frightfully insular and uninquisitive and, hence, it is extremely difficult to see English painting in Paris. But what little I have seen leads me to believe that there must be a lot of interesting work being done. Is any proper effort being made to employ commercially, say, Grant and Kauffer and Walton, and I dare say a lot of others I have never heard of ? Not a bit of it, and instead of trying to get you to put the matter right for yourselves the Tories simply clamour for tariffs so that you can all go about dressed in Empire sackcloth. I'm told that in any case French jumpers are only made for foreigners. This may or may not be so; if it is so, it shows the French understand the meaning of the word export trade. I heard you occasionally mumbling something about silly young nincompoops who were always trotting off to Paris for their ideas. I must say I don't blame them overmuch if they do, and I see no harm in it.

What we want is a corresponding Anglomania on
the Continent like there used to be. As far as I can
see, except for Lytton Strachey, certain sorts
of motor engines, particularly, of course, Rolls
Royce, which is almost worshipped, and gramo-
phone records we have hardly set the pace in
anything since the athletic boom of the early
twentieth century. Golf professionals are, however, among our most valuable invisible exports
and Continental golf club secretaryships afford a
happy retreat to innumerable old Etonians.

I certainly don't sneer at our later literature and
got a real local patriotic thrill when I read how
much Proust had admired our beloved midland
novelist. But where are the latter-day Richard-
sons, who invented French novels, the Byrons, who
made Pushkin, the Dickenses who set Dostoievski
going? Nor can I easily forget the influence of
Constable on Corot, or of Turner on Monet. We
do not perhaps much care nowadays about the
sort of theatre for which Kemble was responsible:
but it was no small achievement for an English
producer to have canalised the art of Delacroix
and released the dramatic genius of Victor Hugo.
I am sure such people still exist but somehow they
get discouraged. But I must give you Joyce—I
will allow him to be an Englishman. And tire-
some as I find most of his *Ulysses*, I see he is a
great figure. And you mayn't even buy a copy in

England. What a country! English society kicked out the physical Byron, but even in the worst moments of the political reaction they didn't stop the sale of Don Juan. I don't believe you recognise for a moment how much harm you do yourselves nationally with your ridiculous censors, official and unofficial. Privately you've all gone mad about Freud (and quite right, too). But this widening of psychological interests is severely cut out of your books and plays. How can you expect anybody to write decently, if he's not allowed to say any of the things he wants to ? The spectacle of your all kowtowing to the daily papers revolts me. And you don't even know you're doing it. You're all hopelessly out-of-date, my dear friend, out-of-date like your own carpet designs, except in the regions of pure thought, where our family cannot hope to penetrate. English people, if they have the ghost of a chance, aren't in the least stupid, and pure thought depends less than any-thing on a helpful social ambiance. Besides Cambridge really has made an effort to keep up with the times (or so I should judge from the few young Cambridge men, whom I have been lucky enough to meet as they were passing through Paris) and hence Cambridge is still the Cambridge of Clerk Maxwell and Cavendish. Cambridge is the one satisfactory English institution, despite my own lamentable degree and the unhealthy

set I got into. As I said before, young English
people aren't the least bit stupider than anyone
else. On the contrary they appear to be extremely
intelligent and utterly open-minded. Yet they
live like exiles in their own country and are always
flying abroad to get a breath of fresh air. I never
see them enjoying themselves with all that
restrained lyricism, of which our race has the
secret, in Paris or on the Riviera or sniffing out
all the most intelligent things in a provincial town,
with their endless good nature, their gift for
foreign languages, their absence of race-preju-
dice, their easy cosmopolitanism, without feeling
an infinite pity for them, as I contrast them with
their often inferior French counterparts, settling
down so happily in their own country and flattered
out of all proportion to their merits.

The way you've all lighted on that word high-
brow (I heard you employ the word more than
once yourself) exasperates me; and it accounts,
I'm certain, for half your troubles. And, at the
risk of appearing Gallophile, I must say I can
hardly imagine the word catching on in France
(though I once met something rather like it in an
article by Clément Vautel in the *Journal*). The
stupidest Frenchman would hardly boast that he
was stupid. You've got to get rid of all that, my
friend, if you want to catch up again. I am sure
Stanley Baldwin is a charming man. But some-

times I think he is even more of a danger to you than the *Daily Mail*. He flatters your weaknesses so terribly, so unconsciously and so high-mindedly. I was reading some awful stuff by him in *The Times* the other day—yes, I economise in order to take in *The Times*; it prevents exiles going native, rather like shaving in the South Seas—about how American was ruining the language of Shakespeare, Baldwin who would not have understood a word of Shakespearian English had he heard it spoken, and who doesn't apparently know that the only places in which it still is spoken are certain parts of America.

Why do you all admire your politicians so tremendously ? But here I am not completely *déraciné* myself, and on Baldwin's advice I laid down a cellar of Mary Webb in the new cheap edition. Christ! Would any nation except the compatriots of Milton and Dryden tolerate such trash ? This, however, is only a parenthesis. Baldwin voiced that preepsy public-school shabby-genteel contempt for America, which is one of your most trying characteristics. You talked yourself a good deal about degrading American films, while I was at Middlemarch, and about the importance of stimulating the British industry, quotas, embargoes, stiffer censorships, of course, and whatnot. So, as there were some British films showing, I went to a few on two or three wet

afternoons. Good God! You dare to pitch into
Hollywood, when you can, yourself, only produce
these miserable photographic versions of worn-out
West-End comedies. American may often be
crude and vulgar, but it is distinctly less fatuous
than the refaned jargon of your English pictures.
The English guttersnipes in the streets all seemed
to be talking good raw screen American. I was
delighted to hear them ; they may renovate the
English language yet. For however much American slang may jar on your nerves, it has at any
rate got some life in it, some joy in language and
in the invention of idiom for its own sake, which I
am sure would have delighted Shakespeare if he
had heard it. Whereas I fail to see what advantage,
moral or linguistic, anybody could possibly derive
from the stuff I saw served up out of the British
studios. You're in danger of becoming an aristocrat, my boy, and an aristocrat is a person who by
some evil chance never finds out about any of the
important things that are going on round him
Give me Gary Cooper or Jack Oakie any day
rather than your suburban actors lisping out the
exhausted formulæ of a tenth rate night club.
America's up-to-date anyhow, and that's what
you need.

Yes, up-to-date like a decent, cheap French or
German hotel with running water in every room
and the family firm's carpets not running to seed

on the floor. I gather that that ingenuous " Visit Britain " organisation is trying to do something about English hotels, which are now admitted to be an abuse, and I don't want to flog a dead horse. But I should like to know when it was that English hotels began to get so frightfully bad. I'd lazily supposed that they always had been bad. But I now perceive that this is not the case. As I can so rarely visit England in person, I do so vicariously in foreign travel books, particularly eighteenth-century books, and I am amazed to read of a very different state of affairs. One and all the travellers declare that they never knew what comfortable inns and decent food meant till they had crossed the narrow strait between Calais and Brighton. Dear, vulgar, noisy, beautiful Brighton, how I used to love it when I lived in Middlemarch—the only town in England where an Englishman feels free and it is the very poetry of esplanades. I must spend a few days there soon if I only can get leave from Aunt Mary and Major McChutney. Now, I don't pretend that our English eighteenth-century hotels would have been bearable to modern taste. But the point is that English hotels were better than other hotels. In this as in so many other things, England led the world. And now the opposite is the case. Why is this ? We are told that it is motor cars. But motor cars, in spite of what a certain sort of

snob says, haven't destroyed French hotels. A
number have inevitably lost their " off-the-road "
charm, but the general standard has been raised,
greatly owing to the admirable activities of the
Touring Club de France, and also because the
French inn keepers want to do a good trade and are
not like you and Jane, above putting their house
in order to meet American standards. I at any
rate am very grateful to American tourists for
having got hot water into my bedroom. One thing
only saddens me. The proud word *confort anglais*
no longer has any meaning and *confort américain*
has taken its place. When was it English land-
lords took to living on tinned soup and meat and
stale cakes from London ? This would not have
been tolerated in the days of Dickens. I suppose
it has something to do with the public schools,
but for the moment, I admit, I can't see what.
But don't you see, you've all fallen off so terribly;
you don't count any longer. You ruled Europe by
pride of intellect for one hundred and fifty years
and now foreigners are beginning to treat you as
a kind of inferior Americans. Or, to use your
own favourite metaphor you're becoming dagoes.
Though expatriated I'm a good patriot and this
makes me sad, but still it's true. Your morals,
your taste in colour, most of your novels, your
historical information, even your scientific chit-
chat are all so damned antiquated. You're so

badly educated, my friend. Try to bring your country up-to-date somehow. Don't snub tiresome young men or sneer at high-brows! This is what I was feeling and was wishing I had explained to you better when I was saying good-bye to you on Middlemarch platform, and my thoughts ran along the same groove in the third-class carriage to London. By the way, it's a mistake to suppose that you can't travel third-class in France. It's quite reasonably comfortable and far cheaper than it is in England. If the pound continues to fall because no one wants your carpets, the *milord anglais* will make many interesting Continental discoveries of this order. And I continued to reflect in this manner through most of the night, till I got up to make the most of my two days *permission* in London. What a wonderful capital you might have made of it, had you liked, and what a splendid place it is, in spite of everything! Most of the things I liked best you have pulled down since my last visit—Regent Street, the Foundlings' Hospital, the best parts of Trafalgar Square, the nice part of Park Lane. What barbarians you are! I don't blame you for pulling things down and certainly I don't want to turn London into a sort of museum like Venice or Ravenna. There is a good deal to be said for rebuilding a city every forty years. It is the old European tradition, which is now observed only in America. Still, if you must pull down all the nicest parts of London, it is a pity you can only put up such fatuous objects in their place. And I have a suspicion that the English are rather proud of their modern architecture. Yet, people really are beginning to know how to build a town. I don't know Germany as well as I should wish, but I have seen enough of it to envy them their civic sense, coming down, I suppose, from the Middle Ages which is now wonderfully made manifest in their workman's dwellings and their swimming-baths, and their sun traps and their planetaria, and their beer gardens. Next time you take your family to Switzerland (that corner of a foreign field, which is for ever England), get out at Basle, have a look round and blush. I haven't been to French Flanders, but I am told that some of the *cités ouvrières* round there are models of modern planning. I wonder whether the French will ever be suitably grateful to the Germans for first burning down the North-Eastern Departments of France and then rebuilding them properly at their own expense. At any rate when the Germans pull down something old they put up something really modern in its place; when your architects pull down a real row of Georgian houses, they erect a pastiche of them on the site, and call the result " Luxury flats." Still, the London squares recalled the good old days, when, as I blush to remember,

I too used to call myself a gentleman—Grosvenor Square and Portman Square and, in spite of everything, Hanover Square. Mr. John Knightly, I recall, lived in Bloomsbury Square (what an absurd object has just gone up all down one side of it). How fine to have been an Englishman then! Mr. John Knightly recalls Southend, which recalls the fact that the English retaught the world sea-bathing from the Arctic Circle. Ours is a goodly heritage. Then I went again and looked at the Elgin Marbles, admired the improvements in the National Gallery and was amazed at the transformation of the Tate—such a fine place compared with the Luxemburg even before the Legs Caillebotte went to the Louvre. I see many of the best pictures were given by the artificial silk man Courtauld. He must be an interesting fellow. I wonder whether Valentine knows him. I hope he is not by any chance of French descent ?

And then on my last evening, I dropped in on a pleasant enough little musical comedy to see Bobby Howes, whose fame had reached me, though I had never seen him; at last I had found what I was looking for, something (besides the Zoo) which was modern and first-rate. What a delightful fantastic hob-goblin Bobby Howes is, so much more spontaneous and lyrical than all the French comics, so utterly and ruthlessly English, too, like the *Midsummer Night's Dream*, the lineal descendant of Kemp and Tarleton. Why ever did Jane not mention him, when she was holding forth on the theatre and all those shoddy plays and actors she had seen ? I suppose as Jane admires Mr. Galsworthy so much, she is too cultured to have heard of Bobby Howes. But a horrid thought assails me. Perhaps it was less ignorance than shame. Perhaps she feels that Bobby Howes has been educated, not at Rugby, but in the nearby Forest of Arden. He certainly does not look as if he had ever represented the Lord's Schools or even the *menu peuple*, jumbled drearily together as " The Rest." I was lucky to have seen him my last night; for, as a result while I was walking home after the performance to my rather dreary hotel there welled up in me a great love for England, the love Lamb says Drayton felt, " the painful love of a son " and I knew that I would willingly give up anything on earth, if, by so doing, I could help the least bit to make my country once more prosperous and happy.

I was so very sorry to have missed Tom, and wish you could have arranged my visit during his holidays. I am glad he is so happy and successful at Rugby. Is he growing up as handsome as you were, John ? I've always had a slight inferiority complex about you, you know, you were so terribly handsome, though I tried to flatter myself it was in rather a boring way. I advise his instant

removal from the school. If he's the least like his
parents, he must already have enough character
to govern a whole continent of backward peoples
single-handed—which won't be much use to him,
as backward peoples don't want us to govern them
any longer and in any case I presume Tom is
going into the family business, that is, if there is
still a family business to go into. I suggest he
comes and stays for a year with me here. " Do
not start, my dear Coleridge." I'm as mild as
milk now and have, in my day, got into enough
trouble to know how to keep other people out of
it. Seriously, I can think of nothing but advantage accruing from such an arrangement. I
imagine that, like all the rest of us, he will be
taking the history tripos, and I am sure we should
all have got better degrees and derived more
benefit from the course if we had learnt one
foreign language first and seen a little bit of a
foreign country, and so not have been compelled
to look at the whole history of the world from the
angle of the school chapel. And then, if he is
going into business, the experience will have been
quite invaluable. As you may know, it is quite
a short train journey from Neauphle to Paris, and
he could go in every day if necessary and study
the present state of textile design which nobody
in England seems to know anything about (I quite
admit that Germany might be nearly as good, but

I happen to live in France). The English section
of the *Arts décoratifs* Fair was a disgrace to
humanity, and must have lost the country millions.
Your ideal still seems to be to make something
which nobody wants, but which will last for ever.
Mark my words, my dear John, you can't get that
nineteenth-century Louis XV across any longer.
Now, if Tom would come and stay with me, I
could easily get him some sort of helping job in
one of the big French houses. You may be surprised to learn that other people besides Valentine
are willing to give me credit for not being quite
hopeless. He could then study both the artistic
and technical side of the business, get some sort of
idea of what's what, and learn something that's
useful and up-to-date. (It would be different if
Tom were a scholar, but I gather from you that
he isn't.) They really employ quite " high-brow "
artists even at large stores like Lafayettes. And in
the meantime Tom would form connections,
which he will always find useful in business and
he would then be in a position to turn your stuffy
old factory upside down before he's thirty. What
in heaven's name can he learn about art in
Middlemarch! I only had to look at your pictures
and wallpapers to make a pretty shrewd guess,
and it isn't easy to get the best instruction even in
London, so I'm told. Of course I can give you
Jane's reply, before she's even formulated it. Tom

is still young. He might just as well stay on at
school another year, go to Cambridge straight, and
then if it's thought advisable, there will still be
heaps of time for him to spend a year fitting himself for business when he is more of a man.
Theoretically, I quite agree. But I know exactly
what will happen. He will go up to Cambridge
artificially " kept back," mismanage his degree,
and be told that he is a grave disappointment after
all the money that's been spent on his education.
So now he " must settle down without any further
delay." In other words he will be pushed into the
business as a punishment for past shortcomings
without having acquired any useful information
whatever.

What will he be like then, poor boy, by the time
he's fifty ? I could answer the question all right,
but you might think it rather rude. Anyhow, the
dear old firm won't last another generation on the
present lines. The once great Middlemarch carpet
works seem to me not such a bad symbol of our
present discontents.

However, I've wasted a great deal of ink and
paper being rude to you and Jane, which is a
poor return for all your forbearance and hospitality. I wonder whether the prodigal son found
fault with the way in which the fatted calf had
been dressed. But I know I was sometimes rather
sulky in the evenings: so I wanted to try and

explain what I felt and how I wasn't being unsympathetic about all the trouble you have been
going through, especially about the monstrous
expenses connected with Harriet's operation.
Your doctors are not only the worst, but the most
expensive in the world. They hardly ever seem to
keep up with the latest scientific method, and use
their position more to push themselves socially
than anything else. Why can't your doctors and
surgeons frankly own their own clinics, instead of
realising the same end by subterfuge and intrigue
with the owners of nursing homes ? Besides the
additional expense, they have to waste half their
day motoring from one nursing home to another.
A friend of mine had a major operation in Paris
for about £20 and was looked after in the surgeon's
own very comfortable clinic and under the
surgeon's own eye for 12s. 6d. a day. But sheer
bankruptcy will destroy this expensive inefficiency
soon. I sympathise with you all right. In fact I
sympathise with everybody all round. Why
shouldn't I ? It's no pleasure to me, the pound
crashing, considering I live so much on remittances
from Aunt Mary.

Well, my dears, good-night. I'd no intention
of writing such a long letter and now it's much too
late to go and look at the cabbages: so I must put
it off till to-morrow and will just go round to the
café and have a drink and a talk before I go to

bed. I suppose that society at Neauphle is not
very thrilling. But I like the shabby cheapness of
the place and the absence of any noticeable
social differences, among the men at any rate.
You see they were all educated at the same sort of
school and did their military service together.
And even the stupidest of them take some rudi-
mentary interest in general ideas. But I dare say
the golf secretaries will alter all that in time.
Meanwhile think seriously about my proposals
for Tom, and for my own part, I am looking
forward tremendously to seeing you again in about
ten years' time.

Your affectionate cousin,
BLACK SHEEP.

P.S.   I found the proofs of my damned book
on the *Assemblée des Notables* waiting for me here
and hope to get the whole thing off my hands in
a fortnight. I should love to dedicate it to Jane.

A LETTER
TO W. B. YEATS

L. A. G. STRONG

My Dear Mr. Yeats,

I am glad to have this opportunity of writing you a longer letter than would pass between us in the ordinary way of correspondence. At the same time, I begin it with diffidence: with even more diffidence than is natural in a young writer addressing the acknowledged head of his profession. I am not afraid of what you will say when you read it, for you will know it is sincere, and will be indulgent to any lack of understanding. Neither am I afraid of partiality, since, except with fools, it is a condition of good criticism: a kindled mind judges better than a cold. What I am afraid of is that I may damage your credit with poor advocacy: that the result of a confessed admiration may persuade those who have small acquaintance with your work that this is the best that can be said for it, and that, therefore, they may safely continue to let it alone. It will be best for me, I think, at the risk of seeming egotistical, to keep within the limits of the first person singular, and try to suggest the significance you have for a reader of my generation, rather than for the world. Your own generation know what to think of you; and, even if they don't, they will hardly apply to me!

You appear before the young men and women of to-day in several characters, but first and last as a poet. They know you as a dramatist, and have heard that you trained actors to speak your

plays. They know that you have written tales and
essays : some of them have read your auto-
biography: a few have heard that you are a
student of magic. They have heard, too, with a
sense of surprise, that you took part in politics and
were a senator: but this seemed a rumour only.
It did not fit with the figure most of them had in
their mind's eye, and they dismissed it. Some of
them have heard you speak in public places. A
few have been in the same room with you, and
heard you talk. Many revere you as the greatest
living writer: many, their eyes fixed upon a
younger man, have read of you only a verse or two
in an anthology, and wonder resentfully what all
the fuss is about. I have something to say to all
these people. I know your work better than most
readers of my age: I have got from it what no
other contemporary work has had to give me: I
have known you personally: and I know a little
about Ireland. What is more, I am under no
illusion about anything I can write here. There is
nothing I can say about your work which your
work has not said infinitely better: still, as that
holds good of most criticism, it need not deter me
from saying what I can.

One disability weighs heavy on me. If I could,
I would not make a single remark about any of
your work without supporting it, chapter and
verse, by quotation. This I cannot do: the scope
of a letter forbids it. A critic's business is not so

much to give his opinion as to draw attention to
those aspects of the subject on which it is based.
To do that with your work would need a full
volume. Here there is room for a sketch only, and
a thumb-nail sketch at that.

The first thing to be borne in mind is that you
are an Irishman. No one who loses sight of this
will understand you. To some characters nationality is not important: they have no striking racial
traits, and one remembers their origin with a
shock of surprise. Others adopt a nationality, and
so vehemently identify themselves with it that
their real birthplace and parentage become mis-
leading. You have always been Irish No other
country could have produced you.

This being so, it is fortunate that the way in
which you could best serve your country has been
to follow unchecked the development of your
personality as an artist. The service has been done
indirectly, in your work, rather than by any
direct part you have played in politics. No one
will say you have no aptitude for politics: you
have a dangerous aptitude.[1] You have the gift of
oratory, you can, as once at Oxford, rouse a
lackadaisical audience to the wildest excitement
with a torrent of passionate words: but Jim
Larkin could do that. You were not born to be

[1] All things can tempt me from this craft of verse:
One time it was a woman's face, or worse—
The seeming needs of my fool-driven land.

a demagogue. Your quarrel has been less with the world than with yourself: and, as you have said, rhetoric, so needful in the Ireland of your time, is made from our quarrel with the world.[1] Besides, sooner or later you would have turned upon your audience that destructive humour that penned the opening of a speech upon Divorce. " There's not a fool can call me friend "[2]: numbers would not have made them more tolerable. The day would have come when you flung their plaudits back in their teeth. Your way was poetry. The world picked quarrels enough when you advanced work that was purely artistic in its aim. The side-plunge into affairs has always been a distraction to you—all the more so since you have a talent for affairs, and could always produce an effect when you took sides. An *interest* in affairs has been essential to you: indeed, it has been one of the chief strengths of your poetry, for it has kept your mind quick and fierce, and has kept you from acquiescence—I cannot think of any other name for that fatty degeneration which attacks so many poets, who were rebels, in their middle years. Some of your best work has sprung from indignation at public affairs.[3] But you are, and always have been, before everything an artist: and, in pressing everything, patriotism as well, into art's regiment,

[1] *Per Amica Silentia Lunae.*   [2] *To a Young Beauty.*
[3] *Responsibilities*, passim.

you have done your country the greatest possible service. A man of genius serves his country best by the fullest possible realisation of his powers. Burns did more for Scotland by singing to his wenches than if he had laboured unselfishly as a district councillor: and your work in Ireland—whether at the Abbey Theatre, in your study, or as " a sixty-year-old smiling public man "—has been valuable to her in proportion as it was the work whereto your genius called you.

The chief duty it laid upon you was to be a poet: and it is for your poetry that you are famous throughout the world. Your life as poet has been unusual in that your poetry has become steadily better as you have grown older. Starting with work that was new and striking and beautiful in one manner, you have passed on to another manner, and another again: and now you are writing a poetry that unites the fire of youth, the power of maturity, and the skill wrung from a lifetime of devotion to that single end. There is no such poetry elsewhere in the world to-day. There is no flame that is engendered from such a heat of conflict: no other mind melts the ore of so many interests: no other fingers are so strong and so merciless to give the metal form: no other eye so fierce to seek a flaw when the work is cold. " Flame is flame," said your chosen master,[1]

[1] William Morris.

" wherever you find it." The flame in your work
burns up other poets if they come too close.

It is an irony which you will be first to appreciate
that, this being so, your earlier work is the best
known: and that by it the impatient younger
generation sometimes judge and find you wanting.
Disliking what you did, for they are hunting very
different quarry, they dislike still more the skill
with which you did it. They have no wish to
wander with Oisin or Aengus; they prefer Mont-
martre to Ben Bulben; and, having little use for
the pieces the anthologists obtrude upon them, they
seek no further. Mr. Eliot has their admiration,
and well he deserves it. If they could only hear
him speak of you, as I have heard him under the
big tree at Garsington, how quickly they would
rush to fill the gap in their knowledge! But that
is neither here nor there. Your work is up for a
longer day. Like the hills, it will have its clouds
and its patches of sunshine, and will finally settle
down to its proper and permanent stature in the
mind-landscape of the travelled generations.

Your achievement in poetry has been precise
and definite. You are a magical poet, and by that
I mean something very different from the ordinary
use of the word. Your bias has always been to
express the things that lie on the farthest edge of
expression: and it will undoubtedly be said of you
in the future that you enlarged the poetic consciousness of your time. It would almost be fair

to say that you have sought to express the inex-
pressible, since your aim, that rim of difficulty
that stops just short of the impossible, would have
been indeed impossible to any shot but yours.
Poets, you have said, are not permitted to shoot
beyond the tangible: but there has been nothing
to forbid their extending the range of consciousness
to include what hitherto had been subjective and
intangible. This was a task for a magician, and
you have gone about it as a practical magician
must. It is in terms of the tangible that the intangible is snared. The significance of your poetry
has been its power to evoke by the hardest and
most precise of symbols the most delicate tones of
beauty and meaning: and in saying this I do not
for an instant overlook its unparalleled music, for
music has been a definite and practical part of
the incantation.

> In vain, in vain: the cataract still cries
> The everlasting taper lights the gloom.
> All wisdom shut into his onyx eyes
> Our Father Rosicross sleeps in his tomb.

What are the tones that verse sets ringing in the
mind ? What is this power, in which you are pre-
eminent, of summoning to our understanding,
with one swift, wrought phrase, a landscape, a
sky, a weather, and a history ? We do not think
about it, till we realise that in the words before us
there is no logical warrant for that rush of feeling

and knowledge—no warrant we can make the words yield up: yet, when we come to them again, the spine prickles, the eyes blur, the soul admires. This wonder which we feel was upon you when you wrote: and you are a magical poet in that you have by ceaseless diligence and labour found a way of arranging concrete symbols that shall awake in us huge shadows of your wonder. It is a precise and definite art: the cutting of an agate. First, the inquisitive spirit, and the shock of perception: then, by long diligence, the magician. No one since Blake has made a few words signify so much. Poets are hard-headed fellows, if the world only knew it. No surgeon has so delicate a task, or needs more stamina. The strength, nervous and physical, the range of feeling, the sheer muscular skill that has gone into your work, is only to be realised by those who themselves have hammered in the poets' workshop. You began amazingly, and your work at sixty is better than your work at thirty. You cry out against growing old, and it is the only thing in which you deceive yourself: for you do not know how to grow old. I have seen you often, at Oxford, in the company of young men, and you were the youngest man in the room, because you had the most inquisitive mind. You have been collecting ammunition—not years. What man who was not young could have written *Sailing to Byzantium* ? Yet no young man could have written it.

You began with Celtic legend and imagery, with
Eastern imagery, with a world remote from your
time: and, as I said, in the general esteem, you
have never succeeded in living down your early
work. It is not that the public did not like it.
They liked and like it only too well. They did not,
of course, realise the quality of the verses. They
had no ear for the new, bold rhythm of *Innisfree*,
for the subtlety of *Down by the Salley Gardens*, for the
perfection of *A Faery Song*. They found an easier
response: and now they cannot forgive you for
hardening into a world that demands thought as
a passport. You have made them no concessions.
Instead, you withdrew into the wilderness,
climbed further and further up the mountain:
those who followed you had to gird up their loins
and make exertions. Thus the anthology readers,
who would gladly follow you from King's Road to
Innisfree, become discouraged, and lament that
your later work is " less beautiful " than those
early poems. Those early poems are indeed
beautiful, so their liking may be counted to them
for righteousness: and as, if you saw a crowd
following you into the wilderness, you would
probably have wanted to throw stones at them,
their defection is no great matter.

Responsibilities, I suppose, marked your de-
parture into the wilderness. Before that, the
love poems in *The Wind Among the Reeds* had
advanced in precision of imagery and syntax on

the earlier work, without any loss of freshness or
suggestion: and the bold use of lonely words
which is one of the astonishments of your poetry
was more authoritative, more perfectly absorbed
into the texture of the individual poem. Then,
with the entry of your muse into contemporary
life—i.e. its withdrawal into the wilderness—you
stripped your lines bare. Like boughs in winter,
they showed the stark perfection of their architecture, the delicate, severe articulation that bound
each word to stem and branch and root: the idea
bitterly flowing out into the bare, clean boughs.

September 1913: *The Cold Heaven* : *The Magi* :
and the terrible

> Toil and grow rich,
> What's that but to lie
> With a foul witch
> And after, drained dry,
> To be brought
> To the chamber where
> Lies one long sought
> With despair. . . .

and, later, *The Scholars*: put these in the antholo-
gies, and the young men will be much astonished.

From the austerities and savagery[1] of this
period, your work has opened into a second glory.
The bare boughs have flowered again. " The

[1] " But was there ever dog that praised his fleas ? "

woods are in their autumn beauty ": autumn is
the finest season of your year. That magnificent
poem of the swans has been the prelude to a
period of work surpassing all that you had done
before. The thought is more compressed, the diction simpler, the vision bolder. You will be represented in the future by poems from every period,
for in each your genius found the peaks of its
expression. (One reason, I think, why the readers of
later days will sometimes reject the corrections you
have made in your early work, and prefer it as it
was.[1] I remember you said that you let those
things alone, fearing some stupidity in your middle
years. but they deserve protection no less for
your wisdom of to-day. The tag about old heads
and young shoulders holds good of poetry as well
as people.) There is, in the poetry of your later
period, an intellectual content, an imagination,
a passion, and a sure control which is not to be
matched in any poet of your generation or of
mine. It is contemporary poetry, yet it transcends
its time. It is aristocratic, yet has all the vigour
coarseness could have given it. It is intellectual,
but its blood runs hot. It is full of anger, yet holds
perfect equilibrium. It mocks, but keeps its
dignity. A magnificent arrogance, your response
to " the fascination of what's difficult " informs it
all. It is wise, without wisdom's chill. There is
no poetry to match it: and, but for a certain

[1] Such as *The Sorrow of Love*.

occasional obscurity, it is a model to any artist in the craft of words.

You will take me up here, I dare say, and tell me that the obscurity is necessary, and that there are things which can only be spoken in riddles. This is true: but if the riddle is too hard, the thing has not been spoken at all. " Hard " and " obscure " are of course comparative terms, and, when you seem obscure, it is for definite reasons[1]: but the poet, who, as you allow, must not shoot beyond the tangible, has to take *some* account of other men's interpretation of that word, unless his poetry is to be a monologue heard only by himself. Suppose that to me an alligator is the symbol of the lover, and a coco-nut the symbol of the beloved: I have no grounds to complain if my poem of the alligator swallowing and then rejecting the coconut is not understood by my brother poets to signify frustrated love: and if, in consequence, they call the poem obscure. This is a silly example—but it leads to an important matter.

You are, as I have said, a magical poet: and you have approached your art as the magician approaches his. For you, to find the word that shall invoke the thought has not been only a

[1] " They take their place in a phantasmagoria in which I endeavour to explain my philosophy of life and death, and till that philosophy has found some detailed expression in prose certain passages in the poems named above may seem obscure." (Note to *The Phases of the Moon*, *The Double Vision of Michael Robartes*, *Michael Robartes and the Dancer*.)

poetic quest. " The collar-bone of the hare " is a
magic symbol, but its magic, and the magic of all
that poem, belongs to poetry. There are symbols,
however, which have a permanent significance:
which have a power of invocation apart from their
context. The cabalistic sign of Death has, for
example, evoked appropriate images in sensitive
minds which were unaware of its significance.
You have grounds for believing in a symbolism
independent of the human period in which we
live: a kind of universal language, such as
Berkeley held the objects of sight to be. When I
brought you two dreams ten years ago, one
dreamed by a boy, the other by a young married
woman: dreams which involved, one a mixture
of the Europa legend with that of Danaë and the
Shower of Gold, the other a history of a war in
which Pan healed the combatants, you were able
to interpret them both. Of the significance of the
first there was no doubt, and time has startlingly
proved how well you read the second. You based
your reading upon the timeless association of
certain figures and objects with certain meanings.
The implications of that belief we need not discuss
here. I am concerned only with one aspect of it,
its effect upon your poetry. It is, I believe, the
source of any obscurity that can be charged
against you: for your syntax is always clear,

> The caterpillar on the leaf
> Reports to thee thy mother's grief.

Your obscurity is often of the same kind as Blake's.
There is no doubt as to what you say. The difficulty is, what does the caterpillar stand for?
" For one throb of the Artery. . . ." You will
hardly believe the number of intelligent readers
who have been stuck by this. That is their fault,
I agree: but the sort of difficulty it presents is one
which you yourself may tend to minimise.

Some time ago, a weekly paper set a competition
inviting versions of Mrs. Leo Hunter's *Ode to an
Expiring Frog* as you might have written it.
Hastily, I improvised this:

> Sighing I gaze upon the brilliant creature,
> The swift dishevelled sides, until my heart
> Burns with a dull, deep anger. What insolent
>   fiend,
> Plotinus' anti-self, coursing him hither
> Far from the sedges and the quiet pool,
> Cast him upon his belly on this log?
> Dim pulse of the great Artery, I bend
> My sorrowful face above your face, and cry,
> Triumph on death: yours is a royal bier,
> For once there was a Log who was your king.

This is crude and hasty caricature: but it is
perhaps not altogether without significance that
I instinctively included a universal symbol, and a
last line that would be unintelligible to anyone
who did not know the fable of King Log and
King Stork.

All that you have written is for initiates, and it is necessary that some of your work be difficult even to them. The other day I saw how so fine a critic as Mr. Desmond MacCarthy complained that something of yours was obscure, which I had read without difficulty: and I doubtless am puzzled by much that would read simply to him. Do not suppose I think that poetry can be easy. I have written a pamphlet insisting on its difficulty, repeating *ad nauseam* that a good poem is the only human way of saying something which otherwise must remain unsaid. I think no more than this, that the belief in permanent symbols has been dangerous to you as an artist. To the poet, all symbols are private symbols. It is difficult to write a good religious poem because the symbols one must use are universal, and lack precision. They are dog's-eared, and thumb-marked with long handling. For just the same reason, it is difficult to handle precisely any universal symbol. It is almost impossible to make it private. Even in the noblest utterance, such symbols are apt to thunder off to a sonorous vagueness. If any of your poetry has a weakness, it is an obscurity of this kind. To introduce into a novel a person one knows is always dangerous, because one takes him for granted from the start, and may omit to make him clear to the reader: i.e. one may fail as an artist. It may be that in your mind certain equations of symbol to meaning are so axiomatic that you have omitted to make the necessary artistic identification which transforms a verse from a riddle to a work of art. If you have made this mistake, it has been very, very seldom: for you are a consummate artist: and I know of no other charge that can be brought against your later work.

The question of Magic comes here, and, though this is no place to talk of it, it cannot be passed altogether. The studies which culminated in your *Vision* have been a part of your life that embarrasses your critics. A text-book, a system of magic: what can they make of that ? Some of them ignore it: others get round it as best they may.[1] Others, like the American critic, Edmund Wilson, whose account of your work is by far the best known to me, face *The Vision*, and write it off as the price we have to pay for one of the greatest intellects in the modern world. I can say nothing here, for I have not the knowledge: but I cannot be content, even from the historical point of view, to regard it as a waste product of your genius— something you had to get off your chest, before you could go on with your work: nor as a conscious parallel to the life of Blake. You, of all men, are entitled to your own pursuits. If you give attention to a thing, the thing is important: and he is a bold man who takes upon him to say

[1] A.E.'s review in the *Irish Statesman* was a masterly circuit of this kind.

that you are wasting your time. I am not sceptical, both because I have seen too much that looks like magic, and because I know that any self-consistent formula in terms of which we examine life will yield its results. If there were nothing to recommend the book but the amazing insight with which you relate together certain of the typical characters, it would deserve respect. Magic is a domain in which I take what you do on trust.

The next character in which you appear before my generation is the character of dramatist. Many of your plays are in verse, and your whole interest has been in poetic rather than realistic drama. As a dramatist, within the four walls of the theatre, you have made no impression to be compared with your fame as poet: but you have done a great deal more than is generally realised. You not only wrote the plays: you called into being a theatre and actors to present them. There were about the turn of the century two brothers in Dublin, Frank and Willie Fay, who had a passion for acting. They and the little company they had assembled passed under your control and that of Lady Gregory: and the result was the Abbey Theatre. Frank Fay followed the path of poetic speech; Willie attended to the racy realistic speech of hill and quayside. With this company your plays, the plays of Synge and Lady Gregory, and many others, were presented to the world.

One thing all your players had in common—they could speak: and one of the most beautiful voices in the theatre of this century, the voice of Sara Allgood, was trained upon the Abbey boards. Her performance in your *Cathleen ni Houlihan* was one of the most beautiful and terrible things I have ever seen on the stage: and it showed how effective your work is, when it is perfectly presented. In this country, your plays are usually badly done, and therefore pronounced ineffective for the stage. Last time I saw *The Land of Heart's Desire*, the fairy child was played by a woman of thirty with fat legs. She reminded me of the musician who wrote to you and said " You should have heard my setting of your *Innisfree* as it was sung in the open here by two thousand Boy Scouts." I have seen *Riders to the Sea*, most effective of one-act plays, brought to nothing by the inability of the two girls who were on first to work up any tension: so that the play started anew with the entrance of each character. The last time I was in Dublin, an actor told me that, when he and his friends read the script of your play on Swift, they said, again and again, " This will never come off on the stage ": yet, when they played it, you were right every time. It is legitimate to suspect, therefore, that you may know more than your critics: but certainly the players of the modern theatre, the actor who fidgets and makes faces, the actress who fidgets and makes eyes, can do nothing for a

drama that demands the power of immobility
and a perfect speech.

Next, you are a writer of prose. From *Red
Hanrahan* by *The Cutting of an Agate* to the *Autobiographies* and the Introduction to Hone and
Rossi's *Berkeley*, the current of your prose has
flowed on with increasing power and stateliness.
It has great flexibility, astonishing force, a studied
architecture, and a noble music. There is no
room here—I wish there were—to analyse its
development and give examples. It is at its best
in *Per Amica Silentia Lunae*, where abstract and
difficult matters are expressed with masterly
clearness.

If I had to compile an anthology of your prose
(Heaven forbid there should be such a thing) I
should think first of all of the end of that chapter in
Autobiographies which tells of the downfall of Oscar
Wilde. Then, immediately, I should think of a
hundred other things. Like your speech, your
prose has a manner very much your own. You
put on your mantle to write as, when there are
more than four people in the room, you put on
your mantle to speak. It is the most amazing
thing about you (next to your genius), that in an
age of change and mechanisation and vulgarism
such as has never been known, you have kept your
artistic life aloof from the age's infection. "The
technique of seeming ": with you, that phrase has
implied neither varnish nor pretence. You took

the one way out for your temperament: hardened yourself in youth, going about everywhere till you had found a cloak for your diffidence, the mantle of the writer: till there was a public manner— genuine, hard-earned, won by blood and sweat— to give the world what was due to it from a poet's person, and to give the man beneath the privacy due to a poet's self. In this age the artist's person is exploited with his work. His credit with the public depends on both, and few personalities can escape adulteration. That soilure never befell you: and the manner that to many has seemed aloof or even haughty, the flow of talk behind which the man they impudently sought escaped them, has been the price of your integrity.

Upon the quality of your talk, whether formal or informal, there have been no two opinions. In a nation of talkers you have belonged always to the front rank. One attribute only you have lacked, the attribute of irresponsibility. The wild ranges of fantasy and satire, the inspired-demented improvisations of a Stephens or a Gogarty, are outside your temperament: but in the conversation of ideas, in breadth and certainty, you have had no superior. The quickness of your intellect to leap into a point of vantage, the accuracy with which you marshal and mount some piece of technical knowledge, has always been the admiration of those who sat around you. I have heard you defeat, upon the date of some Athenian sculpture, a specialist in that study. He laboured for days afterwards to prove you wrong; but you were right. An instinct leads you to the knowledge that belongs to your destiny: and besides this you have like a jackdaw accumulated a most curious and copious collection of facts, and made them serve your purpose. It is hard to imagine you at a loss: and your retort is most formidable.

" Are you not afraid, Sir," asked someone at Oxford once, when you had been speaking, " that your thought will lead you away from the realities of life into some intellectual desert, remote from action ? "

" No," you replied. " Too many of my friends have been shot."

And—you will not remember this, but I shall never forget it!—one night in your Broad Street house, a shy and solemn young man put to you a solemn question.

" What is it, Mr. Yeats," he asked, desperately nerved to speak, " about the writings of Mr. George Moore that makes you read page after page with such delight ? "

" Well," you replied, " as I never read anything of Moore with delight, I am afraid I don't know."

Then you were very kind to the abashed young man: and, as he was thereby cured of asking solemn questions, he got his lesson cheaply. Had the reply come from anyone but yourself, the young man might never have had the courage to return: but he did return: and on the Monday evenings of the next year or so, he learned more than he had ever learned, or, I dare swear, ever will learn.

But we were speaking of your conversation. That first meeting with Oscar Wilde, which you record in *Autobiographies*, must have made a very deep impression upon you: for, when there are more than three people in the room, your talk has a rhythm and a precision which can only come of long practice. You tell the stories, you chant the phrases, with a singer's exact proportion of breath to effort. The last time I was with you, you told at the dinner table the magnificent death of the O'Rahilly. " I helped to wind this clock, and I must be there when it strikes," you repeated, two or three times, and on to the noble conclusion " Here died the O'Rahilly. R.I.P." with every note in the cadence perfect. I do not mean that the effect was studied for conversation, but that your mind speaks its thoughts, and long brooding makes them ready for utterance. If I were tempted to think otherwise, there would rise the memory of the most perfect paragraph I heard you speak, which came, years ago now, in your Merrion Square house, in answer to a remark of A.E. Its form, its complexity, wrapped round a quotation from Wilhelm Meister, showed it to have been ready in your mind: yet a unique occasion called it forth. Your mind speaks its

knowledge to itself, and the utterance is ready for
all occasions. When, after an interval, I hear you
talk once more, I find I have forgotten that life
can be lived at such a pitch: that mind can blaze
with such intensity and not be consumed.

Yet all your conversation is not stately or of
high import. You have, heaven be praised, a
liking for a broad story or an Elizabethan jest.
Once—I seem to be delving too much into my
own memories, but that cannot be helped—once
when I had arrived before other guests, you began
to tell me a marvellous and Rabelaisian story
about a member of the Rhymers' Club. In the
midst of it sounded upon the stair the footfall of a
theologically minded friend.

" Wait," you said. " This will not be suitable.
Wait till afterwards."

In a minute, the talk was all theology. The
theologian brought with him a young man who
wished to be ordained, but had doubts of his
calling. You exhorted him like a prophet of old.
" In religion," you said, " never leave your
father's house till you are kicked down the steps " :
and finally, when it became apparent that the
doubts were grievous, you made a private appoint-
ment with the young man. For hours, then, all
the talk was of visions and the pursuit of wisdom.
At last the guests rose to go. I waited while you
showed them out. The canaries twittered sleepily
under their coverings. In a minute, you returned.

" Now," you said. " The gallipots. . . ."

When, some time later, we heard that the doubter had been to see you, and had gone away confirmed in his faith, we asked what on earth you had said to him.

" Oh," you replied, " I took him through all the Forty-Nine Articles! "

An American journalist who came to interview you a few months ago wrote to his paper that it was you who had interviewed him. This is your secret. This enabled you to deal with the doubting young man, and with a hundred others. A stranger comes into the room. You watch him. For a time you say nothing. Then, in three rapid questions, you penetrate his mystery. You unlock the gates. It is a power of divination. In all the time that you let me visit you, you saw always where I was heading before I knew myself. This I know has been the experience of many others. You do not solve a man's problem for him: you put the means for solution near his hand. It is the greatest service that one human being can do another, and you, with your gift of divination, have done it a thousand times. But gifts of divination do not drop from the sky. They come to those who are *interested*. You have an unending interest in those of your fellow creatures who your instinct tells you are worth your while: and by worth your while I mean susceptible to your interest: people whom that interest will enable for some positive human purpose. Naturally, it is not an indiscriminate interest. " There's not a fool," etc. To fools you would be as useless as they to you. What but this gift of divination enabled you to see Synge's destiny and put him in the path of it ? The world owes you a heavy score there. But for you, those plays would not have been written. You saw what he needed. You sent him to a place where he would hear an idiom not his own: where thought became objective for him, and he could judge it. Synge owed you much: and in that there are many like him.

In some ways, it is safe to judge of others' experience by one's own. I came to see you at Oxford, a silent, awkward young man who had written a few verses. It took an act of faith to connect the young man with the verses, for they were lively, and he was not. I was in poor health, and had a poor conceit of myself. You did for me more than any other human being has done. You allowed me to come and sit and talk with you. You enabled me to discover myself. What self-confidence and strength I have to-day I owe to you. It was, as I said, the greatest service one human being can do another: the one service that never humiliates nor becomes a burden: and what you did for me you must have done a hundred times for others. Your life and work have been the pattern for many an artist: too big to be imitated, too individual to be copied, but a

perpetual bulwark against vulgarity and smallness
of heart.

This letter is over-long, and I must close it. You
stand alone, and unchallenged, as the greatest
living poet and man of letters. More than anyone
of your time, you have upheld the high name of
poetry and the honour of the poet's calling. Everything in your life that did not belong to others
you have brought to the service of your art. You
have made use of all that has happened to you—
and of all that has not happened to you. You
have lived as an artist. You have never asked your
art to fill your pocket. When, twenty years ago,
you won a money prize, you kept of it enough only
for a bookplate, and returned the rest. The image
of a young man in a garret arose to the mind of
one who knew garrets: you would not take what
another might need. The results of this devotion
to your art belong to the world. You have given
poetry new rhythms, new subtleties, and new
precision. You have added a note to blank verse—
a feat which puts you in the great line of poets.
Your fame is such that Dublin must assiduously
call you Willie to show that she is not impressed.
You have claimed your own niche in history:

>   And I may dine at journey's end
>   With Landor and with Donne.

Assuredly you may. After dinner Shelley will look
in. Tom Moore will present his compliments to a

brother Irishman, and there will be a message
from the Dean of St. Patrick's. On the morrow
you will be bidden to Dr. Johnson—" Why, Sir,
I am delighted to see you. Come in, Sir "—but,
at the first moment you can manage, you will be
off to call on William Morris. . . . There will be
an apologetic note from Blake, who has been told
that you have come, but was so busy that the news
slipped his mind. Then the magicians will claim
you for an evening. You will drive in a carriage
to visit Stanislas de Gaetan—and this time, there
will be no fear of its overturning. On the appointed
evening, the Rhymers will be gathered: Beardsley
will have drawn a new Madonna, and Lionel
Johnson will be still astonished at the vulgarity of
those who deny eternal punishment. . . .

They will be keeping your chair warm for you
in Elysium, but never mind that. You are not due
there yet! There is work to be done, there are
evenings to be spent in talk: and your heart is
still young for both.

Believe me always

Yours very sincerely

L. A. G. STRONG.

A LETTER TO
A GRANDFATHER

REBECCA WEST

MY DEAR GRANDFATHER,

It was very foolish of me not to write to you before.
I might have known that you would be aware of
what had happened to me, since it affected me so
greatly, even if it were not what I fear it to be. But
I suppose you are also aware of my reasons for not
writing to you; your letter is very forgiving. It was
partly that the whole business seems such a monstrous
weight for the mind to carry. To start discussing it
with you makes me feel as tired as if we had decided
to run a large stockbroking business together. It was
partly also that I have had no time. Ever since this
happened to me, I have been running about buying
clothes. It has amused me that this confirms a theory
of yours. Do you remember how you once pointed
out to me that all the women who have been most
noted for extravagant dressing—Queen Elizabeth,
Madame Tallien, the Empress Josephine—had been
at some time or other of their lives exposed to great
danger? You argued that the real reason why Paris
made the best clothes in the world was that France
has been the battlefield of Europe. I understand
that now. Fear has made me feel that my substance
may run away like water and be lost in a crack of
the earth, so I build myself up to solidity with rich
stuffs. I command an expenditure of art on these
stuffs which would be absurd if I had not a guarantee
promising perpetual safety to the object they adorn;
and I am not absurd, I am plainly reasonable. It is a

device of self-deception that works well enough if one runs about and gets tired.

I suppose that, strictly speaking, I have not been in danger. But didn't you find, when it happened to you, that it was worse than danger? You aren't afraid of dying, it is true. But you know as soon as it begins that you are going to find out what's what, and you feel as if you had realised all along that half the reasons you have given yourself for thinking this universe a safe place to be born are fraudulent inventions, and that this is the moment when they are going to be exposed as frauds. Of course, if it happened as it used to do, I suppose that was the last unhappy moment one had on earth. But now— if it really was that which happened to me three weeks ago—it is very different. I tell you that ever since I have been going about buying clothes. What a metaphysical action that is! One can't exhaust its implications. Among other things it's so Berkeleyan. One wraps the self in gorgeousness as if to say, " There's nothing but you really, the universe is just a figment you keep on creating, if I give you all these lovely presents will you make me a lovelier universe ? "

I am not sure that you are free to do the only thing that would be of any help to me: to tell me what your experience was like so that I can compare it with this thing that happened to me and see if I have had my share of the vision that comes to each generation of our family. Of course, it may be that this is something which one can't discuss with one's descendants, like one's love-affairs. That there may

be some such shyness is proved by the curious fact
that I do not want to tell Father about it. If I am
asking you something impossible forgive me. But
do tell me what you think: whether it has really
happened to me. I am nearly sure it has. I had all
the signs. A cold wind blew past me, though it was
a hot June day and not a leaf stirred. I felt where
every vein was carrying blood all through my body,
and suddenly the flow seemed to turn backwards.
I felt my bowels as a moving snake, my skin seemed
to slip and then writhe back to where it had been.
Then there was the sense—almost the sound—of the
rent veil. It is not possible that it could have been
anything but that; and I am the right age too.
Didn't you tell me that all the family—except the
ones who took steps to fight it off, and thanks to you
I have never done that—had to go through it before
they were thirty-five?

It isn't, in the least, as you say in your letter, you
fear it may be, that there is anything wrong in the
way the family prepared us for it. I think you all
handled the business most sensibly. For one thing,
I knew from the very beginning—even, I think,
before I could talk—that it was going to happen to
me. Most of the intimations have no words, make
no sense; only they tell one. On a veranda at a
tennis-club or somewhere, when there is going to be
a thunderstorm and it is very still, a strong wind
suddenly begins to tear at the awning over one's
head; *hack-hack-hack* it goes, and a rainspot round
like a penny falls on the hand one is leaning on the
rail; or one is standing by a river at night and they

have been letting off fireworks, filling the sky half-way up and glazing the waters with golden rain and red and green wheels that sizzle as they fall and turn, and then the darkness comes back and is not dispelled, and seems to spread out very softly, filling everywhere, and one knows that it has come back for the last time and will stay. It is at moments like these that for no particular reason one remembers one will some day have to stand in front of the thing which is hidden to all other people all their lives long, and look at it as much as it wants to be looked at, and take just what it wants to give one. The mouth goes dry, a shudder passes over one's scalp and down one's spine, and one's stomach falls and comes up again, but one feels proud.

So, as the knowledge was there and you couldn't disregard it, I think you did quite right in exploiting that feeling of pride. Of course, it's obvious that something's gone wrong in the last few centuries— I was aware of that even before what happened three weeks ago. But you cannot prepare the young for the worst. Look at the pitiful generation that has been prepared for the worst by opening their eyes on a world ravaged by war. I think it was quite right to bring us up to regard the hereditary faculty of vision as a family glory, a sort of perpetual Crusade, an inalienable right of recourse to the Holy Grail, and to make us feel a proprietory complacency in what our ancestors created under its inspiration.

No church that is standing to-day, not even Chartres or Vezelay or my dear Tournus, means as

much to me as the church that Philippe de Beauchamp built to commemorate his vision, though it
can hardly be said to be standing at all. I can hear
your voice as you said that morning, " To-day I
will take you to Beauchamp Abbey." I thought you
were tired and did not really want to go, that you
were forcing yourself to do something which you
hoped would amuse me; I told you not to trouble,
that I would be quite happy playing in the garden.
But you insisted, you suddenly became querulous
as though I had refused to perform a necessary
routine like going to school. So we got into the dog-
cart and drove so far that the roads changed from
red earth to white, we passed Bath lying in a bowl,
fantastic and romantic as a planned city is to the
eyes of a child that has only known towns and
villages which have grown, we followed the rising
tail of a valley up to the high stone houses of Becham
Charterhouse. Then there was a bleak stretch of
road, lodge-gates, and an avenue of elms.

You got out of the dog-cart stiffly, I thought I had
never seen you looking so old. We went down the
avenue and crossed a field. It had been raining all
that spring, the bluebells at the foot of the elms
looked like slate-coloured rags that tramps had cast
off there, the red cows munching the foundered grass
had stars of mud on their flanks. It did not seem
worth while having come all that way, there was
nothing in that field except a black tower in the far
corner, which was not quite a tower, which had an
air of accident about its proportions. You said
something about it having been the great fault of the

Reformation that it broke so many eggs which could not go into that particular omelette; and afterwards, very lazily, almost inaudibly, you said something more intricate about the preservation of the single chapel that was left being one of those special blessings for which one cannot be properly thankful, owing to one's resentment at the general disaster to which they are an exception. Then we opened the mean plank door under the stone portal, and for the first time I participated in the paradox and mystery of the great churches, of the unloving architecture built by the grimness of supreme love.

When we came out again you showed me a broken arch projecting only a few inches from the wall of the building, and you said that from the spring of this arch they knew this must have been a vast abbey, covering at least half of the field. We gaped at the air, which was grey and glassy with unfallen rain, as if it had been a solid medium which had always been there, and must still bear within itself the imprints of the vaults and arches by which Philippe de Beauchamp had tried to copy the harsh and solid and real architecture he had seen in the moment when the veil was rent. He had made too good a copy. I shuddered, being aware that that was why men had destroyed it. Man does not want to know. When he knows very little he plays with the possibility of knowledge, but when he finds that the pieces he has been putting together are going to spell out the answer to the riddle he is frightened, and he throws them in every direction; and another civilisation falls. How I have longed to have that full copy,

and raged at that remaining fragment for being so
small a part of it, and worshipped it for the revelation it made of the quality of the whole! I was miserable that very dry summer when the earth sank and
disclosed foundations we had never suspected, and
we saw that the Abbey must have covered nearly the
whole field. I felt like someone who, having suffered
some great loss, learns from the delirium of a person
concerned in the tragedy that his loss was greater
than he knew.

It dominated all my youth, that chapel, and the
Abbey which was not there: the kind of architecture,
worked in blackish stone, that would have put into
the mind the idea of a man stretched on a cross.
The arches and doorways and sanctuaries give such
a sense of breadth that the consciousness strains
itself to follow right and left as far as it can, like
outstretched arms; the vaults rise to such a height
that the consciousness strains up and down, like a
torso stretched so that the muscles are gnarled in the
recess under the ribs. But a man cannot stretch more
than a certain distance from his head and his belly;
and that makes him a tense and interesting pattern
worked on the surface of infinity. That was Philippe
de Beauchamp's vision, and the commemoration of
it had been destroyed, and in my time I was going to
see something like it. All of it exhilarated me, even
the thought of the destruction, which gave me the
blind, drowning sense of pleasure one has in a very
rough sea, when one swings low in the trough between two great waves. That was specially so after
the later day when we had climbed up the stone

spiral stairs to the dove-cote above the chapel and
the muniment room, and you told me that here was
the reason why this single part of the building had
been spared. The despoilers had feared to disturb
the home of the doves, lest they should fly away and
be lost. The dove, the thing that flies forth, the
logos, the symbol of the spirit, the dove that only
the lords of the manor and the Abbey might possess,
that flew down from its tower and pecked the seed-
corn and ravaged the crops, while the peasants
cursed who had to see the ruin of their labours and
pay a tithe of what was left to maintain their winged
enemy and its owners. Supremely apt symbol of the
spirit, the full life of which is lived only by certain
human beings, and by certain parts of human beings,
which flies forth and pillages the material life with
its sharp, greedy beak of criticism, while the natural
man stands by and curses, seeing his relationship
with his environment ruptured, yet knowing himself
under an ineluctable obligation to support the life
of the spirit. How strange it is that men should pull
down the Abbey but spare the doves; and how
strange it is that though they spared the doves, time
dispersed them. They are gone, save from my mind;
for when I remember the dove-cote, it is as if the
dimness had been full of the harsh wooden whirr of
doves' wings, and as if I had seen hundreds of them
fall forward from the window into space like the
sense of a letter travelling from the writer's mind,
and coming back to post themselves prudently in the
holes in the walls as if they were the material forms
of letters.

I am sorry that the picture Sir John Beauchamp
had painted to commemorate his vision was another
of the eggs that the Reformation broke without
proper regard for the omelette, even though it was
painted two hundred years later and things had been
getting softer every minute. But I learned the contract between him and John Petty the painter by
heart, because of its certainty and pride, as well as
its traces of Froissart-like sweetness.

" First there shall be the likeness of Paradise and
in this Paradise shall be the Holy Trinity, and between Father and Son shall be no difference, both
having fine dark beards, and the Holy Spirit in the
form of an English dove, but with a wider stretch of
wing, more like to a sea-bird, and Our Lady before
them, and she is not to be painted like any earthly
woman known to Master Petty, and on the head of
Our Lady the Holy Trinity shall be placing a crown.

" Item: the vestments shall be very rich, and
those of Our Lady shall be white damask, and around
Our Lady shall be a circle of cherubim and seraphim,
some to be red and some to be blue, for it is true how
they are shown of these colours in our tapestries and
missals.

" Item: on the left side of Our Lady shall be the
angel Gabriel with a certain number of angels, and
on the other side saint Michael, with as many
angels.

" Item: on the other hand, saint John the Baptist
with beside him the confessors, that is to say saint
Gregory in the form of a pope on whose head an
angel shall be holding the earth, and two holy

cardinals, one old and one young, and saint Hugh
and saint Agricola bishops (saint Hugh in the
Carthusian habit) and many other saints.

" Item: on the right side shall be saint Peter and
saint Paul, with a pope martyr on whose head also
an angel shall be holding the earth, and saint
Stephen and saint Martin, in the habit of cardinal
deacons, and the Magdalen and the two Maries, the
mother of James, and Salome, each holding in her
hand that which she ought to hold. . . ."

Definite, definite as a specification for the Lord
Mayor's Show. There are one or two items that must
have driven Master John Petty of Winchester to his
wits' end, but not because they were vague. Sir
John wanted " under the same paradise to be the
heavens, in which shall be the noon sun and the full
moon, and under them the earth, where it shall
seem to be all four seasons of the year," and he
wanted the scene on earth to be a part of the high
road about a hundred yards from Castle Farleigh
and yet also to be the city of Rome. So doubtless it
had seemed in the moment of his vision; his consciousness stretched up and down through time and
out through space. But it was not strained like the
body of a man on the cross. Rather it grew easily,
reaching out from ordinary limited knowledge into
experience of infinity and eternity, like a branch of
may reaching out into the early summer air.

Definite was his vision, but soft and sweet, like the
fine-edged but fragile may-blossom. Do you remember how he directed that there was to be painted the
Church of the Holy Cross of Jerusalem as it stood in

Rome, showing saint Gregory as he was when he was
celebrating mass and Our Lord appeared to him?
" Not," said Sir John, " that I saw him thus, but I
would not have it seem that I am the only man who
has seen a vision." He was sweet within and he saw
sweetness all around him. In all the scenes he be-
speaks to illustrate his cosmography, of the angel
crying He is risen, He is not here, above the sepul-
chure of Our Saviour, and the angel crying She has
been lifted up to the heavenly chamber, above the
sepulchre of Our Lady, and of the three strangers
who came to Abraham's tent, he commands that it
is " to be very joyful." Oh, early summer time of
England! Yet I prefer the bleak spring of Philippe
de Beauchamp, though in his world, as in Byzantium,
halocs would not shine without fuel, and divinity
would not only gild itself with light, but would burn
itself with fire.

Of course, it would have helped me enormously if
the number of articulate Beauchamps had been
greater. Philippe de Beauchamp came about 1230,
didn't he, Sir John Beauchamp about 1453. Then
Richard Beauchamp about 1670. Decidedly it's
been inconvenient, the way that there's a steady
flow through the ages in our family of men of action,
interrupted only every two hundred years or so by a
man of the analytic type who employs artists or is
himself an artist. It makes one think of the Italian
philosopher's theory of the human spiral, which
implies that man passes through alternate phases of
determinism and free will. The idea is that the
universe thrusts a certain number of experiences on

the individual, which for a time overwhelm him. He reacts to them purely mechanically; he is the victim of an obvious determinism. But then he gets these experiences in hand; something emerges from him which regards them as its material, and it manipulates them. He enjoys, in fact, something roughly approximating to free will. But by these manipulations he creates a certain number of new experiences which tumble down on him in an unorganised state and make him again a victim of determinism, until again he controls them and has another taste of free will; and so on for ever. This isn't a theory that can be neatly proved. There are supermen who will make an attempt at free will in any age, and submen who will never renounce the pleasures of a determined existence. But it has the merit of recognising that life is a different thing at different times.

How I wish we could check that theory by knowing exactly what it was that was seen by the Beauchamps who did not call in the aid of art for commemoration! I would give much to know if the visions changed during the Reformation, to know what came to the Beauchamp who was Privy Councillor to Henry VIII and close friend to Erasmus. Did he see, added to the crowds of saints on the right hand and the left hand of Our Lady, a new martyr carrying in his hand a pen the size of a sword, emblem of the means of his martyrdom? And if he had been bespeaking a picture of his vision, would he have been able to order the painter to make that martyr "very joyful"? Or was that crowd not added to but thinned ? Perhaps in each vision the Trinity and Our Lady have lost some of their attendance and stand more alone. Perhaps man, in the whimsicality of some passion not yet defined, has gathered the rose of godhead as he might have gathered any other flower, and has plucked it apart, murmuring, " Loves me, loves me not," till fewer petals hang on the stalk. At any rate not all had gone, there were still some saints in waiting left for Richard Beauchamp to see a hundred years later.

There's another proof of how wise you were in making us proud of the concrete results of our ancestors' visions. In the squeamishness of adolescence I might have shied at the oddity of our family destiny, if I had not found when I went to school that it wasn't only Beauchamps who thought Richard Beauchamp better than Crashaw, nearer Milton. Of course all his work fulfils gloriously the first condition of religious poetry. It makes one feel that a void is being filled; and the void is here, in this world of appearances where we spend our every-day lives, and the material which is filling it up has been brought over the threshold of what we call the world of reality—that is, our intimation of the forces which lie behind these appearances. . . If a poem works the other way round, and one feels that for the writer there's a void in the world of reality and he is filling it up with sensuous material from the world of appearances, then that is cant, that is " devotional verse." When I read Richard Beauchamp's " Ode to Saint Catherine " and see the fragile woman stuffed out by saintliness to majestic contours,

I know he played fair in every line. He saw the
woman and realised that as an individual she presented an insoluble mystery, and accounted for her
as one more example of an ardour that had been
inspiring the universe. If he had said, " Let us not
worry about the universe so long as it produces these
mysterious individuals "—which is the burden of
much nineteenth-century religious verse—he would
have betrayed the argument by closing it. That, of
course, would not have been Richard Beáuchamp's
way, since he was of the Renaissance, and that age
poured all its power into argument. The poem
about saint Catherine is own brother to the panel
on the ceiling of the Sistine Chapel (which, like all
Michael Angelo's work, isn't a picture at all, but
painted literature) which shows God stretching out
His forefinger to Adam and infecting him with life.
The form of God is manifested before us as the very
substance of life; not a grain of that skin, not a drop
of that blood, not a cell of that flesh, but has eternal
existence, incorruptible in its glory and power. This
substance of life is of its charity pouring itself into the
body of man, which is manifested before us as the
very substance of death; and thereby it gives him a
second body of life, which shall survive when his
body of death decays. How Michael Angelo argues
his point with his brush, his brains, his loins! But it
appears, even if one accepts his argument, that God
did not keep his forefinger stretched out quite long
enough. He failed to impart to man His attribute
of tirelessness. The age flagged. We were left
suddenly with more on our hands than we could

possibly need of sacred persons not inspired but
inflated, unattended by cherubim whose cheeks are
swollen not with the spirit but with mumps, and
whose duties are plainly not to choir the godhead
but to slip linen cases on and off the feather-stuffed
clouds. Now, what happened after that? What was
the secret of Geoffrey Beauchamp? Do you know?
Can you find your way about the eighteenth century,
that age which keeps on saying it is obvious and
which keeps on being infinitely mysterious? It calls
itself the Age of Reason, yet its literature is moved
as none other by the yeasty workings of faith; and in
what it chose to regard as causes for joy and fear it
ran stark mad, miles out of reasonable territory.
Think of the horridness of those times. They were
fine, but they were foul. Take two steps out of the
great hall, and one was at the green baize door;
push it back and one's foot slipped on the fat beetles
bred in filthy kitchens, one's eardrums shivered to
the oaths of warring cooks and scullions, flunkeys
and maids. Take two steps out of the great house,
and one was in Gin Lane, where such seeds of sweetness that are in man had been cast out and trodden
in the mud. There the sick and the old screamed under
more than their aches and age, for their irritated kin
rained blows on them. There children grew to but
half-child size till they had reached years when they
could defend for their own use what they earned by
vice; then, galvanised by the electric juice of dread
for Tyburn and transportation, they shot up into an
adulthood prenaturally vital even in the poisonousness
of its leers, the extreme contortion of its defor-

mities. In previous ages there had been poverty, but man could not more be blamed for it than a dog can be beaten for its mange. Since he had not learned to identify it, much less to analyse it, he could not be blamed for failing to cure it. But now that the poor had become articulate, now that literature and art were reporting their plight to the rich, poverty was as disgraceful to man as dirt on his hands when there is soap and water near by and he has learned to wash. How mysterious it was then that the scrupulous of that day, who had leisure to think upon their destiny, who went to bed so pleasantly free from fatigue that they were able to be awake and weep over their sins, did not shed tears over the double beastliness of man—the beasts that were made beastly by poverty, the beasts that, being rich, let their poor brothers be bestialised! How mysterious it was that the common channel of grief ran in such other direction!

Take, for example, that clergyman's widow of whom we know from the diaries of Geoffrey Beauchamp and her nephew. With difficulty, that morning when her history touches our family annals, she was coaxed from the darkened room where, usually on all fours, to show her humility, she had dwelt for the past few months. They had great difficulty in dressing her, for she had made herself a coarse holland shift and had put over it some rags the cook Sukey had thrown out as past wearing, and she would remain so. This was absurd, for she was even above the common station of a clergyman's widow, having been constrained to her marriage by some

prolonged trouble about settlements which had
severed an earlier attachment and left her too long
a spinster. Why, she was the young squire's aunt.
She had the best of clothes hanging in her wardrobe.
But she wept when they put them on her, and most of
all when they crowned her with a neat mobcap of
starched muslin, for she wanted to go bareheaded,
with unpowdered hair, like a Bedlamite or a lost
woman. She wept, too, when they led her out into
the garden, though the stone of the Manor House lay
flushed like a ripening peach before the early sun,
and the spring flowers she had used to tend stood
sturdy-fragile, each with its long, blue morning
shadow on the ground beside it, like a lance given
to defend it. She wept, she wept, even when they
lifted her into the coach, though it was the fine one
that in her sister's lifetime she had always coveted.

Why did she weep? Had she the compensation
some maintain is often given to the witless? Could
she see half a mile across the meadows, down by the
willow-gardens, where her nephew was, that should
have been beside her in the coach? Then might she
well have wept. There, just before the old stone
bridge, the little river broadened and deepened to a
pool that had been useful in the past for ducking
witches. (" You need not be sorry for the stag," I
heard someone say to a child at a meet, " stags have
always been hunted.") Reason had since dawned
on England. There was no witch in the pool,
superstitiously suspected of traffic with the unseen,
only a boy suspect, on the soundest material evidence, of having run away from a workhouse. On

the previous day he had formed an uppish notion
that he might stop being starved and beaten, and he
had overed a wall and lain under a hedge till dusk.
Then, at the end of a night's stumbling, he had come
on this pool, and thought it a pleasant place to rest;
and so it was. Between the water's edge and the
rough fields there was a gardeny bank, and above it
the blossom of an old may tree rose steep and tall as
the sail of a boat. He slept late and was seen by a
labourer, who had heard the beadle rapping at the
village doors and announcing the State's minute
particle of loss. News was sent back, and presently
a party sauntered over the fields behind the beadle,
ready to fall back and listen whenever he turned
about and addressed them, for he was a well-built,
full-bodied, loud-voiced man, who could talk with
authority of wars abroad. The young squire himself
joined them, since Aunt Dolly was such an age at
her toilet. Presently they looked down on the boy,
who was paddling naked in the shallows. The beadle
pressed his finger against his lips, and all stood still
and tittering. A man is ridiculous when he is
watched by his enemies and does not know it. Then
a guffaw forced its way out, and the boy looked up
and saw the beadle tremendous on the skyline of the
grassy bank. He threw up his hands and fell forward into the stream, and was carried under the
bridge. Everyone shouted and ran down the bank,
and peered into the shadow under the arch. It was
thought at first the boy had gone under, but presently
the sharper eyes saw two bent matchstick arms clinging to a cleft in the piers, and a face like a turnip-

ghost's bobbing in the quick water. Two men
stripped to go and find him, and the beadle told
what would be done with him when he was found,
echo spreading out his voice into an open fan of
curses and threats under the dank arch. It is no
wonder that the clergyman's wife shed tears, were
she clairvoyant.

But it is more probable that she was not. For all
of a sudden the matchstick arms, the turnip-ghost,
were gone. The beadle's voice had perhaps sounded
more tremendous, the swimming men even more formidable than those who come to lay hands on one,
because of the cold water, and the green-slimed
stone, and the darkness. They did not find him for
some time, and then he was caught head first in the
weed beyond the bridge. They brought him back
and laid him stomach down on the grass at the
beadle's feet, but though the beadle swore his
loudest he did not move. A vomit of blood and
water poured out of his mouth, but his shoulder-
blades, which were as sharp-edged as if they were
cut out of tin, never stirred, and the pattern of
weals on his ribs and buttocks was steady as if it had
been painted on a wall. Above him the may-
blossom stirred like a bellying sail running before
the wind. Now, if the clergyman's widow were clairvoyant, she would stop weeping. Here is one organism capable of suffering which shall suffer no longer.
But she continues to blubber as hard as ever. Her
nephew has turned back across the fields, shaking his
head as he looks downward and ponders on the
frowardness of the very poor, and gets into the

coach, and though she is glad of his company she is weeping. They bob along for so many a westward mile that the roads turn from white earth to red under their wheels, and the nephew says a hundred times, " Oh, have done, have done, Aunt Dolly, you did nothing wrong," while his eye scours the passing fields and he wonders how it would be to farm such fatter land ; but still her two hanging curds of cheeks wobble in inconsolable woe, and the mobcap loses all its stiffness and is a dishclout hanging limp against her pinkish nose. It is not the sorrow of the workhouse boy that is distressing her. It is her conviction, which she shall not lose till the coach stops and Geoffrey Beauchamp leads her by the hand into his house, that she has committed the sin against the Holy Ghost.

They came to him from all over England, those who had committed this sin: great ladies, scholars, cobblers, farmers' wives, all brought to a common level by their melancholy, all wearing their hose about their ankles and forgetting the proper seasons for clean linen. Not shrinking from the damp hands of the mad, he greeted them like a brother, and took them into the library, and sat them in the high chair that is still by the fire; and he was able to inform them of something he had seen in his vision which utterly dispelled their doubts. They broke into thanks, their fingers groped in embarrassment about the flapping disorder of their attire, they left in haste with a firm step, and returned neat and restored to their families. Now, how did these people come in the first place to believe that they had

sinned against the Holy Ghost? It is a sin that has
been washed up on the shore of the human mind
from the shipwreck of an obscure text. It is an
unthinkable sin. How can the peasant in the fields
harm the dove? If he has a bow and arrow he can
kill doves, but never the dove. At his feet one dove
and another and another may be dead, but he cannot dry up the spurt of doves that jets from the cote
in the tower; and if he persists the keepers of the
birds will close in on him, to take his weapons from
him and punish him. There is nothing more evident in history than the persistence of the life of the
spirit, and its power to raise up defenders, which is
far more amazing than the persistence of brutishness,
since it works against and not with the tendency to
inertia. The spirit is plainly not to be killed. Why,
then, did the clergyman's widow try to kill it, as she
said she did, at nine o'clock on a Monday night in
late November, as she sat in her seat by the fire in
the saloon? And why did hundreds of others, as im-
potent as she was, have this ambitious fear of sin
against the Holy Ghost so successful that it deserved
damnation?

It must, I think, have been the result of some confusion between the spiritual and the ethical worlds.
The eternal factors in the universe were identified
with the rules of human conduct that follow from
recognition of these factors. In the ethical world
the will is—or, at least, seems to be—the most important instrument. Without it we cannot even use
our intellect; before we can think we must choose
whether we wish to know the truth or invent lies.

If one identified the spiritual and ethical worlds one
would be troubled by this paramouncy of the will.
One would see it as able not only to choose or reject
the knowledge of good and evil, truth and lies, but to
work on the very existence of these entities, and even
against them: not to kill them, since the eternal is
the eternal, but to strike at them. Inevitably such
melancholy persons as always fear the worst, as fret
when they are snug in bed that they have left the
lamp alight downstairs, felt that they must have
used this dangerous weapon to the worst purpose, in
the assault on the essence of Holiness. I can conceive that Geoffrey Beauchamp may have cured
these sufferers with a hair of the dog that bit them.
Though he was compelled by his family destiny to
believe in God, there can be hardly any doubt but
that he must have partaken in the certitude of the
faith which upheld the eighteenth-century sceptics;
which gave David Hume his inexhaustible sweetness,
which organised into confident order Rousseau's
vast hordes of ideas and routed the disorder and
despair natural to his mind, which inspired Voltaire
to those decades of interventions between oppressor
and oppressed, liar and dupe, so innumerable and
so vigorous that no biographer has been able to
chronicle them. These infidels also had identified
the spiritual and the ethical world, they dreamed of
an orgasm of the universe when achieved justice,
pity, candour, honesty, and sense, should fuse into a
substitute for God. It may be that Geoffrey Beauchamp saw the flower of the godhead denuded of all
its petals, stripped of its former company of saints,

surrounded with abstractions, names of the blander tendencies in human conduct.

Different the vision his son Arthur had, I would be ready to swear, though he, too, was silent, and our marvel at the hour and place of his enlightenment eclipses our curiosity about its content. It was a dreadful, shuddering kind of luck to have employed Robespierre as lawyer in a suit about a valuable property in the Pas-de-Calais, and therefore both have permission to stay in Paris till late in the Revolution, and be obliged to use it. But it was perhaps even more terrible, and yet still lucky, that his share of the family fate made him transcend that opportunity, when he achieved his vision on the wet, dark morning of January the twenty-first, 1794, as he drove through the Place de la République in obedience to a summons from Robespierre. His carriage had been brought to a halt by the dense crowds that stood in a half-happy, half-sullen lethargy, sensually drowsy because they were about to gratify a lust, but cowed by the fear punishment would follow this gratification; and the last of the Capets was ready on the scaffold. But though Arthur Beauchamp stood up it was not to have a better view of the killing of the king, for his eyes were fixed on a gleam of livid light above the huddled houses. What did he see? What eternal things could be presented that would reconcile him to this monstrous deception of time, when men gathered together in the name of reason and peace and love for the people, had been liberated by the wine of the moment into open confession that they cared for

none of these things so much as they cared for blood ?
Nor were they to be placated with indiscriminately
chosen blood. It must be shed with reference to an
obscure system of symbolism, which has only a
inexact and variable correspondence with reality.
On the scaffold the man who was the next moment
to be the victim of the error attempted to indict it.
" I am not the Great Father, the Bull, the Thief who
has stolen Power, who must be killed if the Son, the
Weak Human Being, the Dispossessed, is to succeed
to his inheritance. I am only a poor fat man, who
has been made to write important letters when he
had hardly the wits to lick the stamps." But he was
not allowed to complete his indictment, for an
officer in charge of the soldiers about the scaffold
lifted his sword and bade the drummers roll their
drums. This was long thought to be Santerre the
demagogue: the truth was far more visceral, far
deeper in the ground where the mad roots of human
motive grow. The officer was the son of a woman
who, when her hair was mouse brown dusted with
gold and her features snub yet delicate with youth,
had been painted by Boucher lying naked on a sofa,
her rounded little hindquarters uppermost. By
showing the spectator the pink sole of one of her feet
the painter indicates to what breadths of indecorum
extended her spreadeagled pose; and her little face
shone with that absolute innocence which can only
be attained when immodesty has swung full circle,
and no naughtiness is meant as naughtiness since
nothing is known that is not naughty. She was then
the mistress of a king, who in his good time married

her to an Auvergnat nobleman. She was a flower for the world to stick in its coat, only duffers could find reason to shake their heads over her story, for her white and her pink and all her several warm little hemispheres were indubitable boons to man. But the viscera of sons are lunatic. To them the Father, the Bull, the Thief of Power, vile at all times, is at his vilest when he uses his strength to pollute the mother, who, they demand, should be inviolate from all embraces save her children's. The King on the scaffold was not the King who had lain with *la petite Morphy*; but a symbol is a symbol. The young officer flung out his sword, the drums rolled, and doubtless Arthur Beauchamp saw in that gleam of lurid light above the housetops a godhead that had changed its company again. It walked neither with the saints, nor with the virtues, but with the passions that are behind human thought and conduct: passions which were luminous as angels or the flames of hell, which looked like sin yet were responsible for so many of the phenomena of life that if they were sin then all is sin, which had their plain part in making all the moments when man is most nearly more than himself. For there was genius here, in this French Revolution, though there was horror. In the sky, in that livid light, must have been a mystery.

It is a family joke that Arthur Beauchamp's son again and again wrote home from Harrow, "There is a boy here called Byron, I hate him," and added no explanatory detail. We know that when Byron used to lie on the tomb in Harrow Churchyard looking northward over the suavely barbered midland plain, young George Beauchamp squatted against the trunk of the elm tree that shadowed it, watching the older boy as a cat watches a mouse, but we have no record of any childish disputes between them. It may have been that there were none, but that anybody was under the necessity of seeing God once in his lifetime would feel a natural hostility towards a destined leader of the Romantic Movement. When one turns over the leaves of any anthology of poetry one gets a sense of loss, as soon as one comes to the nineteenth century, even though the individual poets brought to their task as superb an equipment as the poets of any previous age: even though some, like Emily Brontë, were not themselves losers. It is as if that phase of poetry represented a marvellous army in retreat before some new catastrophe which had nullified all previous theories of tactics and strategy. The human race had gathered what disagreeable facts it was likely to discover about itself if it progressed farther along the path of self-consciousness, facts far more disagreeable than it had ever recognised under the blanket term of sin; and the redemptive power of divine grace no longer seemed credible, nor very respectable in the arbitrary performance that was claimed for it. Therefore it reversed the natural trend of self-consciousness, it frustrated its natural development into the analysis of experience and its synthesis into a coherent vision of life, and it concentrated on its sensations. There was no limit to the ambition of Shelley's thought, but he tried to think

with his skin and not with his mind. Like Keats he
dwells with too much zest on the impressions he
received by the nerves; his conduct of the further
process, by which the nerves telegraph their messages to a central authority, who discovers their
deeper significance by decoding them into other
terms by the light of the human tradition, is too
languid and febrile. There has been a limitation of
interest; and we see the same restricting tendency
in the moral sphere when Byron discloses to us his
hankering after incest. This appeared to be an attempt to extend man's sphere of liberty, but it was
an opposite action, since the prohibition of sexual
relations between the members of the same family
served the purpose of extending man's sphere of
liberty by securing that one of his chief appetites
should drive him out to see the world. Not that I
decry the Romantics. They serve a purpose, for if
now and then a generation did not concentrate on
recording its sensating the actual and passing
experiences of mankind, then later generations would
have nothing on which to base their classicism, their
interpretation of experience. Nevertheless to be a
Romantic is to be limited, to be poorer than one
would wish to be. This state of impoverishment was
not in any way remedied by the people who carried
on through the nineteenth century the error of the
eighteenth century, and confused the spiritual and
ethical worlds. Life is not tolerable unless the clergyman's widow is clairvoyant and can see half a mile
across the meadows to the pool by the bridge, where
the workhouse boy is drowning; unless she can

descend from her coach and walk with such pride on her errand of mercy that the full-bodied beadle is seen by the lowest as the gross silly beast that he is. But she cannot do that if she is blubbering behind a wet frill of muslin, because she has committed the sin against the Holy Ghost. Unless she is calmed by the knowledge that she could not kill the dove however murderous she be, she will be able to devise a flexible and aristocratic technique for treating the passing accidents of the universe in the light of its eternal factors.

Through all this preoccupation with the merely sensuous and this moral fussiness which were the two prime faults of the nineteenth century, the true poets and the scientists went on searching for the eternal. How I hate the people who sneer at the Victorian scientists, how cheap they show themselves! If the land where you live shows signs of being swept by flood and hurricane you build barns to store your grain, and if you can find no other building material but corrugated iron, well then, you use corrugated iron; and if fools who come after choose to regard you as a man who felt for corrugated iron the curious sort of fetish-love which is celebrated in small print at the end of Mr. Havelock Ellis's great work, it does not very much matter. One ought not to reproach the Victorian scientists for their lack of style, for their cocksureness and their illusion that they could propound a complete solution to the problem of destiny, because they were doing something in a hurry to counter the disintegrating effect of romanticism, to insist that life ought to be something

more than an agitated search for the proper opportunities of sacrifice. By fixing man's attention on the
ascertainable facts of his own history and environment they brought back into fashion the idea of
coherence; by insisting that the reality of these
facts had to be tested they warned man of his tendency to lie, and went some way to warning him why
he lied. I do not wonder that you became a scientist,
though it has added to my perplexities that you did.
It was time for our race to become articulate again,
and no doubt you have; but you have insulated
your articulateness within a screen of pure mathe-
matics. The advance of science must mean a certain
loss to humanity as a whole; for the further it goes
the further it withdraws a certain number of first-
rate brains from contact with the common mind. I
know you've had your vision, probably about forty
to fifty years ago, and I am sure that every piece of
work you've ever done since bears the imprint of
that experience. But what good would Dante be to
me, if he had written the Divine Comedy not in
terza-rima but in a drunken ant's script of mathe-
matical symbols?

My perplexities are so many that it is not a little
thing that I had to do without direct enlightenment
from you. Your affection and the invariably exquisite quality of your nature has made me able to
endure what I have experienced of tragedy, and has
confirmed all pleasant events; but I have no knowledge of the one moment when life was presented to
you as a unity. That is, I do not really know that
that moment ever came to you, any more than I

really know that there is a town in Australia named
Adelaide. It is merely a reported fact, and it cannot
speak past my mind to my bowels. As I have said,
I could not speak to Father about this at all. So I
have gone on, contending with what seems to me
a peculiarly detestable phase of existence. My youth
was, of course, shocked and enraged by the war;
but I have been still further shocked and enraged by
my slow discovery that peace is not much better.
I have learned, as we all do during our passage
through life, the truth about the foully corruptible
body of man, which is so carefully kept from us
while we are children; I realise that it might be
better for a man to be dead in No Man's Land than
to go home and be soil for some dreadful flower of
cancer. But I find still worse than the corruptibility
of the body the more precocious rottenness of the
mind. I loathe the way the two cancers of sadism
and masochism eat into the sexual life of humanity,
so that the one lifts the lash and the other offers
blood to the blow, and both are drunken with the
beastly pleasure of misery and do not proceed with
love's business of building a shelter from the cruelty
of the universe. I loathe the mean trick of generation
which makes a contract between the flesh of parents
and child that promises tenderness, and then annuls
it by making the child so jealous of the parents'
strength. Then there is war; and the child knows so
many defeats in its weakness that when it is a parent
undischarged resentments make it revenge them on
its own child. In spite of these things there is love in
the world, but it is not normality, any more than the

painless intervals in the day of a cancer patient.
For the pain and uncertainty of our personal lives
there is compensation in the world of the intellect,
but that seems to me pitted with shell-holes by the
war. People are tired and disoriented, they do not
follow any road to truth, they stand still and gabble.
It seems to me that never at any other time would I
have been obliged to listen to such nonsense as a
condition of living. Tradition has been thrown out
of the window by all parties, even those who pretend
to be traditionalists. Can earth have seen such
idiots as those who declare that they want to sub-
mit to the authority of the Roman Catholic Church,
not because they believe in its supernatural revelation, but because they dislike the disorder of life
lived without authority? How can it escape them
that the Church loses its claim to authority on the
possession of that revelation, and that it must reject
all such disingenuous proselytes unless they dis-
honestly conceal their motives, in which case their
conversions are void? But they are not more fatuous
than those of the Left Wing, who have thrown the
whole tradition of economic idealism out of the window, and babble of nothing but Russia. Some of them
may be excused for talking as if all ideas of social
and economic equality had been invented by the
Bolsheviks by the circumstance that they were not
Socialists before 1914. But they cannot be excused
for their lickerish liking of the harsh effort of Russia.
They are in love with cancer, they want the love of
man for his kind to be eaten away like the love of
man and woman by sadism and masochism. That

justice should be done without passion and stripes would disappoint them, they have not got out of the fateful ring-fence of primitive ideas where every good must be paid for by pain and sacrifice. There is something regressive about it, for they do no work towards making the indigenous revolution for which we are all waiting; since there has died in nearly all of us who are literate, I think, the desire to protect order based on arbitrary social and economic privilege.

Life seemed to me, therefore, like sitting down to a meal of innumerable courses, most of which were bad, though some were delicious. I meant to order again one that I had often eaten and found delicious when I came over to Paris last week. It refreshed me at once with that curious combination of physical and moral medicine which is the gift of France to the rest of the world. I have never been able to understand its physical effect. It is natural enough that one should feel better in Spain or in Italy, because the air is saturated with sunlight; but it is a mystery why any part of France, even the grey North, puts the nerves to sleep. There is real magic here. But the mental refreshment is surely due to the circumstance that the French relax the tension of life by abandoning a certain irksome pretence. They do not attempt to conceal that they are cruel, and they even let it appear that cruelty almost inevitably manifests itself during the operation of the forces that lead to glory, to great deeds, to great art. They do not pretend that man is without his disposition to cancer. That pretence dropped, they can get on

with living. Think how well one always works in
France. I got to Paris on Friday, and on Saturday
I did some work at the Musée Guimet. It's very
wise to get on such terms with museum authorities
that one is allowed to enjoy sculpture in the proper
way, which is not by looking at, but by feeling it.
As I was running my hands over a Cambodian wall
piece I came on one figure that gave me such a sense
of unity, of the gathering up into a whole of such a
myriad of the sculptor's impressions, that I thought
of the vision, I imagined it must be like that. But I
had forgotten about it when I woke up on Sunday
morning. I went and fetched Lisa, and we went a
walk in the gardens of Bagatelle, to see the prim
roses. Then we met Lionel and Ambrose for lunch
at the Château de Madrid, the usual sort of thing,
we women talked more than the men. Ambrose was
rather unhappy, because he has long been toying
with the idea of entering the Roman Catholic
Church, and it had been a great shock for him to
find on his arrival in Paris that the young priest who
had been the special inspiration of his circle had had
a little trouble and had stepped out of his cassock to
become a dealer in negro sculpture in the Rue de
Boétie; and Lionel, of course, never talks very much,
he is too good-looking and does not like to lose his
pose But they were very nice, and we did not want
to separate, so we all went on to the Fête de Neuilly.
I expect you know what that is. It is a fair held in
the long strip of market place outside the Porte
Maillot, two parallel streets of booths and tents and
merry-go-rounds, painted for the most part in the

French colours, red for blood, blue for water, white
for light, all rather dirty, and braying with that
lovely hurdy-gurdy music which grinds with as
beautifully inevitable an accent as nursery rhymes.
A moving stream of people carried us up one of the
streets. It was like Bank Holiday on Hampstead
Heath, an incredibly villagey show to come to even
the outskirts of a great capital; there were lots of
stalls where you had to throw a ring over beautifully
hideous china ornaments, and dingy curtains that
hid medical museums or Siamese twins or mer-
maids, and platforms where men cast in just the same
mould as the great European statesmen sold patent
medicines. The people about us were villagey too,
ugly and formless and full of honest hardihood in the
exhibition of those characteristics. In the hard light
of the June afternoon, the sallowness of their skins,
the impure black of their clothes, appeared as new,
paler, bizarre and even gay colours. We got to the
end of the street of booths and stood for a time looking at the Utrillo-like face of meaner Neuilly: the
houses painted violet-grey like a healing bruise,
their shutters waiting with a patient look for that
hour when they should be shut and each room might
be the ciborium of some dreary copulation, some
murderous assault; a quarter set aside for consum-
mations of the cancerous human need to be cruel
and to suffer. Then we joined the mob that would
take us up the other street of booths, back to the
Porte Maillot; and after we had moved a hundred
yards or so a strong wind suddenly blew. *Hack-
hack-hack* went the awning over the shooting-gallery.

A vase in the ring-throwing stall crashed over as if a stray bullet had shot it down. A dark cloud rode the sky above the fair, fell lower and spread widely. I knew the bright June afternoon had gone for ever. A rainspot round like a penny fell on my hand. The people's sallow skins and black clothes became more common tints and more massive to the eye, the crowd became a solider thing, solid like an audience collected for an indoor, not an outdoor, show.

I turned about. A cold wind blew past me, but this time the awning did not move. I slipped between the booths and looked at a tree on the pavement. It was without motion, yet the cold wind went on chilling my face, my hands. My bowels writhed in me, my skin slid as if I were a snake and going to cast it. I felt fear, but mainly fear that I should not find what I had to see. A man ran into me, and I nearly laid hands on him to keep him still till I had a good look and saw that the bearded shiny oval of his face meant no more to me than a Court Card. Then I turned about and saw that in front of where I was standing was a kind of merry-go-round formed of a circle of little motor-cars, with a sign above it, carved out of crimson gilded wood, that formed the words " Le Dragon," and upheld them with rampant monsters. On the platform in front of this merry-go-round was a narrow platform with a staircase leading to a turnstile to the ground. On the platform in front of this merry-go-round stood a negro, a very tall negro, no longer young, dressed in evening clothes made of faded scarlet cloth, wearing a

top-hat, and carrying a cane with a gold crook for a
handle. There was a dense crowd of people watching
him, and he was calling out in a hoarse voice that
was like the ghost of thunder, "Aux voitures! aux
voitures!" Every now and then some people
obeyed and passed through the turnstile up to the
platform, and he touched them with his cane, direct-
ing them to their proper seats in the automobiles.
He was much taller than anybody who came up to
the platform; and he was so instantly aware of them
as transport problems, of where there was room for
them, that the lack of personal interest in his eyes
seemed like a harsh rejection of them. It was
evidently of immense importance to him that the
merry-go-round should be quite full. As he bent
over his customers, driving them on with his cane,
it seemed absurd to think of them as people volun-
tarily patronising an amusement. When he had
them all in their seats he turned his face to the crowd
below, and threw up his cane in the air and caught
it. At that the hurdy-gurdy music brayed out, and
the merry-go-round began to turn. He smiled at
the crowd, jerking his head back at his customers as
if in derision. Then he held out his cane straight in
front of him. It became a rod of iron, compelling
the will of the people who looked up at it. They
could not move, they cried out asking him to take
this image of necessity so that they could be free.
But he held it rigid until the merry-go-round behind
him had performed a certain number of revolutions,
when a kind of Venetian blind rose from the side of
each automobile and closed right over it, so that for

a minute or two the occupants were hidden from view. Then he shot back his thumb over his shoulder, contorting his face in a leer, over and over again, in perfect time to the music, till one's own thumb began to twitch, one's own cheek muscles to contract. The crowd made twittering, giggling noises; and at length the negro freed his arms by letting his cane dangle from a barrier on the platform and held out his hands before him. With the first finger and thumb of his left hand he described a circle, and into this circle shot the first finger of his right hand. His teeth shone, his rolling eyeballs exhibited the whites of his eyes; it was if a gleaming bird, a dove, shot forth from his face and in its flight became his finger. Then a turn of wrists broke the pattern, and when it was nothing he made it again, all in time to music so that it happened in the muscles, in the blood, of those who watched him. Sometimes they said " Ahhh! " as if they saw a firework cleaving the sky, sometimes they laughed in irresistible nervous shame; but there was always a crowd. It could not be doubted that this was a great sight to be seen, that one would find nothing better wherever one went in the fair.

I had pressed close through the crowd when he dropped his cane, so I was able to watch his blurred movements when he stooped to pick it up. His knees would hardly bend, his fingers scrabbled round it on the planks. I thought, " He is drunk," and then the green tint on his face, the negro's version of pallor, told me that he was only very tired. I looked at my watch and saw that it was now two hours that I had been watching him, getting people on and off this merry-go-round and entertaining the crowd, and he probably did it all day and every day; and now I was near him I noticed that his scarlet evening suit, though it was well cut, was too loose for him, as if a long disease had wasted him. Now his patrons were getting out of the automobiles and going downstairs, and he had a moment to rest before he started his patter to bring up the fresh ones. I was right under the platform now, and I put up my hand and touched his knee. He looked down at me with eyes blindish with fatigue, and with seeing so many people, and I asked, " Do you never make any other gestures? " In a charred whisper he answered, " What other gestures? " We stared at each other for a minute as if through darkness, and I had a sense both of his endurance, and the actual moments that were racing by as I looked at him. I felt time as a discipline, as a cross on which he and I and the events we took part in were crucified. We might stretch as far as we could to right, to left, to the sky, to the ground, but we were bound to our place in this universe. His body slumped in his loose clothes, I thought he might fall, but he straightened himself. His hoarse voice made its ethereal thunder. The fair went on, he beat his flock into their seats, he held out his cane like a rod, he jerked and leered and shared his jerks and leers with the flesh of his audience, his hands made their pattern, and from his teeth and eyes shot forth the dove. As lights came out round the carvings of the dragon overhead, his teeth and the eyes gleamed brighter than ever. The dove flew forth snow white. I turned and walked away through the falling dusk, knowing that I had no need to look at him any longer, since I should always see him.

When I started to write to you I meant to ask you, " Can this be all? " But now I have told you, now that I have made that full admission of experience which is necessary before an experience is complete, that seems a foolish question. It is like asking, " Is all all? " I was ashamed of my revelation because it showed me not as we all like to appear before our elders, before the past, before that only audience we really fear and respect: sweet, full of the acknowledgment of guilt, infantilely ready to admit our corrigibility, free from exaltation in dark things. I feel that in my spiritual apotheosis the nice thing would have been for me to be like the clergyman's mournful widow, muttering about my Waste Lands, moaning because it is Ash Wednesday, or to be a Romantic, melting and guttering with my own heat like a candle, or to be a simmering-pot of ethical activity. But that is cowardice. I am a fool to be ashamed of what I saw. It was almost intolerably without comfort or benignity. But what does that matter ? The splendour that Philippe de Beauchamp saw, when he built his strong, his valid Abbey, must have been grim. In his faith he saw a gaunt figure extended on a cross. In my faith, which seems to some unfaith, so did I. I also saw a gaunt figure extended on a cross, and if the cross was mere existence the pattern was the glorious same, there was the same tension, there was the same heroic attempt to cover all, to know all, to feel all, although fixed to one point in the universe, and thereby pinned to ignorance. I also know that some are born to be saved and some to be damned, that the pulse which is heard through time and space beats to some other rhythm than human justice. That I see the spirit not as holy or independent, but as the white product of dark gestures, the refined descendant of man's primitive play, does not matter; I still revere the dove and its flight. I admit that when I saw my vision a cold wind blew on me, I was in winter. My generation has long known it lived in winter, but it has deplored it. I no longer do. Now the trees are bare, now one can see the form of the land. I exult in being just where I am, in an age where sweetness, that human invention, which can operate only in association with completely comprehended and controlled things, is not imposed on eternal things that have no knowledge of it. The tragic spirit has come back into life. We feel under no necessity to sentimentalise it and pretend it is pleasanter than it is. We can embrace it in its completeness, we can accept the truth. Suddenly the rich clothes I have been buying seem to me trash, like titles or more money than one needs. To be ashamed of the body one is born with is hysteria, and so also it is to be ashamed of the truth as one's position in time shows it to one. I want to see you, I do not know why I have been writing to you apologetically, I will leave Paris to-morrow and come straight down to the country. I was a fool to think that it would be difficult to talk this over with you, that it would

be a burden to our minds. I have accomplished
what Christians call the will to belief: that is I admit
what I believe. That brings, I see, an inevitable
happiness.

Yours ever, with love,
C. B.

A LETTER TO
A YOUNG POET

VIRGINIA WOOLF

My Dear John,

Did you ever meet, or was he before your day, that old gentleman—I forget his name—who used to enliven conversation, especially at breakfast when the post came in, by saying that the art of letter-writing is dead ? The penny post, the old gentleman used to say, has killed the art of letter-writing. Nobody, he continued, examining an envelope through his eye-glasses, has the time even to cross their t's. We rush, he went on, spreading his toast with marmalade, to the telephone. We commit our half-formed thoughts in ungrammatical phrases to the post card. Gray is dead, he continued; Horace Walpole is dead; Madame de Sévigné—she is dead too, I suppose he was about to add, but a fit of choking cut him short, and he had to leave the room before he had time to condemn all the arts, as his pleasure was, to the cemetery. But when the post came in this morning and I opened your letter stuffed with little blue sheets written all over in a cramped but not illegible hand—I regret to say, however, that several t's were uncrossed and the grammar of one sentence seems to me dubious—I replied after all these years to that elderly nekrophilist—Nonsense. The art of letter-writing has only just come into existence. It is the child of the penny post. And there is some truth in that remark, I think.

Naturally when a letter cost half a crown to send,
it had to prove itself a document of some importance; it was read aloud; it was tied up with green
silk; after a certain number of years it was published for the infinite delectation of posterity. But
your letter, on the contrary, will have to be burnt.
It only cost three-halfpence to send. Therefore
you could afford to be intimate, irreticent, indiscreet in the extreme. What you tell me about
poor dear C. and his adventure on the Channel
boat is deadly private; your ribald jests at the
expense of M. would certainly ruin your friendship if they got about; I doubt, too, that posterity,
unless it is much quicker in the wit than I expect,
could follow the line of your thought from the roof
which leaks (" splash, splash, splash into the soap
dish ") past Mrs. Gape, the charwoman, whose
retort to the greengrocer gives me the keenest
pleasure, via Miss Curtis and her odd confidence
on the steps of the omnibus; to Siamese cats
(" Wrap their noses in an old stocking my Aunt
says if they howl "); so to the value of criticism
to a writer; so to Donne; so to Gerard Hopkins;
so to tombstones; so to gold-fish; and so with a
sudden alarming swoop to " Do write and tell
me where poetry's going, or if it's dead ? " No,
your letter, because it is a true letter—one that
can neither be read aloud now, nor printed in

time to come—will have to be burnt. Posterity must live upon Walpole and Madame de Sévigné. The great age of letter-writing, which is, of course, the present, will leave no letters behind it. And in making my reply there is only one question that I can answer or attempt to answer in public; about poetry and its death.

But before I begin, I must own up to those defects, both natural and acquired, which, as you will find, distort and invalidate all that I have to say about poetry. The lack of a sound university training has always made it impossible for me to distinguish between an iambic and a dactyl, and if this were not enough to condemn one for ever, the practice of prose has bred in me, as in most prose writers, a foolish jealousy, a righteous indignation—anyhow, an emotion which the critic should be without. For how, we despised prose writers ask when we get together, could one say what one meant and observe the rules of poetry ? Conceive dragging in " blade " because one had mentioned " maid "; and pairing " sorrow " with " borrow " ? Rhyme is not only childish, but dishonest, we prose writers say. Then we go on to say, And look at their rules! How easy to be a poet! How strait the path is for them, and how strict! This you must do; this you must not. I would rather be a child and walk in a crocodile down a suburban path than write poetry, I have heard prose writers say. It must be like taking the veil and entering a religious order—observing the rites and rigours of metre. That explains why they repeat the same thing over and over again. Whereas we prose writers (I am only telling you the sort of nonsense prose writers talk when they are alone) are masters of language, not its slaves; nobody can teach us; nobody can coerce us; we say what we mean; we have the whole of life for our province. We are the creators, we are the explorers. . . . So we run on—nonsensically enough, I must admit.

Now that I have made a clean breast of these deficiencies, let us proceed. From certain phrases in your letter I gather that you think that poetry is in a parlous way, and that your case as a poet in this particular autumn of 1931 is a great deal harder than Shakespeare's, Dryden's, Pope's, or Tennyson's. In fact it is the hardest case that has ever been known. Here you give me an opening, which I am prompt to seize, for a little lecture. Never think yourself singular, never think your own case much harder than other people's. I admit that the age we live in makes this difficult. For the first time in history there are readers—a large body of people, occupied in business, in sport, in nursing their grandfathers,

in tying up parcels behind counters—they all read
now; and they want to be told how to read and
what to read; and their teachers—the reviewers,
the lecturers, the broadcasters—must in all
humanity make reading easy for them; assure
them that literature is violent and exciting, full of
heroes and villains; of hostile forces perpetually
in conflict; of fields strewn with bones; of solitary
victors riding off on white horses wrapped in black
cloaks to meet their death at the turn of the road.
A pistol shot rings out. " The age of romance was
over. The age of realism had begun "—you know
the sort of thing. Now of course writers themselves
know very well that there is not a word of truth in
all this—there are no battles, and no murders, and
no defeats and no victories. But as it is of the
utmost importance that readers should be amused,
writers acquiesce. They dress themselves up.
They act their parts. One leads; the other
follows. One is romantic, the other realist. One is
advanced, the other out of date. There is no harm
in it, so long as you take it as a joke, but once you
believe in it, once you begin to take yourself
seriously as a leader, or as a follower, as a modern
or as a conservative, then you become a self-
conscious, biting, and scratching little animal
whose work is not of the slightest value or importance to anybody. Think of yourself rather as

something much humbler and less spectacular, but to my mind far more interesting—a poet in whom live all the poets of the past, from whom all poets in time to come will spring. You have a touch of Chaucer in you, and something of Shakespeare; Dryden, Pope, Tennyson—to mention only the respectable among your ancestors— stir in your blood and sometimes move your pen a little to the right or to the left. In short you are an immensely ancient, complex, and continuous character, for which reason please treat yourself with respect and think twice before you dress up as Guy Fawkes and spring out upon timid old ladies at street corners, threatening death and demanding twopence-halfpenny.

However, as you say that you are in a fix ("it has never been so hard to write poetry as it is to-day") and that poetry may be, you think, at its last gasp in England ("the novelists are doing all the interesting things now"), let me while away the time before the post goes in imagining your state and in hazarding one or two guesses which, since this is a letter, need not be taken too seriously or pressed too far. Let me try to put myself in your place; let me try to imagine, with your letter to help me, what it feels like to be a young poet in the autumn of 1931. (And, taking my own advice, I shall treat you not as one poet in particular, but as several poets in one.) On the floor of your mind, then—is it not this that makes you a poet?—rhythm keeps up its perpetual beat. Sometimes it seems to die down to nothing; it lets you eat, sleep, talk like other people. Then again it swells and rises and attempts to sweep all the contents of your mind into one dominant dance. To-night is such an occasion. Although you are alone, and have taken one boot off and are about to undo the other, you cannot go on with the process of undressing, but must instantly write at the bidding of the dance. You snatch pen and paper; you hardly trouble to hold the one or to straighten the other. And while you write, while the first stanzas of the dance are being fastened down, I will withdraw a little and look out of the window. A woman passes, then a man; a car glides to a stop and then—but there is no need to say what I see out of the window, nor indeed is there time, for I am suddenly recalled from my observations by a cry of rage or despair. Your page is crumpled in a ball; your pen sticks upright by the nib in the carpet. If there were a cat to swing or a wife to murder now would be the time. So at least I infer from the ferocity of your expression. You are rasped, jarred, thoroughly out of temper. And if I am to guess the reason, it is, I should say, that the rhythm which was

opening and shutting with a force that sent shocks
of excitement from your head to your heels has
encountered some hard and hostile object upon
which it has smashed itself to pieces. Something
has worked in which cannot be made into poetry;
some foreign body, angular, sharp-edged, gritty,
has refused to join in the dance. Obviously, suspicion attaches to Mrs. Gape; she has asked you
to make a poem of her; then to Miss Curtis and
her confidences on the omnibus; then to C., who
has infected you with a wish to tell his story—and
a very amusing one it was—in verse. But for some
reason you cannot do their bidding. Chaucer
could; Shakespeare could; so could Crabbe,
Byron, and perhaps Robert Browning. But it is
October, 1931, and for a long time now poetry
has shirked contact with—what shall we call it?—
Shall we shortly and no doubt inaccurately call it
life ? And will you come to my help by guessing
what I mean ? Well then, it has left all that
to the novelist. Here you see how easy it would
be for me to write two or three volumes in
honour of prose and in mockery of verse ; to
say how wide and ample is the domain of
the one, how starved and stunted the little
grove of the other. But it would be simpler
and perhaps fairer to check these theories by
opening one of the thin books of modern verse that

lie on your table. I open and I find myself
instantly confuted. Here are the common objects
of daily prose—the bicycle and the omnibus.
Obviously the poet is making his muse face facts.
Listen:

Which of you waking early and watching day-
    break
Will not hasten in heart, handsome, aware of
    wonder
At light unleashed, advancing, a leader of
    movement,
Breaking like surf on turf on road and roof,
Or chasing shadow on downs like whippet
    racing,
The stilled stone, halting at eyelash barrier,
Enforcing in face a profile, marks of misuse,
Beating impatient and importunate on boudoir
    shutters
Where the old life is not up yet, with rays
Exploring through rotting floor a dismantled
    mill—
The old life never to be born again ?

Yes, but how will he get through with it ? I
read on and find:

Whistling as he shuts
His door behind him, travelling to work by tube
Or walking to the park to it to *ease the bowels,*

and read on and find again:

> As a boy lately come up from country to town
> Returns for the day to his village in *expensive*
> *shoes*—

and so on again to:

> Seeking a heaven on earth he chases his shadow,
> Loses his capital and his nerve in pursuing
> What yachtsmen, explorers, climbers and *buggers*
> *are after.*

These lines and the words I have emphasised are enough to confirm me in part of my guess at least. The poet is trying to include Mrs. Gape. He is honestly of opinion that she can be brought into poetry and will do very well there. Poetry, he feels, will be improved by the actual, the colloquial. But though I honour him for the attempt, I doubt that it is wholly successful. I feel a jar. I feel a shock. I feel as if I had stubbed my toe on the corner of the wardrobe. Am I then, I go on to ask, shocked, prudishly and conventionally, by the words themselves? I think not. The shock is literally a shock. The poet as I guess has strained himself to include an emotion that is not domesticated and acclimatised to poetry; the effort has thrown him off his balance; he rights himself, as I am sure I shall find if I turn the page, by a

violent recourse to the poetical—he invokes the
moon or the nightingale. Anyhow, the transition
is sharp. The poem is cracked in the middle.
Look, it comes apart in my hands: here is reality
on one side, here is beauty on the other; and
instead of acquiring a whole object rounded and
entire, I am left with broken parts in my hands
which, since my reason has been roused and my
imagination has not been allowed to take entire
possession of me, I contemplate coldly, critically,
and with distaste.

Such at least is the hasty analysis I make of my
own sensations as a reader; but again I am interrupted. I see that you have overcome your
difficulty, whatever it was; the pen is once more
in action, and having torn up the first poem you
are at work upon another. Now then if I want to
understand your state of mind I must invent
another explanation to account for this return of
fluency. You have dismissed, as I suppose, all
sorts of things that would come naturally to your
pen if you had been writing prose—the charwoman, the omnibus, the incident on the Channel
boat. Your range is restricted—I judge from your
expression—concentrated and intensified. I
hazard a guess that you are thinking now, not
about things in general, but about yourself in
particular. There is a fixity, a gloom, yet an

inner glow that seem to hint that you are looking within and not without. But in order to consolidate these flimsy guesses about the meaning of an expression on a face, let me open another of the books on your table and check it by what I find there. Again I open at random and read this:

To penetrate that room is my desire,
The extreme attic of the mind, that lies
Just beyond the last bend in the corridor.
Writing I do it. Phrases, poems are keys.
Loving's another way (but not so sure).
A fire's in there, I think, there's truth at last
Deep in a lumber chest. Sometimes I'm near,
But draughts puff out the matches, and I'm lost.
Sometimes I'm lucky, find a key to turn,
Open an inch or two—but always then
A bell rings, someone calls, or cries of " fire "
Arrest my hand when nothing's known or seen,
And running down the stairs again I mourn.

and then this:

There is a dark room,
The locked and shuttered womb,
Where negative's made positive.
Another dark room,
The blind and bolted tomb,
Where positives change to negative.

We may not undo that or escape this, who
Have birth and death coiled in our bones,
Nothing we can do
Will sweeten the real rue,
That we begin, and end, with groans.

And then this:

Never being, but always at the edge of Being
My head, like Death mask, is brought into the
    Sun.
The shadow pointing finger across cheek,
I move lips for tasting, I move hands for
    touching,
But never am nearer than touching,
Though the spirit leans outward for seeing.
Observing rose, gold, eyes, an admired land-
    scape,
My senses record the act of wishing
Wishing to be
Rose, gold, landscape or another—
Claiming fulfilment in the act of loving.

Since these quotations are chosen at random and
I have yet found three different poets writing about
nothing, if not about the poet himself, I hold that the
chances are that you too are engaged in the same
occupation. I conclude that self offers no impedi-

ment; self joins in the dance; self lends itself to
the rhythm; it is apparently easier to write a
poem about oneself than about any other subject.
But what does one mean by " oneself " ? Not
the self that Wordsworth, Keats, and Shelley have
described—not the self that loves a woman, or that
hates a tyrant, or that broods over the mystery of
the world. No, the self that you are engaged in
describing is shut out from all that. It is a self that
sits alone in the room at night with the blinds
drawn. In other words the poet is much less
interested in what we have in common than in
what he has apart. Hence I suppose the extreme
difficulty of these poems—and I have to confess
that it would floor me completely to say from one
reading or even from two or three what these
poems mean. The poet is trying honestly and
exactly, to describe a world that has perhaps no
existence except for one particular person at one
particular moment. And the more sincere he is
in keeping to the precise outline of the roses and
cabbages of his private universe, the more he
puzzles us who have agreed in a lazy spirit of
compromise to see roses and cabbages as they are
seen, more or less, by the twenty-six passengers on
the outside of an omnibus. He strains to describe;
we strain to see; he flickers his torch; we catch
a flying gleam. It is exciting; it is stimulating;

but is that a tree, we ask, or is it perhaps an old woman tying up her shoe in the gutter ?

Well, then, if there is any truth in what I am saying—if that is you cannot write about the actual, the colloquial, Mrs. Gape or the Channel boat or Miss Curtis on the omnibus, without straining the machine of poetry, if, therefore, you are driven to contemplate landscapes and emotions within and must render visible to the world at large what you alone can see, then indeed yours is a hard case, and poetry, though still breathing— witness these little books—is drawing her breath in short, sharp gasps. Still, consider the symptoms. They are not the symptoms of death in the least. Death in literature, and I need not tell you how often literature has died in this country or in that, comes gracefully, smoothly, quietly. Lines slip easily down the accustomed grooves. The old designs are copied so glibly that we are half inclined to think them original, save for that very glibness. But here the very opposite is happening: here in my first quotation the poet breaks his machine because he will clog it with raw fact. In my second, he is unintelligible because of his desperate determination to tell the truth about himself. Thus I cannot help thinking that though you may be right in talking of the difficulty of the time, you are wrong to despair.

Is there not, alas, good reason to hope ? I say
" alas," because then I must give my reasons,
which are bound to be foolish and certain also to
cause pain to the large and highly respectable
society of nekrophils—Mr. Peabody, and his like—
who much prefer death to life and are even now
intoning the sacred and comfortable words, Keats
is dead, Shelley is dead, Byron is dead. But it is
late: nekrophily induces slumber; the old gentlemen have fallen asleep over their classics, and if
what I am about to say takes a sanguine tone—
and for my part I do not believe in poets dying;
Keats, Shelley, Byron, are alive here in this room
in you and you and you—I can take comfort from
the thought that my hoping will not disturb their
snoring. So to continue—why should not poetry,
now that it has so honestly scraped itself free from
certain falsities, the wreckage of the great Victorian age, now that it has so sincerely gone down
into the mind of the poet and verified its outlines—
a work of renovation that has to be done from time
to time and was certainly needed, for bad poetry
is almost always the result of forgetting oneself—
all becomes distorted and impure if you lose sight
of that central reality—now, I say, that poetry has
done all this, why should it not once more open
its eyes, look out of the window and write about
other people ? Two or three hundred years ago

you were always writing about other people. Your
pages were crammed with characters of the most
opposite and various kinds—Hamlet, Cleopatra,
Falstaff. Not only did we go to you for drama, and
for the subtleties of human character, but we also
went to you, incredible though this now seems, for
laughter. You made us roar with laughter. Then
later, not more than a hundred years ago, you
were lashing our follies, trouncing our hypocrisies,
and dashing off the most brilliant of satires. You
were Byron, remember; you wrote *Don Juan*.
You were Crabbe also; you took the most sordid
details of the lives of peasants for your theme.
Clearly therefore you have it in you to deal with a
vast variety of subjects; it is only a temporary
necessity that has shut you up in one room, alone,
by yourself.

But how are you going to get out, into the world
of other people ? That is your problem now, if I
may hazard a guess—to find the right relationship,
now that you know yourself, between the self that
you know and the world outside. It is a difficult
problem. No living poet has, I think, altogether
solved it. And there are a thousand voices
prophesying despair. Science, they say, has made
poetry impossible; there is no poetry in motor
cars and wireless. And we have no religion. All
is tumultuous and transitional. Therefore, so

people say, there can be no relation between the poet and the present age. But surely that is nonsense. These accidents are superficial; they do not go nearly deep enough to destroy the most profound and primitive of instincts, the instinct of rhythm. All you need now is to stand at the window and let your rhythmical sense open and shut, open, and shut, boldly and freely, until one thing melts in another, until the taxis are dancing with the daffodils, until a whole has been made from all these separate fragments. I am talking nonsense, I know. What I mean is, summon all your courage, exert all your vigilance, invoke all the gifts that Nature has been induced to bestow. Then let your rhythmical sense wind itself in and out among men and women, omnibuses, sparrows—whatever come along the street—until it has strung them together in one harmonious whole. That perhaps is your task—to find the relation between things that seem incompatible yet have a mysterious affinity, to absorb every experience that comes your way fearlessly and saturate it completely so that your poem is a whole, not a fragment; to re-think human life into poetry and so give us tragedy again and comedy by means of characters not spun out at length in the novelist's way, but condensed and synthesised in the poet's way—that is what we look to you to do now. But as I do not know what I mean by rhythm nor what I mean by life, and as most certainly I cannot tell you which objects can properly be combined together in a poem—that is entirely your affair—and as I cannot tell a dactyl from an iambic, and am therefore unable to say how you must modify and expand the rites and ceremonies of your ancient and mysterious art—I will move on to safer ground and turn again to these little books themselves.

When, then, I return to them I am, as I have admitted, filled, not with forebodings of death, but with hopes for the future. But one does not always want to be thinking of the future, if, as sometimes happens, one is living in the present. When I read these poems, now, at the present moment, I find myself—reading, you know, is rather like opening the door to a horde of rebels who swarm out attacking one in twenty places at once—hit, roused, scraped, bared, swung through the air, so that life seems to flash by; then again blinded, knocked on the head—all of which are agreeable sensations for a reader (since nothing is more dismal than to open the door and get no response), and all I believe certain proof that this poet is alive and kicking. And yet mingling with these cries of delight, of jubilation, I record also, as I read, the repetition in the bass of one word

intoned over and over again by some malcontent.
At last then, silencing the others, I say to this
malcontent, " Well, and what do *you* want ? "
Whereupon he bursts out, rather to my discomfort,
" Beauty." Let me repeat, I take no responsibi-
lity for what my senses say when I read; I merely
record the fact that there is a malcontent in me
who complains that it seems to him odd, considering that English is a mixed language, a rich
language; a language unmatched for its sound
and colour, for its power of imagery and suggestion—it seems to him odd that these modern poets
should write as if they had neither ears nor eyes,
neither soles to their feet nor palms to their hands,
but only honest enterprising book-fed brains, uni-
sexual bodies and—but here I interrupted him.
For when it comes to saying that a poet should be
bi-sexual, and that I think is what he was about to
say, even I, who have had no scientific training
whatsoever, draw the line and tell that voice to be
silent.

But how far, if we discount these obvious
absurdities, do you think that there is truth in this
complaint ? For my own part now that I have
stopped reading, and can see the poems more or
less as a whole, I think it is true that the eye and
the ear are starved of their rights. There is no
sense of riches held in reserve behind the admir-

able exactitude of the lines I have quoted, as there is, for example, behind the exactitude of Mr. Yeats. The poet clings to his one word, his only word, as a drowning man to a spar. And if this is so, I am ready to hazard a reason for it all the more readily because I think it bears out what I have just been saying. The art of writing, and that is perhaps what my malcontent means by " beauty," the art of having at one's beck and call every word in the language, of knowing their weights, colours, sounds, associations, and thus making them, as is so necessary in English, suggest more than they can state, can be learnt of course to some extent by reading —it is impossible to read too much; but much more drastically and effectively by imagining that one is not oneself but somebody different. How can you learn to write if you write only about one single person? To take the obvious example. Can you doubt that the reason why Shakespeare knew every sound and syllable in the language and · could do precisely what he liked with grammar and syntax, was that Hamlet, Falstaff and Cleopatra rushed him into this knowledge; that the lords, officers, dependants, murderers and common soldiers of the plays insisted that he should say exactly what they felt in the words expressing their feelings ? It was they who taught him to write, not the begetter of the Sonnets. So that if you want to

satisfy all those senses that rise in a swarm whenever we drop a poem among them—the reason,
the imagination, the eyes, the ears, the palms of
the hands and the soles of the feet, not to mention
a million more that the psychologists have yet to
name, you will do well to embark upon a long
poem in which people as unlike yourself as possible talk at the tops of their voices. And for
heaven's sake, publish nothing before you are
thirty.

That, I am sure, is of very great importance.
Most of the faults in the poems I have been
reading can be explained, I think, by the fact that
they have been exposed to the fierce light of
publicity while they were still too young to stand
the strain. It has shrivelled them into a skeleton
austerity, both emotional and verbal, which
should not be the characteristic of youth. The
poet writes very well; he writes for the eye of
a severe and intelligent public; but how much
better he would have written if for ten years he
had written for no eye but his own! After all, the
years from twenty to thirty are years (let me refer
to your letter again) of emotional excitement. The
rain dripping, a wing flashing, someone passing—
the commonest sounds and sights have power to
fling one, as I seem to remember, from the
heights of rapture to the depths of despair. And

if the actual life is thus extreme, the visionary life
should be free to follow. Write then, now that
you are young, nonsense by the ream. Be silly,
be sentimental, imitate Shelley, imitate Samuel
Smiles; give the rein to every impulse; commit
every fault of style, grammar, taste, and syntax;
pour out; tumble over; loose anger, love, satire,
in whatever words you can catch, coerce or
create, in whatever metre, prose, poetry, or
gibberish that comes to hand. Thus you will
learn to write. But if you publish, your freedom
will be checked; you will be thinking what
people will say; you will write for others when
you ought only to be writing for yourself. And
what point can there be in curbing the wild
torrent of spontaneous nonsense which is now, for
a few years only, your divine gift in order to publish
prim little books of experimental verses ? To
make money ? That, we both know, is out of the
question. To get criticism ? But your friends will
pepper your manuscripts with far more serious and
searching criticism than any you will get from the
reviewers. As for fame, look I implore you at
famous people; see how the waters of dullness
spread around them as they enter; observe their
pomposity, their prophetic airs; reflect that the
greatest poets were anonymous; think how
Shakespeare cared nothing for fame; how Donne

tossed his poems into the waste-paper basket; write an essay giving a single instance of any modern English writer who has survived the disciples and the admirers, the autograph hunters and the interviewers, the dinners and the luncheons, the celebrations and the commemorations with which English society so effectively stops the mouths of its singers and silences their songs.

But enough. I, at any rate, refuse to be nekrophilus. So long as you and you and you, venerable and ancient representatives of Sappho, Shakespeare, and Shelley are aged precisely twenty-three and propose—O enviable lot!—to spend the next fifty years of your lives in writing poetry, I refuse to think that the art is dead. And if ever the temptation to nekrophilise comes over you, be warned by the fate of that old gentleman whose name I forget, but I think that it was Peabody. In the very act of consigning all the arts to the grave he choked over a large piece of hot buttered toast and the consolation then offered him that he was about to join the elder Pliny in the shades gave him, I am told, no sort of satisfaction whatsoever.

And now for the intimate, the indiscreet, and indeed, the only really interesting parts of this letter. . . .

A LETTER TO A
MODERN NOVELIST

HUGH WALPOLE

On a Boat from Tunis to Gabes,
North Africa.

March 17th 1932.

MY DEAR RICHARD,

I received your letter yesterday before leaving
Tunis. I was touched, I must confess, that you
should take the trouble to write to me at such
length because you have often told me that you
detest to write letters and have never ceased to
wonder that my great-great-Uncle Horace found
so much leisure to amuse himself in that fashion.
But what frankly astonishes me yet more is that
you should care to have my opinion on your book.
I received it, as I wrote and told you, an hour
before leaving London and I read it between
Calais and Marseilles. I would have written to
you before this, burdening you with my honest
if not very original opinions, had it not been that
I doubted quite frankly whether you would be
interested to have them. It is true that you sent
me the book, that you even inscribed in it: " For
Hugh Walpole from a Beginner "—but forgive
me if my sensitive spirit saw even in those simple
words a good-natured and only too inevitable
patronage. Don't misunderstand me. I was
pleased and touched that you should think of me

at all. I have my full share of the pathetic nostalgia on the part of the aged for the tender consideration of the young. But I could not believe that you cared whether I read the book or no.

Now it seems from your letter that you do. You say that it has been well received, that all your friends like it, that your publisher has given a luncheon and that Mr. Agate, the dramatic critic, has awarded it two columns in the *Express* although, with regard to that last, why you should care what a dramatic critic has to say to your novel I cannot understand. However, when we are young we care what *everyone* has to say, although we pretend not to—and when we are old, too, perhaps! Of the sensitiveness and vanity of authors there is no end nor ever will be! However, with all this success flaming about your ears you still want my opinion although, as you quite honestly confessed to me at Seabrook when we were there together last month: " All that *your* school of novelists has to say about the novel seems to us nonsense "—by " us " meaning I suppose your entire generation and by " *my* school " meaning two or three doddery old fellows who have shamefully outstayed their welcome. All the same I'm only forty-eight, you know, and *feel* as though I were just beginning, so in a way we step out together and can be as frank with one another as the Siamese twins! Well, I *will* be frank! Now that you have all this praise, frankness won't disturb you and as in *any* case *all* my opinions are nonsense one or two of them, honestly delivered, won't damage you a bit!

From all this you will think that I have nothing but curses for your *Camel with Four Humps* —not at all; I have quite a number of blessings. But I am able, happily, to write in the most comfortably detached fashion. I feel at the moment completely removed both from heaven and earth, for the small cargo-boat on which I am travelling from Tunis to Gabes is floating along towards Sousse in a quite immaterial fashion like a little grey cloud swimming between other clouds. It is true that there is a large brown horse, destined for some Tripoli sportsman, tethered on the deck just outside the Saloon and every once and again he stamps with his hoofs just to reassure himself against the sea; there is a group of Arabs squatting on the other side of the funnel and eagerly excited in some mysterious gamble; the little Japanese steward has just brought me some tea in the grimmest most steel-clad teapot I have ever beheld outside a London boarding-house. Turgenev's *Smoke* and Dr. Donne's poems and the last romance of Miss

Dorothy Sayers are piled together on the shelf opposite just to prove that even now, after thirty years of literature, I am still cultured: but these, and more than these, fail to bring me to earth. I am in perfect state to survey your *Camel* without prejudice, without that enthusiasm for which I am so unjustly famous, without that condescension inherited by me from a hundred schoolmasters, without that sentiment that would drive me to placate the younger generation at all costs.

There is another reason, too, why this is an excellent moment to tell you what I think of your *Camel*. I have in these last few days read yet once again Anthony Trollope's *Barchester Towers*, a book I remember that you told me you *could* not read in spite of the present Trollope revival and the excellent works on that gentleman by Mr. Michael Sadleir and myself. The fact that I had written a book about him made him, I fancy, all the harder for you to read, but the sentence from you that sticks in my memory ran something like this: " You see what makes all those old boys impossible is that they leave off where Proust and Joyce and Lawrence begin." I remember that I enquired whether you included Flaubert, Tolstoi, Dostoeffsky, Turgenev and Stendhal among those same " old boys " and that you answered airily: " Oh! I'm talking about the *English* novel!" I recollect that I wanted then to say a lot of things, but was most fortunately interrupted by the dressing-bell. I can still see your look of relief when you heard it! But what I wanted to say *then* I can pour out to you *now*—being, as I have told you, so completely detached with only the champing horse, the gambling Arabs and the thin red line of the African coast to prejudice me, and your *Camel* and Trollope's Mrs. Proudie lying down so decently together in my parochial mind.

Well, in the first place, as you have never read *Barchester Towers* I will very briefly give you its subject. It is the story of a battle for power in an English cathedral-town. The battle is engaged between a number of different persons—a Bishop, his wife, the Bishop's secretary, a proud Arch-deacon, a Beauty from Italy, a mild and humble little clergyman. An important London news-paper lends its aid and there is a chorus of gentle country gossip. The issues involved are small com-pared with the fate of nations or Einstein, but they are also symbolic, although Trollope knew little and cared less about symbolism. The battle fought in Barchester for wealth, position, lust of the flesh, is being fought at this instance between China and Japan, between Hitler and Hinden-burg, and between, I don't doubt, the two Arabs who are at this moment wildly gesticulating on the

Quay of Sousse whither we have now arrived. Such is the theme of *Barchester Towers*. What, dear Richard, is the theme of *Camel with Four Humps* ?

At first I must confess that, accustomed as I am to the present school of English novelists from Joyce to, shall I say, Richard Benson, I find it difficult *exactly* to state your theme. You would doubtless prefer that it should be difficult. Henry James used to say that it should be possible to state the theme of any novel in one short quick sentence. " That," he expected you to say, " is the pattern in *this* carpet." I think perhaps he was right; at any rate he himself obeyed his own law faithfully, and even that most mysterious of all novels *The Sacred Fount* can be defined in a word or two. But *yours*!

The theme, if you will permit me, seems a little uncertain. At first it was, I thought, the one customary to the novelists of your generation, namely that Flesh is as Grass and All is Vanity. Then, as the book developed I fancied with some anticipatory pleasure that the charm of solitude, the contemplative life, the desert, its great advantage over the noise, the chatter and restlessness of contemporary London was your pattern. But no. The desert—as symbolised in the picture of the elegant Camel hanging over the mantelpiece of the drawing-room at Lady Clancarty's—

proves most desperately disappointing and it
seems for a moment as though Matrimony,
decent, conventionalised Victorian Matrimony, is
after all the cure for modern malaise. But your
Matrimony is worse than your Desert. No one in
your novel is married for more than five minutes.
At the last there is a touch, a suggestion, of something mystical. Is there, after all, a Soul in Man,
and will we all be religious again in another year
or two ? No, the Soul rises for an instant only to
sink at once before a barrage of mockery and we
are left gazing as it seems to me rather emptily on
the portrait of the Camel, the broken remnants of
the dinner-table, the old family nurse asleep in
her chair and Lady Clancarty counting her gains
from Contract.

Now to all this you will say at once: " But of
course—the Theme of my book is that there *is* no
Theme. Life has no Theme. Do you not know
that we have got beyond that *arrangement* of the
older novelists, the placing of things in order, the
punctual rising of the sun, the crisis at its proper
time, the ending neatly rounded off ? Life was
never like that. What we have to do is to render
life as it is. To be Real."

Very well. Granted. But let us look again at
Barchester Towers. Trollope begins his book with
this sentence:

"In the latter days of July in the year 185—, a most important question was for ten days hourly asked in the cathedral city of Barchester, and answered every hour in various ways. Who was to be the new Bishop?"

You will, of course, observe the childish meticulousness of that statement. We have the month, and, nearly, the year. We have the place and we have the question that sets all the narrative going. I contend that, having due regard to the obvious old-fashionedness of the method, that is a masterly commencement to any novel. You may say that you are not interested in cathedral towns nor in ecclesiastical dignitaries. No. Quite so. But you *are*, you *must* be interested in human beings. Here is a situation in which there will be inevitably disappointments, jealousies, antagonisms, plots and intrigues. It does not matter whether the impetus that sets this ball rolling is the succession to the Crown, the engagement of an ironical Débutante, the selling of a farm, the betrayal of a young village beauty. It is the passions that spell the plot and there is room for all the passions here.

What, on the other hand, is the opening sentence of your *Camel* ?

" The bell whose echoes broke the symmetry of the quartet round the bridge-table ceased its sharp querulous

anger only just in time, for Lady Clancarty's maid had the colic—indestructibly fugitive and the result of a country passion for sheep's head."

I admit that your opening sentence is intriguing. Its grammar I find to be a little weak, but then I have never been strong on grammar myself. I do not *exactly* understand *what* was "indestructibly fugitive." Do you mean that Lady Clancarty's maid was doomed to colic, off and on, so to speak, for the rest of her days ? But no matter. The point is, does this sentence stir eager curiosity in the reader's breast ? In a sense, yes. The reader must feel that he (or she in all probability) is in the hands of a clever and interesting guide. This should be an amusing world, this world of bridge, bells and indigestion. The silly irony of life is already conveyed. The scene is set. Yes, but there is, I think, something further.

The effect upon the reader of Trollope's opening sentence is exactly the effect of a newspaper paragraph. " Hullo! " you cry, " The Bishop of Barchester is dead! I wonder who his successor will be? " But it is more than that. You not only read the newspaper paragraph, but you are assured that you are about to be informed of all the details of that affair. " Thanks to Mr. Trollope," you are told, " we will be able to take you right *inside*! He was there from the very be-

ginning. There is nothing that he won't be able
to tell you."

You, yourself, on the other hand, say to the
reader: " I have something interesting here—
something curious and amusing. I shall investigate
it, but purely for my own interest remember. If
you listen intently you may pick up a thing or
two, but I care very little whether you do or no.
My interest is in my art. I give you the chance of
watching an artist at work."

Now I am not for a moment comparing these
two methods of approach with the notion that one
is preferable to the other. Not at all. Both I don't
doubt are excellent. I would only suggest that
when our mutual friend, Harold Nicolson, and
others suggest that the novel of the new school in
England has not all the readers that it ought to
have, there *may* be a reason! Readers are both
arrogant and lazy. New novels are flung at their
heads every minute of the livelong day. " Read
us! Read us! Read us! " the novelists cry and
the booksellers, more languidly, cry. Yes, the
reader is spoilt and flattered, things are made far
too easy for him; it is wrong that he should not
respect more ardently the sensitive ambition of the
artist. Very good. All, alas! too true. But remember that *because* the general reader is spoilt
and lazy and *because* you are clever and sensitive—

therefore there is sometimes a gulf, a sad gulf that
hinders the proper circulation of cash and notor-
iety. It is a pity. What will you do about it?
Surrender some of your sensitiveness ? No, never.
The public must be educated. Well—good luck
to your ambition!

And now consider, dear Richard (this letter is
becoming, I don't doubt, intolerable to you),
Barchester Towers a little further. In my proper
pompous schoolmastery manner let me say something about technique. Here I am at a great disadvantage because, although *you* know well
enough what *I* mean by that old-fashioned word,
I have not the least notion whether you mean
anything at all by it! That is to say, is there
any arrangement of any kind in the *Camel* ?
Does any one incident, conversation, detail of
dress or furniture or scene prepare for any other ?
Have you a plan simply in not having a plan ?
Well, first, before you answer these questions (and
it is night now: we are leaving Sousse under a full,
yellow African moon; the sea streams like silk
away from our boat) let me say one thing about
technique in the novel. That there have been
until the post-war period, two kinds, conscious
and unconscious—and mostly unconscious. Trollope and Turgenev. Although you haven't read
Trollope you *have* read Turgenev. I remember

that at Seabrook you told me that *Fumée* was like
a nice neat sampler worked a hundred years ago
by a clean little schoolgirl. *Fumée* ! at the heart of
which, thirty years ago, for me Irina burnt like a
flame! In any case, disregarding these sentimentalities, you will remember how Litvinov returns to his hotel in Baden to find Irina's gift of
heliotrope scenting his room and you will remember too how that same heliotrope haunts,
with its melancholy and sinister fatality, every
page of that book ? That seems to me technique
of the very finest. Technique, moreover, of which
Trollope, of course, is altogether incapable. *His*
technique is of the simplest; very often there is
none at all. Many of his novels were ruined by
that ghastly Victorian necessity that they should
stretch to eternity for serial purposes. And stretch
they did! Often they are beaten out so thin that a
careless breath of the wind and they are torn into
shreds! But it happens that *Barchester Towers* was
not serialised and it remains with *The Warden* and
The Last Chronicle and *The Claverings*, the *tightest* of
all the Trollopes. (And am I not perhaps forgetting one of the best in *Framley Parsonage*, a book
so fresh and charming and natural that it might
stretch out for ever and ever, and yet not weary!)
There is in this *Barchester Towers*, I swear, not a
single dull moment, although there are several

shy-making ones, as when the Widow Bold plays
with her infant or yields to the Oxford importuni-
ties of Mr. Arabin! Trollope's technique here,
though, is quite rightly despised by you or would
be had you the tolerance to observe it, for it is
nothing more than the simple succession of one
incident by another! First, he gives you the
arrival of the new Bishop, Dr. Proudie; with him,
in attendance, Mrs. Proudie and the red-haired
chaplain, Mr. Slope. These three assembled, who
is to rule—Mrs. Proudie or Mr. Slope? A simple
question but fraught with drama for the cathedral
and town whose fates are immediately involved.
There is, of course, the Opposition. Trollope was
too wary a hand at his business not to know that
all you need to awaken the reader's interest is to
have two opposing forces, whether they be
Napoleon and Wellington at Waterloo or Swann
and the hero's grandmother in M. Proust's endless
chronicle. The opposition to the Proudies in
Barchester is the arrogant Archdeacon on the male
side, and the lovely a-moral Signora Neroni on
the female. The stage is set. The battle joined.
All that is needed after that is a concrete cause for
the battle and the position of Warden—for Hiram's
Hospital is, following on *The Warden*, ready to
hand. Could anything be more simple? A child
could do it. I don't at all wonder that your gener-

ation, Richard, find it all too naïf for your self-importance. It is right that you should do so, and I agree absolutely with you that the novel ought always to be moving on. Moving on—yes. But, while moving, need it discard so completely gifts that surely add, even now, to its charms ? This steady march of event, this move upon move as in a good chess game, when Mrs. Proudie first threatens with her Bishop, Mr. Slope replies with his castle (the *Times* newspaper), Mrs. Proudie screams " Check! " Mr. Slope, sniggering, shows her to be premature, only because of his over-weening ambitions to be checkmated after all! Is this simple genius for story-telling altogether so negligible ? Homer had it, Chaucer had it, Dante had it, Shakespeare had it—mixed beautifully with other and possibly greater gifts but, all the same, none of those geniuses disdained it!

Of this particular art there is no sign whatever in your *Camel*. There was a moment when your hero, Nathaniel Peace, shrinking from the lady who loves him, is tempted to succumb to the lady who detests him; for an instant I fancied that an event of some sort would be born! But no! Illusory hopes! All that occurs is that the clock strikes, the visit to the Camargo Ballet is a dreadful failure and Nathaniel gives a cup of coffee at a shelter to a prostitute!

My pulse slackens again. Nothing leads me from page to page, although I perceive the cleverness, even the beauty of many occasional sentences. And of that other *conscious* technique, the technique of *Fumée, Bovary, Boule de Suif,* even of *The Man of Property* that you despise so consumedly, there is also not a trace! Here I suspect quite frankly that you are too lazy. To create a work like *Fumée* in which, through all the apparently idle and silly chatter of Baden, the love episode of Irina and Litvinov is woven into a perfect and completed pattern needs an intense concentration, a fastidious power of rejection, the deepest emotional feeling. In all these things you are, at present, lacking. You have little concentration, a poor power of rejection and no emotional feeling at all. But then you are very young—there are pieces of dialogue and description in *The Camel* amazing for one so tender! I would not be disturbed if it were not that you have no intention of acquiring these gifts. The artist, you say, must not be too deeply concentrated or he shows too clearly his hand; life, real life, will do the rejecting and accepting for him, and as to emotion you dare not show any lest you should be betrayed into sentimentality.

Were you ever to read *Barchester Towers* you would triumphantly display to me the fearful abysses

into which Trollope's sentimentality tumbles
him! I will admit them at once: his appalling
appeals to the reader, for instance, so that at one
point he actually exclaims: " Do not be disturbed,
dear reader. Neither Mr. Smith nor Mr. Jones
will marry my heroine—for, if they did, where
would my novel be ? " Or the dreadful scenes in
which this same heroine, who is for ever weeping,
plays her part ? I admit that the Widow Bold
offers in her single person an example of all the
horrors, sentimental and nauseating, into which
the Victorian novel could be betrayed. But no
one is asking you to return to such things, dear
Richard. Only on a single page in your next
novel give me something of the emotions that
Tanya's farewell to her lover in *Fumée* gives me
(it is a matter of a few lines of dialogue) and I will
say no more about emotion.

But here I perceive that I must betray to you
my innocent notion of the importance of
character-creation in the novel. What a sentence!
How portentous! Without a wink, a smile, an
ironic nod of the head! I am quite aware of it.
I am but just returned (it is Palm Sunday and
there is not a ripple on the harbour waters) from
the Sfax souks bearing with me a silver whip, a
crimson leather blotting-book and a pair of green
slippers. Just as, at an inordinate price, I have,

once again (after how many earlier resolutions ?) bought these tawdry sops to tourists, so in the same fashion I anxiously peer for character into the contemporary novel. It is part of my child-like and always optimistic nature. It leads me again and again to cry : " Ah, this at last is the blotting-book for which I have so long been searching! " òr " Into *this* work of art at last I shall plunge my hand and bring out a character! "

From *Barchester Towers* at any rate I am certain of three—three whom nobody, of whatever age, whatever school or country, could possibly deny. Goethe, Sainte-Beuve, Anatole France, Peacock, Amanda Ros (my list is entirely haphazard) faced with Mrs. Proudie, Bishop Proudie and Mr. Harding, must at once acclaim them as living and real persons. No period, no literary fashion, no question of age or youth can make these less real. They are not, perhaps, of the great select company of immortals; I ought not possibly to place them beside the Wife of Bath, Falstaff, Emma Bovary, Old Grandet, Sarah Gamp and the rest. And yet I do not know. Mrs. Proudie at least would not be shy in such company and would send the Wife of Bath and Falstaff to Prayer Meeting without a tremor. Among the greatest or no these three are, within their range, absolutely created.

Now in the *Camel* is there any character of

whom honestly I can say this? Honestly and
naturally, no. Naturally, because these supremely
successful creations are rare and it would be
astonishing indeed if you, at your first attempt,
were able to provide us with one. All the same, I
plunge in my fist and what do I bring forth? Your
hero, Nathaniel, your (I suppose) heroine, Miss
Winchester, your Lady Clancarty—these three.
Now here is a point worth, I am sure, attention:
that you have from the beginning handicapped
yourself as so many of your generation are doing.
Nathaniel is a homosexual, or would be if he had
the courage of his unwilling convictions. Miss
Winchester is, I understand, a Lesbian. Now I
have nothing whatever to urge, on the moral
ground, against such a choice. The artist is free
to pick where he pleases; every possible element
in human nature is at his service. You have in
fact shown much insight and delicacy in your
analysis of Nathaniel's nature. You have not
slobbered him with sentimentality nor have you
pretended that his unhappy handicap is an added
virtue. Nevertheless you have, I am convinced,
halved your chances by choosing for your principal
figures the abnormal. The abnormal is the minority and always, so long as this race peoples the
earth, will be. You have analysed (with much
delicacy I repeat) instincts and emotions that

must be foreign to two-thirds of your readers as
though you had, in fact, given your heroine a hare-
lip, your hero no legs. I am not pleading for the
normal; I am not saying that there have not been
in fiction magnificent interpretations of the
abnormal, as for example the Alyosha of Dostoeffsky, the Vathek of Beckford, the Heathcliffe of
Emily Brontë. I am, nevertheless, certain that in
the main, it is the great normal figures that
triumph through the world's literature—Othello,
Carmen, Bazarov, Dandie Dinmont, Clarissa,
M. Bergeret, Cousin Pons, Prince Andrew, Anna
Karenina, Tess and all the others. Trollope is the
most normal novelist who ever lived. It is one of
his great lucks, in his " Barchester " series, that he
gives us no insight into the spiritual conflicts that
must have beset his characters. Archdeacon
Grantley discovered by Balzac—*what* a character
he would have been! Bishop Proudie is a little
man intimidated by a dominating wife. Had
Turgenev interpreted him to what depths of
pathos he might have led us! In Mr. Harding
Trollope delves a little deeper: that scene at the
close of *Barchester Towers*, so brief and simple when
Mr. Harding introduces Mr. Quiverful into the
hospital, is worthy of the greatest masters and we
feel here, as we sometimes do with Trollope, that
it was only the reticences and decencies of his time

that prevented him from showing us another and deeper world. Let that be as it may. A novelist's faults and weaknesses belong so finally to his character that they are as important and valuable as his strengths and virtues. A primrose by the river's brim was simply a primrose to Trollope, but for that very reason when he speaks he is sure of touching something that he knows to be true. Mrs. Proudie is real, because we have something of Mrs. Proudie in all of us, but your Nathaniel can be real to a few only and those few not always the most interesting.

Trollope, by his very pedestrianism, is betrayed into exaggerations of which you could never be guilty. How ashamed, for example, you would be to name in a novel of yours the father of a large family Mr. Quiverful, although that crime does not in fact seem to me a greater one than the cheap satire of Ford in Aldous Huxley's recent novel. You reveal your character by a hundred delicate touches. Trollope frequently uses the blunderbuss. He allows Mr. Slope—an admirable creation—to slip into caricature. You are as afraid of over-emphasis as you are of sentiment.

The Proudies nevertheless exist *beyond* Trollope. We might meet him at any turn of the street; we speculate on their actions, their fortunes, both before and after the volumes that tell us of them.

Your Nathaniel and Miss Winchester do not exist except when you tell us of them. It is Richard Benson who is interesting, not his creations. They interest only *because* of him!

And here your old and dogmatic friend comes to *the* question of all questions. What is reality in the novel? A question surely worth asking once a day at least seeing that for the last twenty years the English novel has been struggling to be nothing else but real—real at all costs, real whatever happens. " Let us throw everything else over but at least achieve reality! "

Now what are we to do in this little matter between you and me? *Barchester Towers* seems altogether real to me (except for certain moments of caricature, and even they smell of the Period, the Hooks, the Hawley Smarts, the Barhams and the rest) while *Camel with Four Humps* seems not real to me at all. You may say that this is a weak " tu quoque," because you have told me, most politely, that it is the unreality of my own romantic novels that makes them so unreadable to yourself. But let us not be personal. Here is a question of the first interest, something that demands a volume rather than the tail-end of a letter like this. We arrive at least at this: that I find your novel unreal just as you find mine to be so, but we *both* agree that *Barchester Towers* is real. (You *would* do

so if you read it and I think that after this long
pleading letter you really must do so.) Everyone,
I fancy, will grant the reality of the Trollope novel.
Yes, but you will at once say—" A cheap, easy
newspaper reality. I read this morning in the
Daily Herald that Mr. MacDonald's eyesight is improved and that his daughter, Ishbel, entertained
yesterday his friends at luncheon. It is *that* kind
of reality. No more and no less." A little more, I
think. Mrs. Proudie and Mr. Harding go beyond
the *Herald's* creative power—but I will grant you
that Trollope's art *is* a sort of newspaper reality.
Dichtung und Wahrheit—the Dream and the
Business. There *are* two realities and you are not
even attempting Trollope's *Wahrheit*. You are a
poet. Granted. Every novelist to-day *must* be a
poet. In that at least you may maintain we have
advanced since Trollope's day. And the poet will
certainly find it more difficult to create a general
reality than a simple recorder will. A very good
chapter in *Barchester Towers* describes the opening
of the Ullathorne Sports, the preparations, the
anxieties of host and hostess, the too-early arrival
of certain guests, the somewhat snobbish distinc-
tions between class and class, local jealousies and
so on. All as clear and sharply defined as a summer
morning in an English vicarage. I take a chapter
at random from your *Camel*, and what is con-

tained in it ? A description of a lady's dress, the
scent of flowers, nostalgia on the part of your hero
for the black rocks of Assouan, a reflection on
François Mauriac, a sniff of Paris, the maid-
servant's colic, a brilliant jade necklace, two
cocktails and a burst of ill-temper on the part of
Miss Winchester. This is, I think you will agree,
an unprejudiced description of Chapter VIII of
your book. Some of the things you give me are
beautiful—the rocks of Assouan, the jade necklace,
the hot smell of carnations and morning coffee on
a summer's morning in Paris. Trollope could give
me none of these things. But instead he gives me
something that, whether he is there or no, must
always be real. Miss Thorne and her brother,
their anxieties, their feudalism, their generosities,
their obstinacies—here is a fragment of English
character true for ever and a real possession.
Whereas you, dear Richard, have given me only
a part of yourself, and even then yourself in the
theatre, on the platform, doing your damnedest
in public.

I will admit at once that we novelists of to-day
are trying for something rarer and more difficult
to catch than Trollope did. He did not even know
that such things were to be caught. I will admit
also that the creator should not disturb himself as
to whether others find his creation real or no. He

will never be satisfied. If only the stupid and imperceptive found him unreal how agreeable it would be!—or if on the other hand it were the unperceptive alone who find him real he could at least say: " I have my public. They may not be of the finest taste but they are in the end the most faithful and affectionate."

But the novelist will always be bewildered by his readers. A young man from Oxford—obviously of the finest intelligence—calls you magnanimous but cannot do with your unreality. A critic, wise, ironic, blasé, most surprisingly blesses you for that very romantic quality! A creator works first for himself—he gives his notion of the universe through the shape and colour of his personality. He can, poor devil, do none other. Afterwards his work collects round it the citizens of the same world as himself. Be they deaf and blind, halt and maim, it is no matter. He must not be disturbed. He can do only what he can.

Trollope's reality is altogether a slighter, smaller thing than Balzac's, Turgenev's, Tolstoi's—but he is never false to himself. If I see life like one of those toy-theatres beloved to me in my youth, well, it is the world of the toy-theatre that I create. Even that little stage of coloured paper and dancing marionettes has its virtues.

So I am not criticising you because I find your

world unreal. I am only asking you that, your
world being what it is, you should fill it as full as
you can. Trollope did that. He knew nothing of
the rocks of Assouan, but he *did* know of the
terrors of the Quiverful family when they thought
that the hospital would, after all, slip their grasp;
of Mr. Slope's lust for the Signora; of Mr. Harding's delicate conscience.

And here for a moment, at the very last, I will
tread on most dangerous ground. Trollope's men
and women are engaged in a battle, a battle that
seems at any rate to themselves of the first importance. Your characters are concerned in no sort
of conflict. Conflicts are, I am well aware, old-
fashioned. The hero has been banished from the
novel and, you are well assured, will never return.
I am not so certain. I believe that there *is* a moral
world and that the novelists of your generation
are losing a great deal by disregarding it.

Behold, dear Richard, how entirely I have given
myself away; a thing that you are pledged never,
never to do. Nevertheless—when you are forty-
eight. . . !

I am,
Your affectionate friend,
HUGH WALPOLE.

A LETTER TO AN ARCHBISHOP

J. C. HARDWICK

YOUR GRACE,

Permit me to address to you from a cure in a remote parish, some reflections upon the present state of the Church of England, which are offered in all humility. True it is that your Grace cannot but perceive the tendencies which prevail, but viewed from the standpoint of an obscure person they may take on a new interest and perhaps a new shape.

Like myself, your Grace is now sufficiently advanced in years to remember the closing decades of the Victorian epoch, and will probably, with me, look back upon that astonishing time with admiration and regret. We remember its solidity, its industry, and above all its optimism—to all appearance so securely grounded. Most of all may churchmen lament the passing of those halcyon days, for if the Victorian fabric was imposing, the Church occupied a conspicuous place in it, and was universally respected and admired. And if the Church was well thought of by others, it had few misgivings, but was sure of its own ideals and methods, and above all it was sure of itself. It shared in full measure the optimism of an age of expansion, activity and progress. Nor was its prestige undeserved. It was a remarkably successful institution, and its good fortune was due to sound qualities—to devotion, to enthusiasm, and to organising ability.

Your Grace will forgive my recollections of the past which must always be tedious. Yet your own thoughts, like mine, must often revert to those days, so fortunate, so successful, so undimmed by despair.

Like myself, no doubt, you cherish a deep admiration
for John Henry Newman, one of the few saints of
the nineteenth century, a man born out of due time.
Yet it is easy to exaggerate the influence of this great
man upon the Church of England of our youth.
The true inspirer of the Church of the eighties
and nineties of the last century was not the author of
" Lead kindly light," but Samuel Wilberforce, the
energetic and bustling Bishop of Oxford, admired by
countless Englishmen under the affectionate title of
" Soapy Sam."

Your Grace, a comparison of these two men (I am
loath to weary you) is exceedingly illuminating.
Newman had raised the terrible question whether
our beloved Church had any right to exist at all, and
thus shook the faith of many devout souls, including
that of Archdeacon Manning, Wilberforce's own
brother-in-law. But Wilberforce took the view that
an efficient church has every right to exist, so long
as it is a going concern, a religious institution like
any other, justifies itself. Thus, while Newman the
saint looked back into the past with longing and
into the future with despair, Samuel Wilberforce the
practical man surveyed the field of the present with
energetic confidence. He incarnated an ideal, the
ideal of efficient religion. In his parish at Alverstoke
he showed what could be done, and Englishmen who
distrusted Newman as an apostle of principles and
ideas, could understand Wilberforce quite well and
took him to their hearts. He had accepted and
sanctified their business methods and standards of
success, and inaugurated a new epoch of Church

history. While Newman was anxiously meditating his passage to Rome, Wilberforce was busy with bricks and mortar and organisation; and it was in the year that the saint seceded to Rome that the practical man became Dean of Westminster. The apostle of ideas was a failure, the apostle of boost and efficiency a success.

This Wilberforce efficiency-cult may best be regarded in the light of a Counter-Reformation. Just as the Roman Catholic Church after the earthquake of the Reformation needed purging and pulling together, so also with the Church of England, after the devastating questionings of Newman which had shocked, not only Thomas Arnold, but bishops on the bench, dons in their Senior Common Rooms, and the clergy in their country vicarages. There had been nothing in Oxford so startling since the youthful Gibbon declared himself a papist. It may have the appearance of a frivolity, your Grace, to compare Samuel Wilberforce to Ignatius Loyola, yet the two played not dissimilar parts in the ecclesiastical arena. For just as the Society of Jesus set the Roman Church upon its legs again after the assaults of Luther, so the energetic Bishop of Oxford repaired the breaches made by Newman. And just as post-Tridentine catholicism differed from the mediæval Church with its delightful anomalies and abuses, so the refurbished and refitted Church of England differed from the easy-going Church of the old days when parsons rode to hounds and read the classics in painful ignorance of the apostolic and post-apostolic Fathers.

It is true that to work the miracle of reconstruction, Samuel Wilberforce borrowed a certain amount of Newman's mortar, for example the doctrine of the Apostolical Succession, and the enhanced estimate of the sacerdotal office upon which the Puseyites laid so much emphasis. And besides this a good deal of the liturgical and devotional stock in trade of the Tractarians was taken over. Furthermore the new efficiency would have been impossible but for the ecclesiastical reconstruction carried out by the impious Reform Parliament, and denounced by Newman and Keble from the pulpit of St. Mary's, Oxford, as " National Apostasy." The redistribution of financial resources which these compulsory reforms involved alone made the Wilberforce renaissance possible, for endowments, like manures, are not fruitful unless they are well spread. But it sheds light upon the genius of Wilberforce that he was able to take advantage of contributions coming from such diverse sources as the pious Newmanites and the profane Radicals. All was fish that came to his net.

Thanks to the redoubtable " Soapy Sam " the English Church of our youth was emphatically a going concern, full of energy, bustle and optimism. The social position of the beneficed clergy was high, the British public was behind them, and there was no shortage of men or of money. Parishes light-heartedly went in for expensive plant—schools, mission halls, parish rooms, and so on; all of which were destined to become a menagerie of white elephants when the religious tide turned. There was no shortage of anything, save of that commodity to which no loyal Englishman attached any importance—ideas. But what need has a machine of ideas ? A machine runs itself, a machine has no doubts or hesitations. The Church was indeed like a gigantic locomotive going full steam ahead with Samuel upon the footplate. Where were they going ? Who cared ? The engine was a good goer and the driver a good fellow, and there was plenty of coal in the tender. To arrive, after all, is less important than to travel ; and meanwhile the passengers, full of satisfaction with the directors, might look out of the windows and admire the view and gasp delightedly at the speed of Sam's locomotive which was pulling them bravely along, whistling loudly and emitting immense clouds of smoke and steam. Those were indeed good days and the steam-engine symbolises their spirit. The gospel of work and production was being assiduously preached and practised. Carlyle was busy with tongue and pen; Ruskin was lecturing; even æsthetes like Disraeli were founding the Conservative party instead of retiring, like Byron and Shelley, to Italy and despair. Does your Grace remember ? Ah, we older ones remember it all too well! From the bishop on his throne to the newly-ordained deacon in his lads' club the spirit was the same.

And so, your Grace, the century drew to its close— the century of hope, of expansion, of ecclesiastical efficiency, of the Wilberforce renaissance. No shadows, even so big as a man's hand, appeared upon the horizon. England and its Church basked in the sun of contentment and prosperity. Bishops shared and sanctified the optimism of the Queen's Jubilee. Yet history was beginning to move. In the autumn of 1899, thousands of miles away from Lambeth, a few Dutch farmers crossed a frontier and motor cars in the previous year had startled the streets of London.

Your Grace will remember the years which followed, and how the first cracks appeared in the imposing fabric.

First was the Education Act of 1902, which transformed the old Church-governed Grammar Schools into efficient secular Secondary Schools with expensive science laboratories but without Greek Testaments. The sixth forms of these establishments no longer bred clergymen, but chemists, engineers, motor salesmen and commission agents. Thus one product of the new educational régime was an entirely new class of middle-class child. Efficiently educated, but steeped in materialistic and utilitarian ideals, schooled but uncultivated, disciplined but irreligious, interested not in books but in mechanical contrivances this class of product had only to await the coming of the cheap motor car to become entirely pagan. With regard to the Primary Schools, the situation now was that the Church schools were faced with expanding numbers of highly efficient competitors, staffed by teachers increasingly impatient of clerical control, and rendered intractable by a new professional self-consciousness. Thus schools of both grades began to turn out a population indifferent or hostile to the claims of the Church of England, which were neither recognised nor understood. This severing of the link which for centuries had bound together the Church and the nation's education, was a serious blow. The Church as a cultural pilot had been dropped.

So much, your Grace, for education. But meanwhile the lives of the proletariat were being shaped by influences over which the Church had little or no control. During the South African War a new popular Press had come into existence which catered for the new partially educated public. Though this new Press was in no sense anti-clerical, its educative influence rivalled and outstripped that of the Church, and taught a different set of values. It gave to the masses a new "this-worldly" outlook, and its gospel was crudely and narrowly nationalistic. Its influence helped to create a cocksure attitude, and the standards of the half-educated were erected into canons of truth.

Your Grace will also remember that social developments were now taking place which helped to reduce the influence of the Church with large masses of the community. The products of Liberal social legislation such as Old Age Pensions, and above all the Lloyd George Insurance Act, radically transformed the lives and outlook of the working class by making them look to the State rather than to the Church for the amelioration of their lot. Nine-tenths of the Church's social work among the poorer working class was now rendered unnecessary. Thus the parson was side-tracked and his charity short-circuited. This is not to say, of course, that both the Church and the proletariat were not both better off for this abolition of the call for charity. But the point is that the Church now became a redundant institution in the eyes of many who previously had found its existence extremely useful. The parson's place in the scheme of things was now radically altered; he had been deposed and the insurance official reigned in his stead. Needless to say the further extension of unemployment insurance still further diminished the utility of the parson in the eyes of those numerous individuals who had patronised religion for what could be got out of it.

But education, the new Press and the new social legislation were not the only influences which helped to undermine the position of the Church of England. About 1909 certain "youth movements" became popular and tended to draw off the young of both sexes from denominational influences. Chief amongst these was the Scout Movement which, vaguely religious and definitely patriotic, tended to secularise the idealism which finds an outlet in work amongst lads. Nor must the steady rise of inexpensive commercialised amusements for the masses be overlooked. In the first decade of the present century the cinema was still in its infancy; but even its beginnings revealed to the far-sighted the fact that a serious rival had now appeared which would gradually displace the religious and moralistic lantern services and lectures which constituted a considerable part of the entertainment offered in mission rooms and similar haunts of hearty religion. Such too homely forms of evangelistic effort would have to give way before large-scale, Americanised, popular forms of entertainment which offered all the latest sensations, and provided the public with seats far more comfortable than the hard and dusty benches of an ill-ventilated mission room. In fact, even before the war cheap commercialised shows were already competing successfully with the old type of parochial entertainment run by the popular curate and his lady workers. Even muscular Christianity itself, with the glove-bout followed by the soul-talk, was fast being knocked on the head by temperance billiard halls, working-men's clubs, and so on. In fact, as State aid was displacing Church charity, so cheap amusements on a commercial basis were short-circuiting the lighter sorts of parochial activity. As the Vicar's half-crown and grocery tickets were no longer needed, so the curate's piano playing and the choirman's bass solo failed to draw an audience, save perhaps of a few children on their off-nights from the pictures. Church charity and Church entertainments were alike out of demand.

Even before the war the short and the long of the situation was that the multiform organisations of the Wilberforce renaissance were fast becoming redundant. Nor, as the fruits of the new secular secondary education began to materialise, were the men to be found to run them. There began to be a shortage both of Church workers and of clergy. Thus all the elaborate parochial plant which had sprung up during the Wilberforce boom was reduced to scrap value. Much of the machinery was still kept uselessly working, out of consideration for those whose money had provided it, and out of pure inertia, for the

Church was slow in adapting itself to the new situation. Though the populace deserted the mission churches, these were often frequented by small groups of devout persons who preferred their quiet atmosphere to the noisy worship of the parish churches with their new chancels occupied by distressing organs and pretentious choirs. But more often than not these back-street bethels became centres of disaffection, and thus many parishes were rent by factions which were far more wearing to the parochial clergyman than the hard work and incessant rush of the Wilberforce period. Indeed the pluck of the clergy who carried on during the slow disintegration of the fabric of the Victorian Church elicits the admiration always bestowed upon those who champion lost causes. But beaten they were at every point.

There were indeed, as your Grace will remember, some futile if well-meant endeavours to apply a little cement to the cracking fabric, such as the founding of the Church of England Men's Society, the rules of which were made as lax as possible, if by any means it might stem the drift of men away from the Church. And meanwhile the women were no longer to be counted upon. A sinister omen of the new century was the beginning of Feminism. The prophet of the new evangel was Mr. George Bernard Shaw, and its ideals squared ill with those of the Mothers' Union. The female sex was now taking the bit between its teeth and was becoming emancipated from the Church with a vengeance; and when the more devout sex begins to desert a religion the outlook is bad. And as it was the more intelligent women who got involved in this crusade, the Church now had to seek its helpers from the lower strata of female intelligence.

Meanwhile, concurrently with the grave weakening of the Church in the sphere of active labour amongst the masses, certain ominous cracks began to appear in its theological fabric. Mr. (now Dr.) R. J. Campbell published his *New Theology* in 1907, and though the late Dr. Gore, that hammer of heretics, speedily refuted it, and the writer himself afterwards repented of it and withdrew it, yet the book had a considerable effect, especially among the theologically inexpert, who must always form the majority in any community. But in 1911 appeared another volume which also merited and received the censure of Dr. Gore—Mr. J. M. Thompson's *Miracles in the New Testament*. This book was said to have been the death of the author's uncle, Dr. Paget, Bishop of Oxford, just as Dr. Gore's own *Lux Mundi* was said to have been the death of Dr. Liddon. Your Grace will recollect the scandal caused by Mr. Thompson's too drastic application of the new methods of historical study to the Gospel miracles, and how distasteful to ecclesiastical authority his conclusions were. The Bishops both of Winchester and of London signified their disapprobation by taking steps against the author—steps which were indeed necessary since his book could not be refuted so easily as the more innocent volume of Mr. Campbell. In fact, your Grace, it has not yet been refuted, and after more than twenty years the field is still open for a careful

archiepiscopal examination of this disturbing work,
which very few clergy (and it is to be hoped no laity)
would venture to read.

Assailed thus by social forces and intellectual
criticism, the ark of the Church was ill equipped to
meet the storm which in 1914 broke over us. The
Great War completed what the previous ten years
had begun. It is true that our ecclesiastical authorities manfully strove to make religious capital out of
this calamity, and indeed, to many of the clergy the
war was in some respects a godsend. For the past
ten years or more they had been feeling more and
more redundant, more and more side-tracked, more
and more that they were piping to a world which
would not dance; and now at last the nation seemed
to have some use for them. They were needed on
committees, they could help the dependants of men
serving, they could visit in the hospitals, they could
comfort the bereaved and anxious, they could help
recruiting. Their usefulness was at once increased
tenfold, and people even began to come to church.
This temporary filling of churches could be accounted
for in a number of ways. There was on the part of
some people a renewed appreciation of the value of
religion and of the place it ought to occupy in life.
Amongst these capable of reflection, too, there was a
certain collapse of the shallow optimism which had
been so prevalent for a couple of generations, and
which was now being replaced by a feeling of being
adrift in a strange world. Besides this, amongst a
wider public, there was a genuine if groundless hope
that by a return to religion, the end of the war, and

of their own discomfort, might somehow be hastened. Besides these more or less genuinely religious considerations, there were other not less effective causes. The censorship of news, and above all the partial cessation of congenial distractions (such as excursion trains and other amenities at week-ends, besides the extreme dearness of petrol) drove people to church for lack of anything else to occupy them. Then there was the darkness of the streets which sent people indoors, where there was often a scarcity of coal in the domestic grate, so that a comparatively warm church had its attractions. Then there was a wholesale and perfectly natural dread of being left alone with one's worries, for it is very depressing to have leisure but no distractions. The Church was for the time being able to supply real attractions— warmth, light, and fellowship; things which, during the war, were a godsend to many lonely, restless and worried people.

Nevertheless, in spite of their obviously increased utility at home, the happiest clergy were those who became honorary chaplains to the troops. There was a great rush to be taken on, for many clergy were heartily weary of their parishes, besides being anxious to " do their bit " and to be seen wearing khaki. A certain number of the younger clergy, sorely disillusioned after a few years of the futilities of parochial life, enlisted as combatants. But this natural course was, as your Grace remembers, heavily frowned upon by bishops, and was calculated sorely to prejudice a man's prospects if, as usually did not happen, he came out of the inferno alive. In this matter the bishops' attitude seemed, to the eye of the profane, thoroughly inconsistent. For if it was right for a layman to kill Germans, it was right for a priest to do the same, save on the principle of a differential morality, which none of the bishops was prepared openly to advocate. But of course it was not a time for principles, only for expedients; and standardised and conventionalised rules of conduct had to take the place of ideals. No one had any leisure to think; the chief thing was to get on with the war. Those who stopped to ask questions were swept aside and were lucky to escape being trampled underfoot. Few clergy or bishops troubled themselves over the theoretical question of the duty of an official of a supra-national institution at a time of national crisis. The sacred character of the priest was sufficiently established by his exemption from military service. Thus the Church was able to make the best of both worlds. Bishops and clergy had all the satisfactions of patriotism without its personal sacrifices; and they solved all the difficult issues by ignoring them. The Church meanwhile was engulfed by the universal craze for activity. All independent thinking for the time being ceased entirely. The clergy were busier and happier than they had been for years; and a moratorium for all intellectual liabilities was declared.

It is an invariable consequence of absolute abstention from the practice of thought that the abstainer flings himself into pointless activities with absolute *abandon*, and although the clergy had their hands pretty full, the bishops, as your Grace will remember, struck upon the device of filling them still further with something quite useless, and announced a National Mission of Repentance and Hope. The nation was too busy to smile or even to take much notice of the stunt, which proved a miserable fiasco. However, in the intervals of criticising the Government and hating the Germans the public was alive to the fact that the gaitered clergy were making fools of themselves by ignoring the sound rule that if a leader perceives that nothing useful can be done, he should be content to do nothing.

Your Grace will recollect, no doubt with a blush, how during those painful years the inquirer for moral guidance was put off by the Church's official spokesmen with evasions and platitudes; how clergy from the pulpit used their best efforts to explain away the plain sense of the New Testament, and showed indecent haste to repudiate Christianity without surrendering their privileges and emoluments. This supernaturally inspired institution, the Church, seemed somehow to have nothing to say but what was already being said, with far more lucidity and point, by the evening newspapers. The most distressing sentimentalities of a pseudo-religious, hundred per cent patriotism were ladled out wholesale, and almost without a protest. Our spiritual currency, your Grace, was more debased than that of the Central Powers subsequently became. Nothing could have more clearly revealed the religious and mental penury wherewith we were afflicted than the forms of prayer which were issued from time to time by authority, and which the parochial clergy were

required to read during divine service for the edification and encouragement of the faithful. I cannot
but believe, your Grace, that the bishops, owing to
the multitude of their engagements, entrusted the
composition of these prayers to their young lady
secretaries. They expressed unctuous insincerities in
the feeblest language, and were depressing alike to
utter and to hear. Their content, your Grace, was
as thin as their English.

It has been necessary to dwell upon these painful
facts because they serve to indicate the state of affairs
to which the Church had been reduced by the habit,
developed during the pre-war years, of running away
from ideas into the endless activities of the Wilberforce régime. And even when, owing to social
changes, all these activities had become quite pointless, enthusiasm for them did not diminish. They
constituted that prime necessity for a Church which
had lost touch—an escape from reality. While
turning the prayer-wheel, playing with Boy Scouts
or Guides, talking to the Mothers' Union, organising
sales of work and whist drives, the vicar and his
curate could forget Mr. Thompson's book, could
close their eyes to the rising tide of infidelity, could,
in short, inhabit a fool's paradise. And even bishops,
as your Grace would admit, are always far too busy
to read or to think. The machine makes such
demands upon them. A bishop has less time for
quiet thought or meditation than a film star or a
prime grade politician. As for his trying to do any
serious work, that is frankly impossible. And in any
case it would be thought unworthy of a bishop to

expend upon intellectual labour energies which should be reserved for diocesan committees. It is of interest to note that the one bishop on the bench who has attained the distinction of being an F.R.S. is far from popular with his colleagues, has been snubbed by an Archbishop, and is perpetually being assailed in the Church Press.

But theological and ethical problems do not cease to exist merely because they are continually being shelved by those who are too frightened to tackle them or too stupid to see that they will grow graver than ever by being shelved. All that happens is that those who run away get into the fugitive habit, so that when a crisis comes along, they are found wanting. Hence it was entirely natural that when the war came, clergy and bishops were stampeded along with everybody else, in spite of their ridiculous claims to possess superior spiritual enlightenment. There is a Nemesis which awaits the runaway; he misses the most precious of opportunities through not being on the spot.

The pre-war policy of the Church having been such as I have ventured to describe to your Grace, what sort of policy prevailed when the war was over? Before the war had ended, and before it was at all certain that it would end successfully, a small but active band of clerical idealists, conscious like every intelligent person, that something would have to be done, started a reformist agitation for which they improvised the happy title of the " Life and Liberty Movement." The phrase was a stroke of genius, and embodied just that touch of counterfeit idealism which appealed strongly to a public too tired to help taking words at their face value, and well accustomed during four years of intellectual degradation, to catchwords and slogans. The programme of this reformist strategy boiled down to two points, namely, democratic control and more efficient management in the Church. By such original methods it was hoped to arrange for a revival of spiritual life within the Church, and to increase its effectiveness in dealing with the world at large. The public was not unwilling to accept the reformers' diagnosis of the Church's ills—that they were due in large part to lack of the democratic spirit and to antiquated machinery. Had not democracy defeated autocracy when after four years of attrition the Hindenburg line gave way ? Had not the war been won by the efficiency of business men, by mechanisation, by mass production of munitions, and by the card-index system ? The principle of success in religion as in war was efficient organisation. Was not the parallel between Britain at war and the Church Militant an exact one ? The Church must resemble a brand new munition factory staffed by willing but disciplined workers and run by an efficient secretarial department.

England, at this initial post-war period, presented a not unnatural combination of weariness and hopefulness. The average man felt that if the Church thought it could reform itself it ought to be allowed to try. After all it might succeed, for while the brief infection of Wilsonian idealism lasted, it almost seemed as if the age of miracles had returned. Thus, your Grace, the Life and Liberty agitators with their contagious optimism had their way and the Enabling Act became law.

The reformers were not wholly representative of Church opinion. Indeed, reform is a thing that the clergy instinctively mistrust. But the new programme was accepted and supported for a variety of reasons. There were those who felt that a self-inflicted reform might well be preferable to a compulsory one imposed from without by possibly unsympathetic politicians. There were others who hoped that the evils and scandals of Erastianism could be ended without sacrificing the solid benefits of Establishment. Such speculators hoped that through the new machinery of self-government, the clergy with the willing help of the ecclesiastically minded laity, would be able to impose their ideals and superstitions upon the Church at large. A greater strictness of discipline, and some wholesome and necessary restriction of doctrinal latitude, which had of late become a scandal, might be secured. Thus the dangerous and rapid growth of Modernism might be nipped.

I would not deny, your Grace, that sincere idealism and honest conviction did leaven the dough of the Life and Liberty movement. Amongst the children of this world who so successfully ran it there was also a small sprinkling of children of light, apart from whose participation in it, possibly, the public would hardly have trusted it to the limited extent that they did, or have let the thing go through. And a quite genuine feeling that the Church could, and should, do better, was widespread. The mistake was to suppose that the primary trouble was defective machinery and organisation. This was an entirely superficial and unreal view to take of the Church's troubles, which were not to be cured by any such simple expedients as were proposed.

The fact was that the solution proposed by the Life and Liberty clique had already been tried out long before the war, and after succeeding for a time, had failed to meet changed conditions and had therefore proved vain. It is possible that your Grace will be able to perceive a very close parallel between the leader of the Life and Liberty movement and the protagonist of efficient religion in the nineteenth century. The head of Life and Liberty, who holds high office in the Church to-day and must be extremely well known to your Grace, was neither more nor less than Wilberforce *Redivivus*. Yet if Wilberforce's methods in the end proved unavailing to stem the drift away from religion, it is hardly likely that the same methods, brought up to date a little, could do much better in times when the difficulties facing the Church were so much greater. If these belauded business methods failed in the nineteenth century, before people became so critical of established institutions, is it likely that they will succeed to-day ? The post-war environment was ten times more difficult as future events were to show. The Wilberforce policy had proved bankrupt once, to try it on again under far less favourable conditions argued either conceit or ignorance. This resurrection of the bankrupt efficiency-cult indicated that in reality the post-war reformers were lacking in useful ideas and utterly devoid of originality. The place of ideas was being taken by slogans and clap-trap, and by silly enthusiasm for details of organisation.

The Life and Liberty corps had wrongly diagnosed the trouble. The weakness of the Church had not in fact been a weakness of organisation. On the whole, the machinery had not worked too badly; and if it fell short of perfection, what weakness there was might easily have been remedied without inaugurating the pseudo-democratic machinery of the Enabling Act. The real weakness of the Church, ever since Newman had issued his challenge, had not been mechanical or even moral (for the intentions of the Church were often laudable), but intellectual. No one knew where it stood. The fundamental issues which were raised first by Newman, and then in an even more challenging form by Darwin, were studiously evaded by the Church of Wilberforce, which was too busy building mission churches and schools to ask what should be taught in them when they were built. And the pre-war Church carried on the tradition, being afraid to tackle the questions raised by the critical study of the New Testament. And these new issues were in reality far more challenging than anything that Wilberforce or Liddon had dreamed of. Thus the post-war arrears of intellectual liabilities were quite sufficient in themselves to have occupied all the energies of Wilberforce *Redivivus* and his friends. But in order to escape meeting Apollyon by the way, they led the Church down a by-path, and busied themselves with details of organisation, with efficiency, and with the card-index. Once more the Church of England had practised its time-honoured policy of evasion.

All of us are agreed, your Grace, that the task of the Church has become much more difficult since the war. It is not merely that the frivolous have become openly irreligious, but unbelief and indifference or hostility to the Church have spread to a disturbing extent amongst thoughtful, well-informed, intelligent, and often idealistic people. And it is indisputable that numbers base their loyalty to the Church upon the professed belief that it makes for social stability, and not upon any lively faith in its doctrines. But it is hardly safe for the Church to count upon even such support as this for very much longer, since it is now recognised that sport and cheap amusements are far more efficient social sedatives than a religion which is losing its grip.

Thus the pre-war and post-war policy of efficiency combined with the shirking of intellectual and moral issues must be accounted a failure. It will soon be half a generation since the war ended—a long enough time to prove that neither defective organisation nor even defective discipline, were our root troubles. The dry rot has been far more deep-seated than this. We seem to be suffering from religious and mental debility, and so long as this condition lasts the reorganisation of finance, the building of churches and schools, an increase in the number of bishoprics, and so forth, will do less than nothing to help us. For by distracting our attention from the real trouble, all this fuss will do far more harm than good.

It would be both painful and tedious, your Grace, to dwell at length upon the symptoms of our disease, but I may mention two—the pre-occupation of the clergy with trifles and privileges, and our declining intellectual standards. A careful study of the correspondence columns of the religious press will reveal the astonishing narrowness of the circle within which the minds of the majority of clergy move. Extraordinary interest and enthusiasm will be displayed over such questions as the proper place of the ablutions at Mass and other similar liturgical details. And what at a lower social level would be termed trade union interests will engage their minds. But beyond these topics, local gossip would seem to form the staple subject of clerical intercourse. All theological questions are approached with the most cautious wariness, lest any man should let anything slip to injure his reputation for true orthodoxy. Everybody is pathetically anxious to be thought " sound," as prospects of promotion are known to depend upon it.

Its reputation for learning, as your Grace is well aware, was formerly the proud boast of the Church of England. Its position of privilege at the two older universities, where the most important theological professorships are limited to men in holy orders, has contributed thereto. Nor must we forget the existence of those numerous and amply endowed cathedral Chapters, which should provide leisure and opportunity for a regiment of scholars. A Church which could not make a fair show of learning under these circumstances would constitute a scandal. And in addition there are a good number of country livings up and down the Kingdom with quite adequate incomes and extremely light duties, the incumbents whereof have every opportunity for a life of quiet study. Yet in spite of these privileges, unique in the world at present, what do we see ? If a census were taken of members of cathedral bodies, apart from those such as Ely and Christ Church, Oxford, which are in close connection with some university, we should discover only an insignificant minority who had made any important contribution to learning, and not very many who had published anything at all. Even deans for the most part do not use their expensive leisure in trying to bridge the gulf which yawns between the Church and contemporary knowledge, and the finest contemporary ideals. The fashion at present is for a dean to act with mock humility as a sort of glorified verger, to transform his cathedral into a pseudo-mediæval arts and crafts emporium, and to seek a cheap popularity by playing to the gallery upon every conceivable occasion. These decanal mountebanks make our Church ridiculous. Thus, in spite of endowments and opportunities, little in the way of serious study or serious thought is undertaken, and the summit of a dean's or a canon's mental activity in the course of a year may be to preach a sermon to the diocesan branch of the Mothers' Union—a task which could be done with far better results by a doctor, a psychologist, or a student of economics; and best of all, perhaps by the mother of a family.

It is not as if much work were not waiting to be

done. Is it not a fact, your Grace, that no Anglican clergyman can be found at present either learned or bold or industrious enough to write a scientific commentary upon the fourth Gospel, perhaps the most crucial book in the whole of Christian literature, ancient or modern ? The standard work at present is by a distinguished French scholar, which it would be safe to say that not a score of Anglican clergy have read. They would no more have Loisy's book upon their shelves than Strauss's *Life of Jesus*. The timidity and ineffectiveness of nearly all clerical Anglican scholarship is notorious.

This narrowness of outlook, combined with this timidity and fundamental insincerity, is, your Grace, a symptom that our Church, instead of being the vehicle and instrument of a living religious tradition, has become imitative only. It can no longer originate or create; it can only repeat and copy. And like all merely conservative agencies, wherever it sees life stirring, and the vital tradition (which it claims to embody) striving to find new forms of expression, it frowns upon them and if possible nips them in the bud. The Church has thus become the enemy of the religious tradition which it claims to embody. Experience teaches that a religious tradition which is alive, in the same way as an artistic tradition, will continually produce new manifestations of itself as the generations pass. The emergence of such fresh manifestations is the only evidence that a religious or artistic tradition is still alive. When life has evaporated, imitation and slavish repetition take the place of creation and

spontaneity. It is a mistake to imagine that faithful-
ness to tradition means a surrender of originality.
On the contrary, a tradition can only be kept alive
by individuals gifted with some amount of originality
which they are not too frightened to express. "All
the great innovators in art were in the great tradition, you cannot quote one exception, however much
they may have been considered rebels by their contemporaries," says Jacob Epstein. The truth about
religion is the same. It is the innovators who are
faithful to the tradition to which they owe everything, and which they enrich. "Tradition implies
progress. To stop is to lose sight of it." All genuine
religion, like all genuine art, is kept alive by change;
and where change is discouraged by academies or
Churches, one of two things must happen. Either
religion and art become conventional and lose
vitality, whilst the academies and Churches appear
to flourish by exploiting the conventions of a past
age. Or, alternatively, art and religion break with
the Churches and academies which seek to suppress
free development, originality, spontaneity, and in
short the living tradition itself. In this case Churches
and academies survive as empty shells from which
the life has departed. The true rôle of an academy
or Church should be to preserve the life of the tradition which it embodies, and this is best done by
adding to it. A tradition can be kept alive only by
lifting every restriction upon experiment and
novelty; nothing can grow unless it is given room.
To be afraid of change is to be afraid of life. Thus a
Church which resists change has become the enemy

of living, and the exponent of dead, religion, which
at its best is a barren convention, and at its worst a
degrading superstition. And the fact that the organisation and management of such a Church was
efficient and up to date would make it all the more
formidable an enemy to living religion. An inefficient
Church can never do a great deal of harm, but what
Wilberforce picturesquely termed "the compact
phalanx of the Church" may be a terrible menace.

Not that I recommend a return, your Grace, to
the Church of Anthony Trollope. I only suggest that
the Wilberforce advance was made down a *cul de sac*,
and that our post-war zeal for finance, advertisement
and organisation is no better. A Church which fears
and discourages change cannot possibly promote the
vitality of religion, and if it had the organisation of an
oil combine (as it already has the wealth of one), this
would avail little. Progress in religion, as in art,
comes not through machinery, but through the
creative individual whom the machinery crushes.
At present all such individuals know full well that
the Church is no place for them; they cannot breathe
stale air.

As things now are, your Grace, the younger
generation, which embodies the religious, artistic
and intellectual life of the future, passes your Church
by. True it is that your Grace and your Grace's
episcopal colleagues can secure for ordination a
number of worthy young men by subsidising their
education. But these malleable seminarists, though
willing to co-operate in running the ecclesiastical
machine and the futile activities of the average

parish, are not at all typical of the post-war generation. The cream of this generation, your Grace, are
aware that you have little to offer them in the way
of compensation for the surrender of mental freedom.
And apart from these young men, who repudiate you
and your Church, you can do very little. Your
Church cannot keep alive without them. And your
Grace would be far better employed in making it
possible for these young men to devote themselves to
the Church, than in perfecting your organisation and
finance. I admit that the presence of these young
men amongst us in the Church would be extremely
disturbing. They would seek to change the Church
from what it now is—a society for the preservation
of old opinions and customs out of which the life
has departed—into a society for experiment and for
the attainment of new knowledge and new and better
modes of behaviour. They would wish to create new
embodiments of the religious spirit, and some of their
attempts might be as startling to you or me, your
Grace, as futurism in art. There would be no restrain-
ing these young men, who would undoubtedly upset
everything and everybody. Their presence amongst
us would be a very unpleasant tonic, but it would do
much to cure the spiritual debility from which we now
suffer. Their activities, for all their strangeness and
extravagance, would not be merely capricious or
irresponsible. These young men would be embody-
ing the life of their time, and as such an embodiment
they would be expressing thoughts and aspirations
which already exist, perhaps vaguely (half-expressed
and half-understood) in innumerable minds.

To have the growing points of the community *inside* the Church would, as I say, be very upsetting for all of us, but to have them *outside* the Church as they now are, though this leaves us in peace, is far more disastrous. This peace which we now enjoy by isolating ourselves from the stirrings of new ideas, is in reality the peace of death.

I do not wish to suggest, your Grace, that religion is solely, or even chiefly, a matter of the intellect, and certainly none of the rising generation would take this view. They are far less " intellectualist," probably, than you or I. Yet it is also true that the individual who suffers from mental inhibitions, is less likely to be creative in religion, or in art, or in any other form of activity, than one who is free from such inhibitions, and whose mind works normally. How is it, your Grace, that many a clergyman who at twenty-five was an intelligent, interested, normal man, at fifty is either a dullard or a sophist, dwelling in some mental prison, and afraid to step out of doors ? This lamentable transformation is the natural result of a system which discourages the free use of the intelligence. Our post-war young men do not wish to get caught in any such trap, and this is why they fight shy of the Church. Can we disarm their suspicions, and show them that the Church is not a trap at all, but a " large room " where a man can stretch his legs and freely exercise all his powers ? A place where he can be creative if he has it in him, and where he can feel at home as well as at liberty ?

Your Grace, we need these young men very badly, not because we wish to exploit them, but because they are the growing-point of the community, and therefore indispensable to us. Apart from them we cannot keep alive, and all our elaborate organisation will only be a body of death. It is indeed fortunate that it is no longer possible for our Church to dissipate its energies over substitutes for religion. As I have ventured to remind your Grace, our non-religious activities, formerly useful, are now out of place and redundant. These activities were not evidence of religious or intellectual life, they were only a means of escape. We are now being forced back upon religion: unless we can make good here, we may as well close down and cease making ourselves ridiculous. The difficulties are great; for religion, like art, cannot be "managed"—it is not a matter for devices and shifts, for opportunism and ecclesiastical *finesse*. Even sound business acumen, or political adroitness will not carry us far. The sort of spirit which animated our recent attempt at Prayer Book revision, when every doctrinal issue was studiously evaded, and discipline was to be based, not on beliefs, but on regulations, will have to give place to a greater sincerity. We shall have to consider seriously the Gospel precept of the single eye.

That our age needs religion, and will get it from some other quarter if we do not give it them, seems evident. The call for it may not be loud, but it is insistent. It would appear that reality is about to invade once more the sphere of religion. This, your Grace, is a very serious matter for you and me. Perhaps after all they will insist that the old wine-skins are not good enough ? And where shall we be then ?

What about our prestige, our emoluments, our elaborate organisation, our alleged supernatural powers and knowledge ? Is it all destined for the scrap heap ? Has the life gone out of the whole bag of tricks ? Is the Church a corpse, and you and I morsels of putrefying matter ? It would almost appear so. And yet . . . ? One would like to believe, if one could, that the Church had a future, that somehow, in spite of such manifest appearances of death, it still lives. Almost incredible, I admit. But you and I, your Grace, are well used to believing the incredible; it is part of our trade to do so. One can but hope. And meanwhile, craving your benediction and your prayers, I remain your Grace's must obedient and humble servant.

                              J. C. HARDWICK,
                                      Priest.

A LETTER TO ADOLF HITLER

LOUIS GOLDING

DEAR HERR HITLER,

I address this letter to you not with the desire to tempt you into controversy, but because I flatter myself that its matter will be of interest to you. You are a German. (I am right, am I not, in suggesting that you are now become a German ?) And being so, you may care to beguile a few moments of your leisure with the exposition which here follows of an attempt to attain an Absolute.

It is the specific variety of Absolute (if I do not use an expression revolting to a German and a metaphysician) which might, or even must, commend itself to your attention. I, Herr Hitler, am a Jew, or a Semite, as I think you would put it. From stage to stage of my career I have been compelled to become aware of a race of beings called Antisemites. You are a Gentile. You are more than that. You are without doubt the most celebrated of contemporary Antisemites. I wonder if you have ever had leisure to meditate on the ultimate, the as it were quintessential, Semite ? I think it hardly likely, of late years, at any rate; for soon after you ceased to be a soldier you became a politician, and in neither capacity could you have had much time for so tenuous an occupation.

But I, for one reason or another, and for more than a score of years, have attempted to isolate the obverse, or the reverse, concept—the ultimate, the quintessential, Antisemite. And having found It at length, I do now commit to musical notation and to your indulgence this symphony of Antisemites.

I say "symphony," I would have you understand, less to indicate any precise technical correspondence in the direction of themes and movements, than to convey immediately my sense of the aesthetic coherence of my experience. I mean that I conceive the Antisemites of my wayfaring not merely as fortuitous persons and episodes, but an organic adventure, which has culminated but lately in the Fräulein Hertha Grossman, the "It" from which and to which this essay proceeds. There is a suggestion of triviality about that brief expression in English, but that is because the English language, like the English people, does not take the Absolute as seriously as it ought. If I were writing in the language of the Fräulein Hertha Grossman and of yourself, I should refer to her and to " It " as " *das Ding an sich*," a more appropriately portentous expression. For, as I have said, it was precisely the Antisemite on the metaphysical plane, the Jew-hater perfect and abstract and absolute, which was the object of my passion. And she it was who consummates it, the Fräulein Hertha, the benignant, the rotund, that chubby Venice whose canals are all brimful of the milk of human kindness.

Two bogies darkly impended over my childhood in the dark city of Doomington. Their lordship was disputed from epoch to epoch by the murderer of the moment. That is to say, that while the murderer of twenty or fifty years earlier, a Jack-the-Ripper, for instance, could not hold a candle to them, they tottered briefly on their spectral thrones when a Crippen was abroad, lurking in narrow entries and hiding in coal-cellars. Their names were King Cossack and King Antisemite.

The first was indeed a *monstrum horrendum, informe, ingens,* a bristling monster, formless, huge. His beard soughed like the pine-forests of the country he ravaged. He tore babes from their mothers' arms and spitted them upon spikes. He performed certain other outrages to which death was preferable, though they sometimes involved death. I could not divine their nature. Altogether he was a noble, swaggering fellow. I should have hated to meet him thundering down the cobbles of my street on his white charger; but there were moments of childish despondency when the prospect of being trampled into the mire by those incomparable hoofs was not without its charms.

And yet King Cossack, in those earlier as in these later days, by no means confined his attentions to his Jewish countrymen. That was why the distinction was drawn between him and that other royal bogey, King Antisemite. I was to apply to him that resonant series of Virgilian adjectives which Salmasius had applied to Milton. He certainly was *horrendum*. My hair bristles now at the thought of him. He was no less surely *ingens*. Sometimes he leaned over my bed and blotted out the sun and half the sky with his hugeness. But he was not *informe*. That was inapt. He was etched with diamond clarity against the synagogues he had enkindled. Sometimes I awoke in the dead hour before dawn to stare straight into his eyeballs and the scarlet scythe of his lips. I knew his eyelashes by heart.

He was at his worst when he presented himself in nightmare. In my day-dreams he seemed a gay dog rather. And in the moments when I felt less certain than usual that I should shortly be appointed Prime Minister of England, I entertained ambitions of being Hetman of all the Cossacks. I should be a virtuous Cossack, a Jewish Cossack. I would have no babes immolated nor women ravaged. It would be important to conduct an occasional pogrom, of course, but they should be non-sectarian pogroms.

The Cossack, then, was not *informe*. He was
clearer in my mind than my own father, whose
outlines were a little blurred in the mist of his own
majesty. It was the Antisemite who was formless;
or he was Protean, rather. There was no fixing
him. You could not say of him that he wore a
beard, which you could so promptly say of his
colleague. Nor that he wore knee-boots. You
caught glimpses of him. Sometimes you thought
you had him, but you found he was not truly, not
essentially, It. He was pretending he was the
metaphysical Antisemite, when he was merely
angry because Reuben Levine had tricked him by
a halfpenny per hundredweight of sugar. Or because our Mr. Belloc had told him that, mystically
speaking, Abraham Myer of Golder's Green did
actually crucify his saviour. Or because a parvenu
Jewish gentleman had eaten asparagus with his
spoon and fork at Claridge's, as doubtless another
Jewish gentleman did only yesterday in the Adlon
Hotel. No, no, the angry gentleman was not *das
Ding an sich*. He voiced a relative, not an absolute,
Antisemitism. It was not in itself a Cause, like
love, like truth. It merely had a cause. No, no,
he was an impostor.

For years and years, I say, he eluded me. But
at length he stands before me, apparent, but not
naked. He wears the camel-brown frock of the

female section of the Bavarian semi-intelligentsia,
a tie and collar, and sandals. His name is Hertha
Grossman.

Bavarian, you will observe, dear Herr Hitler.
For which reason it would have been ungracious
to seek among the ranks of international Antisemites any other Antisemite than yourself. I do
not doubt she drank the swart Hackerbräu in
those same Munich beer-gardens where you
jumped up on to the tables and, shaking your
fist, cried: The Jews! Down with the Jews! But
it was not you, not you, who made her Antisemite. Antisemite she was, is, will be, *in saecula
saeculorum*. That is, in fact, the argument of this
letter.

Many years were to elapse before the vision of
Hertha was at length granted me in quite the
most *gemütlich* of the pensions in Capri. Let me return to the kitchen of my father's small house in
Doomington. The wickednesses of King Cossack
were vehement in character, but, if the truth were
told, they were limited in scope and unimaginative. But there seemed no limit at all to the
subtlety of King Antisemite. No irritating triviality was too mean for him to perform, and no
shape too humble to assume. Not that he had not
also his grandiose conceptions, executed with the
most tremendous breadth and generosity. He was

not averse to sinking an Atlantic liner if he knew
that some poor and pious Jew were travelling
steerage in it. King Antisemite's effects were not
a wit less spectacular than King Cossack's. He
was quite ready to burn down the enormous
waterproof factory owned by Mr. Sager, merely
because Mr. Sager a week ago had presented a new
Scroll of the Law to the Synagogue. There was
no greater expert upon his nature and atrocities
than the ancient beldame who lived at the bottom
of the street. Her name was Mimma Rochel. So
far as our scholars could ascertain she was the
first Iraelite to return to the shores of England
after Oliver Cromwell had lifted the secular
embargo. It was rumoured, even, that she had
witnessed the Second Destruction of the Temple.
She is aware of your lack of affection for her, dear
Herr Hitler; for she is extant to this day. She
will doubtless witness the Temple's re-erection.
I mention her mainly because she had the answer
to that vexed question which so many polemists
have attempted so vainly to answer. Who caused
the Great War ? Ask Mimma Rochel. She knows.
She told me. It was Antisemite. He brought
about the Great War in order to punish the Jews
of Doomington for riding upon tramcars on the
Sabbath, and neglecting to salt their meat carefully. She lost her own two grandsons in the War,

though they had never ridden upon tramcars on the Sabbath, and though their wives had never neglected to salt their meat carefully. But Antisemite had not merely brought about the Great War. He had the managing of it. The War presented no problem to Mimma Rochel which was not clear as day.

There is only one other person in the world who has an answer as precise as hers. That is yourself, of course. Who caused the Great War? Ask Adolf Hitler. He knows. It was Semite. And your reasoning, is it a whit less forceful than hers?

I have seen charabanc-loads of Nazi boys hurtling along the arid Pomeranian roads. They waved high the black swastika embroidered on banners. "Heil Hitler!" they cried to your absent shade. "Down with the Jews!" they cried. They are more antisemitic than the small Lancashire lads were, at my infant school in Doomington, though the name of Christ rarely falls from their Teuton lips. Your bronzed blonde novices remember that half the blood in Christ's veins, if not the whole of it, was Jewish. But my Lancashire colleagues were not prejudiced by that. "Sheeny!" they said. "Who killed Christ?"

Yet I do not believe that they shared Mr. Belloc's transcendental conviction that we did,

namely, Isaac and Barney and myself. Nor did
we ourselves. They asked a rhetorical question.
We replied rhetorically. " Who killed Christ ? "
Swift came the reply. " We did, with a butcher's
knife! " It is, of course, painful to me as I look
back upon these playground skirmishes. But it
was, I am certain, less painful then. Our man-
oeuvres were thrust and counter-thrust in a game
hallowed by tradition, but by no sacerdotal fury.
That particular game ended, the " smoggy van"
Jews and the virtuous little Christian apologists
joined forces in a game of tig or rounders or leap-
frog. Hertha Grossman, who would have preferred a game of pogrom, would have found leap-
frog an anti-climax.

As we moved forward into adolescence and our
horizons extended beyond synagogue and school
to include the area of the great factories of
Doomington and the mines on its fringes, once
more we heard from sallow pit-boys and shrill,
shawled maidens the jibe, the jeer. There seemed
to be more venom in their voices now. But that
was merely because life in so few years had become
so much bitterer for them. They wondered in
their brief respites why it was now so much more
joyless; and they blamed this alien, palpable
race thrust down in their midst. It was an auto-
matic reaction of harassed nerves rather than a

deliberate exercise of evil will. They blamed the
alien race, not because Barney and Isaac and I
had any more direct influence at fourteen over
their destinies than we had exerted seven years
earlier, but because somehow Barney and Isaac
and I had escaped their incarceration in the
pounding factories and the black mines. But we
had all been caught up, had they known the truth,
in tyrannies no less inexorable. Barney and Isaac
pressed trousers in prisons smaller but just as
noisome, and my own subjection to Latin pre-
positions imposed on me hours of labour which
would have filled any trade union with fury.

It is certain that the jeering mill-hands cannot
be accepted as Antisemite absolute. The emotion,
the ecstasy, must be engendered in the void. No
wonder that in the fecund darkness of their factories weeds of lovelessness opened their blotchy
flowers.

Yet I cannot disguise from myself that during
this period, before the Antisemites of my young
manhood overtook me, one certain incident occurred which I must pinnacle dim in the intense
Inane, which I must exalt into that dark crystalline firmament where the Ptolemy of Antisemitism,
perfect and abstract and absolute, resides before
and after Time. (Do I solemnise a petty hatred
of certain numerous midges for certain fewer

midges with a false and factitious Eternity ? What
else shall be eternal then, if it be not hate absolute,
love absolute, without reference to the grossness
or sublimity of the thing hated or loved ?)

I speak of the incident on the brick-croft, which
took place in my sixteenth year. A bleak cavalcade
was ascending the gritty slopes of Longton in the
direction of the Jewish cemetery on the outer
fringes of Doomington. The hearse that preceded
us bore my mother in her coffin. We followed in
the shabby sumptuousness of the four-wheelers to
which our so many pence per week, paid over so
many years, entitled us upon any such melancholy occasion. There was no doubt we were a
Jewish procession, partly because there was no
other cemetery saving of the Jews in this direction,
partly because we displayed no Gentile pomp of
flowers. Moreover, the Hebrew lettering on the
black panels of the hearse told the tale explicitly.

The age of fifteen is perhaps of all ages the one
in which such a loss can least easily be borne. The
young human has attained a faculty for suffering
which his future will not refine upon; nor has he
yet acquired any such philosophy as later may
temper it. It is not necessary, therefore, to expati-
ate upon the condition of the forlorn youth seated
in the four-wheeler nearest to the hearse. He
looked out upon the landscape to his left hand, but

that conveyed no solace. It had not rained that day, but it had rained the day before, and the next day it would rain again. Slushy streams meandered about the brick-croft to a central cesspool. Further away the tall chimneys impended against a blank sky. And then of a sudden three figures of youths about his own age were substantiate before his eyes, on the rim of that loveless field. They gesticulated, they leered, they screamed.

"Smoggy van Jew! Sheeny! Sheeny! Who killed Christ?"

They stuck their tongues out towards the supine corpse, as if there, in that gentle dust, the criminal was at length apprehended. They seemed the principle of evil incarnate, illustrating its essential nature with apt gesture. They were not, therefore, such demons as had fallen from Heaven with Lucifer, but such as Hell's own heart had engendered. So they seemed to that lad following to her grave the mother he loved well. It was not rage that possessed him then, such as later should often seize him till his eyes started. A sort of awe held him, similar in intensity but opposite in quality to the awe he had sometimes experienced upon gazing into the Ark of the Law when it was flung open on the Day of Atonement, and God seemed manifest. He could not see the faces of

the three youths, for a mist was on his eyes. That
is why he has once and again deemed that perhaps they were not there at all. Could such
mortal creatures as we know and are, have behaved so ?

I do not doubt it. Hertha Grossman has since
assured me that I need not.

At school, now, and some years later, at Oxford,
a new type of Antisemitics manifested itself; new
in my experience, that is to say, because of the
limited nature of my social contacts till that time.
The Antisemitics of good form is a constant
variant of the prime instinct in all the polite
countries—unknown in Abyssinia, it has a doctrine both subtle and scrupulous in the Faubourg
Saint Germain and the Hildebrandstrasse. I became acquainted with a breed of young gentlemen who considered it doggy to utter scurrilities
concerning Jews in general and any Jew in particular who happened to be at hand. They used
the verb " to Jew," sanctioned by the editors of
the *Oxford Dictionary*, first out of deliberate malice,
and then, mechanically, to express a particular
concept. The sting was extracted from the witti-
cism by the entirely spontaneous way in which their
own Jewish friends made use of the expression,
stating how Froggie had jewed them out of an
hour of their half-holiday, or how Smithers had

jewed them in the matter of that Guatemala stamp. The doggy young gentleman was, it should be stated, particularly amenable to Jewish companionship. The Jewish athletes and the sons of Jewish bankers were counted among his dearest friends; these, for their part, valued his friendship a hundred times more than the friendship of any vague Shelleyan or fierce Marxian, to whom differences in race and creed were less than motes of dust. When the doggy gentleman uttered his fashionable antisemitic strictures, the Jewish athletes and the budding bankers blushed with a wild pleasure. They felt themselves a step nearer election to membership of Brooks's or the Bachelors' Club.

The Great War hereupon intrudes into this narrative, but during its actual prosecution you must remember, it contributed little palpable substance to the encyclopaedia of Antisemitism. It did not matter during this period what was the shape of a man's nose if he was your enemy and you could confuse it with his eyeballs and bowels and brains in a sticky non-sectarian pulp. The Jewish observer (who no longer had any time to observe the present or still less to anticipate the future, for he was not certain whether there would be a future, individually or collectively) was deceived into believing that the Great War could not but prove the acid dissolvent of Antisemitism. Being in its essence an unreal thing, however viciously real in its effects, he did not believe that Antisemitism could survive so naked and monstrous a reality as the War. Considering the matter sentimentally, he saw his fellows on every front, second neither to Lutherans nor to Freemasons nor to High Anglicans in the fervour of their heroism. His illusion did not long survive the end of the Great War. As if to make up in a few days for the slackness of antisemitic history during the four years, such a fury of Jew-hatred broke out as the world has never before witnessed. Yet it is of particular importance to note that this post-war Antisemitism was a product in the defeated countries of the psychology of defeat. As, indeed, none knows better than yourself, dear Herr Hitler. Rich as it is, therefore, in episode and literature, it stands outside that culminant Antisemitism which is baseless, causeless, unconditioned.

But, for my own part, I ceased to share with more optimistic observers the conviction that Antisemitism would be dissipated like a puff of dust by the tempest of the war, although I, too, retained the rosy phantasy till two or more years of it had passed.

Having returned from less healthy territories, the duty was imposed on me, during the last year, of lecturing to soldiers in camps and to munition-workers in English factories. It was during a swift luncheon lecture in a large arsenal in the Midlands, to the accompaniment of shrieking sirens and moaning wheels and the hellish clatter of thousands of plates, that the disillusion came upon me. I became aware, even as I urged my cracking voice above that pandemonium, of a focus of unrest and hostility. Gradually the face of a man isolated itself across the fumes of soup and fog. There was a twist in his lips I instinct-ively appraised before my mind received any clear message, and a basilisk glare in his eyes, and an ecstasy in his complete pallor. The words: "Jew! Jew! Jew!" at length slid like serpents into my ears. He was sick with hatred of me and everything that pertained to me. I realised that, in one respect at least, all ardours had been in vain and all blood of less worth than sewage conducted into a drain. On that particular morning the realisation was particularly hard to bear. I had learned, two hours ago, of a young brother killed on the Somme on his first day there.

Will it cause you some displeasure to learn that the sallow man did not have it all his own way? I am afraid he did not. A small number of his colleagues quite furiously disposed of him, though they were not aware that the lecturer was lecturing on that particular day against more subtle difficulties than noise and bad manners. When at length the wet murk engulfed the Antisemite, I saw beyond the glare of his eyes other eyes more youthful, more humorous, upon which sunlight would never slant again, nor their own eyelids be drawn when they were tired.

The sallow man was not to be seen again, as the youths that spat at my mother's coffin were not to be seen again. Hertha Grossman was. She was the man in the factory and the boys on the brick-croft. She was the pure lust of Jew-hatred, she was serene in her abomination as Ashtaroth, as precise as a table of logarithms.

And she is so genial and so corpulent a little lady. And she drinks the black Hackerbräu of your Munich, the Munich that pampered you and now spits upon you, with great zest. And her ingenuous cheeks are dimpled with delight when lambs skip and birds twitter. And she is more terrible, more austere, than any plague, for plague is induced by this thing and that thing, and may be countered and at length annulled by this thing and that thing, but her hatred was before the beginning and shall endure after the end.

May I propound to you one sole question ? Do you believe that it is within the nature of the modern civilised man, deliberately and with pride, to permit himself to loathe a whole community *for the mere sake of loathing it* ? Another question arises out of that. Is it, perhaps, a little vain to indulge oneself with such sad sweet phrases as " modern civilised man ? " I fear lest I should flog you with a hail of questions. Let myself answer that I do not believe even your Nazis loathe the Jews for the mere sake of loathing them. There are Americans who loathe negroes as such and Catholics as such; but the sentiment is based, however mistakenly, on a profound fear. It is frequently based on a certain amount of experience of negroes or Catholics. It is not self-engendered out of the ambient void. There are Europeans who detest (I blush to record) all Belgians as such, not a few to whom the concept, Czech, is anathema. Here, again, some sort of direct experience, however unfortunate, however unjustly interpreted, will be found to have some connection with the origin of the detestation. No American and no European burdened with such a hostility as I have described will not confess: " Oh, yes: but there are exceptions to my rule, generously, abundantly. If all Czechs were as agreeable as my friend the lawyer Polaczek, and all negroes as amiable and humble as the liftboy at the Hotel Astoria in Minneapolis—oh, yes; oh, yes, I should sing a different song! "

And your Nazis, too, I say. You loathe the
Jews for certain reasons you have. For example:
They killed Christ, they gave birth to Christ.
They are the granite bulwarks of Capitalism, they
are the acid dissolvents of Capitalism. They are
repulsive to look at, they seduce to their perdition
the Nordic youth and maiden.

That is where your Antisemitism differs from the
Antisemitism of Hertha Grossman. Her hatred is
not related with any unhappy experience of Jews.
She has for most of her life grown lettuces and
tended a succession of sick donkeys by the edge of
a lake in the Bavarian Highlands. She does not
maintain as one of your own more bucolic followers might, that swarthy Jews, under cover of
the darkness, have stolen her lettuces; nor that
the agents of the elders of Zion have poisoned her
donkeys. Nor are there any such exceptions to her
rule as the Belgian-hater warmly claims to his.
Que dis-je? Does not even the Nazi make exceptions ? Am I not correctly informed that a few
Jews have been deemed in their souls so essentially
blonde that they have been accepted into your
communion ? But no Jew, by the very conditions
of his essential being, can be an exception to
Hertha Grossman's rule. She admits that it is
merely a limitation in her knowledge of natural
history which prevents her from expounding

accurately what beneficent functions such beasts
as rats, mosquitoes and vipers perform to compensate for their evil offices. But though she agrees
demurely that certain specific Jews have performed
noble deeds as palpable as rats' and vipers'
wicked deeds, no amount of finite good performance can compensate for that infinity of evil
which is a direct paraphrase of the term, Jew.

You perceive, I am sure, that she must not be
confused with that type of Antisemite who hates
Jews for crucifying Christ, and believes that every
Jewish seamstress or revue-artiste is just as responsible for the crucifixion as her ancestors,
direct or collateral, on Golgotha. No such Antisemite would be so naughty a Christian as to
believe that that stain would not be cleansed in
the waters of true baptism. But for Hertha Grossman not all the multitudinous seas incarnadine
will expunge the evil from the Jew. There is only
one way to expunge that evil. The Jew must be
expunged. Not the Jew who staggered in across
the Eastern frontiers since the year 1914, bleeding
and dazed beneath the blows of bandit rabbles
and banded armies. The Jew, the whole Jew, all
Jews, must be expunged.

You observe that Hertha is no good Protestant,
nor even a good Christian. She was born a Roman
Catholic; but I have heard her declare that the

Prayer for the Jews (which you will find sand-
wiched in the Missal between the Prayer for the
Heretics and the Prayer for the Pagans) takes its
place among the most venomous and the most
comical documents in history. Her eyes twinkled
delightfully as she made the declaration, her
chubby cheeks were pitted with dimples. The
prayer reads: " Oh, Almighty and everlasting
God, who repellest not from Thy mercy even the
perfidious Jews, hear the prayer which we offer
for the blindness of that people . . ."
That " even," she chuckled, was peculiarly
rich in its logical implications. So was the co-
existence of the two qualities, perfidy and blindness. But she wouldn't have the prayer removed
from the Missal for anything, though Roman
dogma is not her province. For her own part, she
likes to play, in what you and many of your
followers imagine is the Arian manner, with the
beards of Thor and Wodin. She forgets, for instance, that the Arians of India have no knowledge of these divinities. In all this, of course, she
is a good Nazi, and one of the most competent of
your lieutenants. She has at her command, therefore, all the amiable technical language of modern
German Antisemitics. But, in fact, her religion, as
it is older than Christ, is older than Wodin. It
belongs to the dark, original God, whom no arctic

or tropic continent confines, who co-existed with the white original God in both Hell and Heaven. She is the high priestess of the unspeakable Manichaean heresy.

Her religion, being based on a foundation older than these upstart creeds of Wodin and Christ, can afford her some charities. She can avow quite playfully that the few concrete Jews she has met are (without exception, she was kind enough to insist) genial people—genial, that is to say, in their superimposed and unessential qualities; which qualities she would describe as protective Nordic coloration. The ludicrous idea occurred to one of these genial Jews of her acquaintance, myself namely, to attempt argument with her. I retired as Canute retired, but like Canute, I had a feeling that my retirement was foredoomed.

I might describe the situation with a humbler metaphor: that as a sufferer from gout will feel the pangs from his foot in this toe so intensely, and in that toe so intensely, after his leg has been amputated from the knee (for the pangs are the condition of his whole organism, and not merely of this toe and that toe) so, despite any sort of spiritual surgery, Hertha Grossman would writhe with the pangs of her Antisemitism. There is only one distinction between the sufferer from gout and the gentle Hertha. Should sufficient surgery be performed on the first, namely, should his thigh be removed from the groin, and shortly after his head from his neck, there is no doubt that then, finally, he would no longer experience the pain of gout in this toe and that toe. Whatever else constitutes the organism called Hertha Grossman, physically and spiritually, might with the exercise upon her body and soul of progressive violence be at length disintegrated. But after the end of her, even as before her beginning, a Thing would detach itself from her ruin, even as it then attached itself to her integral atom. On wings, at first unsteady in that first moment of this new liberation, and shortly on wings assured and magnificent, the Thing would make its way into the recesses of the firmament until such time as its dark, original God directed it once more to inhabit priest or peasant, gaolbird or emperor.

But why this new incarnation again and once again, patient Herr Hitler ? Because, do you not agree, there must be an opposite quintessence, an antipodean absolute, a Thing called Semite ? And over your boyhood, as over mine, did a bristling monster, formless, huge, impend, whose name was Semite as mine was Antisemite ? And did you consecrate yourself to an exorcism as early as I, poor fool, did ? You were not in those days so scientifically-minded as you are now. Now you undertake to sterilise Semite's women when you shall rule the destinies of Heine's country. But I do not think an absolute can so crudely as by emasculation or sterilisation be eradicated. Antisemite will elude me and Semite you till time ceases.

A LETTER TO
MRS. VIRGINIA WOOLF

PETER QUENNELL

DEAR MRS. WOOLF,

Thank you for your letter. I hope that the actual recipient of your advice—after all, it was not addressed to me, and I can only answer by a stretch of imagination—enjoyed getting and reading it as much as I did, that the anxious note which has found its way into your style aroused his conscience to the same guilty throb. . . .

You like his verses even less than you admit. Incidentally, if the work of this young poet bears any resemblance to certain extracts which you quote—I found myself wondering if you'd made them up: they seemed to me so brilliant as sheer parody oughtn't you to change the tenor of your counsels? Wouldn't it be kinder to "give it him straight" and advise him to become a critic on a weekly review?

Let's assume, though, that your dilemma is fundamental. You don't and you can't enjoy his work, yet in spite of everything you believe in the poet's talent. His poems strike your ear as tuneless and dull, yet you prefer to think of him not as simply a bad writer but as a victim of contemporary circumstance. How good he *might* be, if he made the effort, if he could throw himself back in spirit to a happier time!

But can he ? That is the question I am moved to ask. You complain that your friend is out of touch with life and refer him to the great achievements of another epoch which illustrate a more spacious conception of poetry, a bolder and less self-conscious mode of feeling. Poor poet, I have no doubt he will do his best! But it is possible that notwithstanding his sternest endeavour he will recoil with added vehemence on his wretched self. He *is*—he exclaims miserably—a child of his age; you can't drink sack or canary from a modern cocktail glass.

He would like to; but history intervenes. If I may say so, I feel that your advice neglects this sad but necessary perspective. Every poet, as you point out in a different context, is an extremely ancient and delicately balanced organism who has for background the whole mass of poetic literature. He re-incarnates in his single person the huge body of it—tendencies, restrictions, acquired liberties. He cannot choose the pedestal from which he writes. He is hoisted up there, chained by the leg like a cockatoo.

And his pedestal grows narrower day by day
—this, at least, is the view I have to state and
which will provide the basis of any hypothesis I
may evolve—narrower, more elevated, less
comfortable. The poet has been deprived of his
mappin terrace. Steadily, during a long course
of years, it has been split up and given away to
the other arts. You, yourself, as a distinguished
modern novelist, one who excels in the semi-
poetic method, have received a large slice of
his ancient domain.

Time was when he roamed the entire zoo.
There was nothing then that could not be said
in verse. From science to theology all was poetic,
since the most convenient vehicle of information was still the traditional rhythmic form.
Glance at Lucretius and afterwards turn to
Dr. Bridges:

.... Far rather our moods,
  influences and spiritual affections are like
  those many organic substances which, tho' to
    sense
  wholly dissimilar and incomparable in kind,
  are yet all combinations of the same simples,
  and even in like proportions differently dis-
    posed;

so that whether it be starch, oil, sugar or
alcohol
'tis ever our old customers, carbon and
hydrogen,
pirouetting with oxygen in their morris
antics;
the chemist booketh all of them as CHO,
and his art is as mine when I but figurate
the twin persistent semitones of my Grand
Chant.

—I'm sure you'll agree that, putting aside
questions of magnitude—and the late Laureate,
one must allow, was a clever versifier—some
extraordinary change has occurred during the
interval. No modern poet, however gifted in
his degree, can afford to make science the food
of art.

The same exclusion has been practised in
every sphere. . . . But lest this preamble
should begin to affect you as tedious, I propose
that we take a chronological stride; let us
hurry forward to the Elizabethan heyday when
our island, we are told, was a nest of singing
birds.

Even so, there were many cuckoos in the

nest. Curiously enough, our greatest dramatic poet had a large hand in the disruption of the poetic play. Shakespeare's incomparable prose passages, his habit of breaking up blank verse into periods that almost anticipate *vers libre*, revolutionised its originally close structure; while a corresponding emotional change slowly developed.—It is a long way from the lofty melodrama of *Faustus* and *Tamburlaine* to the domestic realism of Heywood's *Woman Killed by Kindness*. . . .

But then Dryden and Otway ?—I hear you protest. Much as I admire both those poets, I can't help thinking that they fought a losing battle and that their weapons, though splendidly tempered, were growing blunt. They were survivors, courageous antediluvians—for the once magnificent supremacy of the poetic drama had been sapped by the appeal of opera and comedy; music and dancing eked out the heroic play, and the comedy of manners came into its own.

Soon Defoe was to emerge as the prophet of naturalism. I seem to remember that, in your volume of collected essays, you have eloquently done justice to his claims—homage which was

first rendered by the Goncourts who record
somewhere or other among their jottings that
they look on him as the patriarch of their tribe.

Could naturalism and the poetic drama co-
exist ? The last gurgling agonies of its demise,
painfully protracted through the eighteenth
century, answer that the two won't go together:

O Sophonisba, Sophonisba O!

—and with these sounds the genius of the stage
succumbs to the bow-string of the modern
novelist. In future there might be lyric or
didactic poetry; but a Queen of Egypt would
never again speak from the boards.

Blank verse—all too much of it—was still
written. I wonder if you have ever read *The
Borderers*—or *Osorio*—or *Otho the Great*—or *Mary
Stuart* ? Good things, it goes without saying,
are embedded in them—but at what a depth
and how hard they are to find, buried under a
mass of remorseless rhythm, of pounding dogged
" poetry " in the worst sense!

Their creation, however, had one excuse.
In the days when every poet who deserved the
name—as well as a large number, inevitably,
who did not—felt obliged to launch out into

poetic drama, the reading public had an appetite for poetry which has long ago declined and disappeared. People *read* poetry in those days —young ladies read Byron with dangling curls and young gentlemen with wild eyes and looscned neck-cloths; earnest Victorian circles perused Browning—but to *taste* a poem for the modern reader is quite sufficient. Delights, which were then purveyed by poetry, can be procured at less expense from the contemporary novel. . . .

I do not intend to suggest that the decay of poetry—and I am not sure that we need regard it as a decay—is connected with the mechanical turn of modern life or with the hurry and bustle said to characterise our civilisation, though these are features that must be taken into account. I see the process from an entirely different angle—poetry as the matrix of literary forms, a nebula which goes whirling through the void and detaches new planets in its course, growing smaller with each system that it begets —smaller but, I like to imagine, more intense.

Fiction and drama are both descended from the epic—that is to say, they have their origin in poetry. And, as the novel during the last hundred years has gradually extended and altered its scope, it has continued in its sure but unwieldy fashion to borrow fresh interest from poetic modes, till with Proust it has stretched to include the prose-poem and become digressive and allusive as never before.

Let me tick off some of the elements verse has lost—the dramatic; that went early in the day —the didactic, the narrative and the descriptive; for I doubt whether you would advise your young friend to attempt a narrative poem in fifteen cantos, describing the events of the General Strike, or a modern *Prelude*, or a new *Ring and the Book*, narrating the Bywaters and Thompson tragedy.

He couldn't if he would: the form is dead. And, since he is young and has no desire to waste his time, he will agree with you that the poetic exercises of the nineteenth century have nowadays exhausted their justification—that to indulge in them is to beat the empty air, to beat it rhythmically, perhaps, but to beat in vain.

He can't muse aloud with Matthew Arnold. He may add that the great masters of Victorian poetry had precisely this failing which he hopes to avoid—a tendency to muse aloud in verse,

to chew the cud with an air of august decorum.
. . . August cogitation is not for him. Then
what *does* he want ?—I imagine you asking,
rather sharply; you are becoming a little
irritated. If it is true that the goddess of poetry
has grown so poor, if she can no longer tell us
tales or read us sermons, show us kings and
heroes on the stage, meditate superbly on the
meaning of life, set her words to the tune of
common speech, hadn't she better retire and
count her rosary, or dwindle out her decrepi-
tude in a cheap hotel ?

Is there anything left for her to do ? Surely
there is; for the elements which I have cata-
logued were but secondarily part of the poet's
rôle. The most difficult function he can still
accomplish. Admitting that poetry once and
for all has abdicated from the pulpit and the
stage, the story-teller's stool and the philosopher's dais, he can still exploit the irreducible
minimum which is poetry—pure poetry—and
nothing besides.

There are certain emotions which only poetry
can meet. . . . We have all of us had the experience when reading verse, some arid and
over-ingenious composition, of stumbling across

a passage or single line that leaps up like a jet
of translucent water, like a fountain in the
wilderness of a public square, otherwise harsh
asphalt and begoniaed beds:

> The modest halcyon comes in sight,
> Flying betwixt the day and night;
> And such a horror calm and dumb
> Admiring Nature does benumb;
> The viscous air, whereso'er she fly,
> Follows and sucks her azure dye;
> The jellying stream compacts below,
> If it might fix her shadow so;
> The stupid fishes hang, as plain
> As flies in crystal overta'en.
> And men the silent scene assist,
> Charmed with the sapphire-wingèd mist.

This is poetry one cries with instant pleasure;
this is what poetry should be, felt in the brain
and along the nerves; the mysterious stillness
of the river-bank beneath the after-glow; the
pure flash of the silently flying kingfisher which
relieves and yet accentuates the tension. The
rest is mere poetising, expense of language,
rhetorical avoidance of the real issue—to write

with this crystalline sense of words, to elicit a clear fountain from the intractable rock.

A sense of words—is not that the first requirement ? As poets find less and less to *say*—for instruction and edification we look elsewhere—let's hope that they will say it with greater delicacy, that they will realise that their vocabulary, and the use they make of it, is more important than all the rest of their poetic baggage.

A sense of words ranks first in the poet's panoply. What you find so distressing in your friend's work is, I hazard, the dogged effort which he makes—often it produces dullness and obscurity—to freshen up his use of the English language by the introduction of strange terms and novel rhythms. *Il faut être absolument moderne.* . . . I expect that he read Rimbaud at the University and I dare say that, like Rimbaud in his time, he wishes to give new colours to the old vowels.

He is dull; he would rather be that than meretricious—tuneless; it is a new music he hopes to sound—obscure and harsh; he prefers to call it experimental; for language, the medium through which he operates, is nowa-

days in the midst of a severe crisis—a crisis
probably more disturbing than has occurred
since the Elizabethan Age.

Somehow the continuity has been broken.
One has only to glance at an anthology of
modern verse, which includes specimens of
verse written before the War as well as produc-
tions of the post-war period, to see the bankruptcy of traditional poetic forms. Even the
Poet, as a legendary figure, is now extinct.
Those splendid wonderfully exuberant young
men, airily sustained by the consciousness of
their own charm, on whose shoulders reposed
the mantle of Shelley and Keats—I needn't
particularise; you know their names—are dead
or have taken to cultivating their cabbage-
patches. Your friend is a young man of a
different type; I do not envisage him dabbling
in the dew or tossing back a Hyacinthine
chevelure, preparatory to his early morning
bathe. He is less picturesque and far more
ponderous. The attitude has mysteriously
" let him down."

He reads *The Criterion* once a quarter; and no
man who makes it a duty to read that journal
but bears its mark inscribed across his brow. I

do not imply that he is necessarily an Anglo-Catholic; for all I can tell he may be a Communist or a young Hitlerite. But I feel certain that the prodigious melodrama of modern Europe casts its shadows in some form on to his mind.

Be indulgent if he seems to you somewhat solemn! Remember that of the placid pre-war universe—how tranquil and how olympian it must have been! Was the pound really worth twenty shillings, and were there parties every night and hansom cabs? Did noblemen not write for the Sunday Press?—he can recall barely five or six summers; then the War to End Wars and so good-bye. . . .

Strange things happened in his adolescence. Life grows " curiouser and curiouser," as Alice said; and, when you tell your poet to stand at his window and " let your rhythmical sense open and shut, open and shut," he may retort that, if he opens it too wide, such a torrent of extraordinary sights and noises will come flooding in and clamouring for recognition that he will fall back with his head between his hands and give up all hope of work for the day.

A poet's brain must be exclusive as well as

inclusive, selective as well as avidly receptive.
. . . And, now I think of it, when you spoke of
standing at windows, I found myself for the
first time as I read your letter in almost violent
opposition to your point of view. Hasn't it
perhaps much the same ring as a piece of advice
we have many of us received, ungratefully,
grudgingly, from older critics—to wit, that we
are to look into our hearts and write ?

Which begs the question as to whether the
contents are worth writing about. "The
heart " includes an enormous deal of rubbish;
and it is only when the mass has been carefully
sifted—a business demanding patience, time
and skill—that our discoveries there acquire
any real value. Similarly, " the street "—it
contains everything and nothing. One could
post oneself at all the windows in the world and
be none the wiser or less self-conscious for the
attempt, since what is important is not the
street that the dustman knows, that your
friend's charwoman crosses on her way to
work, so much as *his* street—or yours or mine—
" reality " as far as he can come to terms with
it.

Caught in the lens of his sensibility, the

street may wear a portentous and novel meaning. But a sensibility has first to be arrived at;
and this is by no means easy in the present day.
The hurry and vibration of constant change
leave little time for such delicate manœuvres.

Shall we search the past for its lost secrets?
T. S. Eliot is considerably older than your
friend; but it is to Eliot, if he has an enthusiastic
temperament, that he probably looks up with
the greatest regard. Have you noticed how the
author of *The Waste Land* makes use of quotation and allusion and reference very much as
the *contadini* of an Italian picture employ the
massy fragments of the antique world, building
a cottage from the debris of a Roman shrine.—
" These fragments I have shored against my
ruins." . . . You remember it comes at the end
of *What The Thunder Said*. Well, your friend,
too, in his more hesitating way, is feverishly at
work among the debris, borrowing a phrase
here and a phrase there, imitating, adapting,
sometimes parodying, always doing what he
can from an old literature to quarry the rough
materials of a new style.

The result, naturally, is very often far from
pleasant. I don't defend your protégé's work

on the grounds of charm; I admit that it is difficult and crabbed, archaistic and modernistic in the same breath. But I feel strongly that these shortcomings are not his, so much as the general property of his period which itself lacks spontaneous charm and an easy style, the grand manner and indeed manners in any shape,— so plainly is it a period of transition, though tending towards what heaven knows. . .

He is the creature of his social and political setting. Whether your friend is directly concerned with politics or more sagaciously, perhaps, passes them by—he is an artist and politicians are politicians—he cannot escape the backwash which they raise and cannot be expected in an atmosphere of turmoil to preserve the equanimity of an Augustan poet.

Nor could he do so and remain faithful to himself. " Difficulty " is one of the by-products of modern literature; and, as experience becomes more and more complex—and more complex it plainly *must* become, failing some cataclysmic simplification—literature cannot choose but follow suit, growing always more allusive and indirect.

And then verse is the most sensitive of literary

forms; it is also—to return to my original
starting-point—a kind of Lear which has
given away its heritage and is now—I won't
say in charge of an idiot wandering in its frenzy
through the blizzard—but considerably impoverished as a means of expression, stripped
of the outward signs of power.

Impoverished but necessarily enfeebled. . . .
A modern poet may put the blame on his surroundings—and to some extent, as I have
attempted to show, he is probably justified—
yet, within himself, the acute pangs of a guilty
conscience keep up their intolerable nagging
rhythm: " Granted that your case is doubly
hard—you are involved in the general fate of
literature, and bewildered by the catastrophe
of your whole age—you can't shirk the major
obligation." " What is it ? " " To write
poetry." " And what is poetry ? " . . . But,
as you have observed the angelic voices which
haunt one's pillow prefer to give advice and
leave it at that. " Write poetry! " they command the nascent poet; then vanish ere he
has time for repartee.

So he sits down and thinks out his expostu-
lation. What *is* poetry ? he repeats a second

time. We recognise the effect but seldom the cause. It is the product—so much is obvious—of devoted labour. Yet no amount of labour and good-will can avail to produce poetry in the wrong conditions. It is as difficult as lighting a bonfire with a burning-glass. . . . I have already introduced a number of images, have allowed them to inter-breed with disreputable lavishness, picked them up and dropped them as I went on. A last image and I can promise it shall have no sequel.—I imagine the predicament of the modern poet as being that of a forlorn traveller in an autumn wood, desperately anxious to kindle a fire from the twigs he has gathered, but without any means of striking a flame.

The twigs are damp. Some are rotten and slightly mildewed; some are still green and full of sap. He has very little properly seasoned material; but he stacks his fire and, finding a morsel of broken glass, tries to focus the watery brightness of the sun—not a very genial or sanguine ray—in a pale intense spot on a dead leaf. Theoretically, he knows it can be managed. The poet knows that if he can focus his own emotion long and steadily enough on the material of life, narrowing the beam down to a radiant pinprick, he will be able—he *should* be able—to produce poetry, like the faint flame hissing and trembling among the twigs.

The burning-glass is his faculty of expression . . . On the other hand, whereas the firemakers of an earlier day came, if not provided with a pocket burning-glass, at least comfortably equipped with the means of making one—a language far fresher and stronger than ours—he must utilise the chipped fragments they left behind, when he has scratched, rubbed and burnished them to suit his purpose.

Naturally, he is slow-fingered and unimpressive. . . . Most verse written in the twentieth century, whether the poet is prepared to admit it or not, represents a frenzied effort to gain time, mere " business " till the fire begins to kindle. The burning-glass may not prevail against damp twigs; but meanwhile, cocked knowingly to one side, it can be made to flash the sun in the audience's face. Look, I've started a blaze, he calls exultantly. We rub our eyelids, but the pyre is still unlit.

Your friend, let us hope, is the destined Prometheus. . . . I wish I thought there was

anything one could do that would help him
forward on the road of self-discovery, any sacrifice collective or separate one could make, such
as re-writing his verses with a red pencil or seeing to it that they were kindly noticed in the
weekly papers!

But there is nothing; it will be all the same
to him. Patience—I am sure patience is a
requisite. Five or ten years may lumber by;
and even so, when his masterpiece takes shape
as the result of long struggles with his obscure
problem, mayn't we expect that its advent will
slightly shock us, that on a first reading we shall
be petulant rather than glad ? The beautiful!
Give us " beauty," we shall groan. It will be a
long while before this spare dynamic elegance
—more " cerebral," perhaps, than the verse we
know, harmonised in a different and subtler
way—impresses us as the prolongation of a
great line, before we recognise between your
poet and his predecessors the continuity of
which to-day we have lost sight. . . .

Till then—

yours ever,

PETER QUENNELL.

THE CONTRIBUTORS TO
THE HOGARTH LETTERS

E. M. FORSTER (1879–1970) Novelist, short story writer, biographer, essayist, librettist, travel writer, and Fellow of King's College, Cambridge. His novels, *Where Angels Fear to Tread* (1905), *A Room with a View* (1908), *Howards End* (1910), *A Passage to India* (1913) and *Maurice* (1913–14, published 1971), were all completed before he wrote his *Hogarth Letter*.

LORD ROBERT CECIL (1864–1958) Educated at Eton and Oxford, MP for East Marylebone 1906–1910, Parliamentary Under-secretary for Foreign Affairs 1915–16, Minister of Blockade 1916–1918, Lord Privy Seal 1923–24, President of the League of Nations Union 1923–45, Chancellor of the Duchy of Lancaster 1924–27, Nobel Peace Prize 1937. Publications included *The Way of Peace* (1928) and many speeches and pamphlets about disarmament and the League.

ROSAMOND LEHMANN (b. 1901) Novelist and short story writer. Sister of Beatrix, the actress, and John, poet and editor. Her first novel, *Dusty Answer*, was written in her early twenties; others include *A Note in Music* (1930), *Invitation to the Waltz* (1932), *The Weather in the Streets* (1936), *The Ballad and the Source* (1944) and *The Echoing Grove* (1953).

RAYMOND MORTIMER (1895–1980) Critic, literary journalist, Francophile, and friend of Bloomsbury and Nicolson circles. Literary editor of the *New Statesman* in the 1930s, broadcaster to France for the Ministry of Information in World War II, regular reviewer for the *Sunday Times* until his death. *Try Anything Once* (1976) is a collection of essays with an autobiographical introduction.

FRANCIS BIRRELL (1889–1935) Critic and belle-lettrist, elder son of Augustine Birrell, the Liberal statesman and essayist. In 1919 he set up a bookshop with David Garnett. He regularly contributed to the *Nation and Athenaeum*. Publications included translations of Diderot and Plato, a book on Gladstone (1933), a biography, *La Duchesse du Maine* (1929), and an anthology of last words, *The Art of Dying* (1930). In 1932, the year in which his *Hogarth Letter* appeared, he had an operation for a brain tumour, and was very ill in the last years of his life.

LEONARD ALFRED GEORGE STRONG (1896–1958) Poet, novelist, biographer and detective story writer. Grew up near Dublin and in Devon; schoolmaster in the 1920s. Publications included books on Tom Moore (1937), John Synge (1941) and Joyce (1949) as well as volumes of verse and *Commonsense about Poetry* (1931). One of his collections of short stories, *The Travellers* (1945) won the James Tait Black Memorial Prize.

REBECCA WEST (1892–1983) Pseudonym of Cecily Isabel Fairfield, journalist and political writer, feminist, critic, novelist, biographer, historian and travel writer. Her novels include *The Return of the Soldier* (1918), *The Thinking Reed* (1936), *The Fountain Overflows* (1956) and *The Birds Fall Down* (1966). Other major works include a biography of St Augustine (1933), a book on the trial of William Joyce (Lord Haw-Haw) entitled *The Meaning of Treason* (1949) and a two-volume history of Yugoslavia, *Black Lamb and Grey Falcon* (1937).

VIRGINIA WOOLF (1882–1941) Novelist, essayist and, with Leonard Woolf, founder of the Hogarth Press in 1917. While her *Hogarth Letter* was being written, *The Waves* (1931) came out and she began work on what would be *The Years* (1937) and *Three Guineas* (1938). Her last novel, *Between the Acts*, was published posthumously.

HUGH WALPOLE (1884–1941) Novelist. Born in New Zealand, son of a clergyman who became Bishop of Edinburgh, educated at King's School, Canterbury, and Cambridge, knighted in 1937. Books include *Mr Perrin and Mr Traill* (1911), *Jeremy* (1919), *Jeremy and Hamlet* (1923) and *Jeremy at Crale* (1927), *The Herries Chronicle* (1930–1933) and books on Conrad (1916) and Trollope (1928).

JOHN CHARLTON HARDWICK (1885–1953) Vicar and writer. Schoolmaster from 1908–1911, Chaplain of Ripon Hall, Oxford (1921–23) and then Vicar of Partington, Cheshire. He wrote extensively on the condition of the church in the modern world – *Religion and Science* (1925), *Institutional Religion* (1930), *Freedom and Authority in Religion* (1932), etc. – and also books on the Oxford Movement, *The Light That Failed* (1933), and on Samuel Wilberforce, *Lawn Sleeves* (1933).

LOUIS GOLDING (1895–1958) Novelist, reviewer and travel writer. Born in Manchester in the Jewish immigrant quarter (which is called

"Doomington" in his novels, *Magnolia Street, Mr Emanuel* and others). Educated at Manchester Grammar School and Oxford. Writings on anti-semitism included *The Jewish Problem* (1938) and *Hitler through the Ages* (1939). He wrote two autobiographical books, *Adventures in Living Dangerously* (1930) and *The World I Knew* (1940).

PETER QUENNELL (b. 1905) Son of Marjorie and Charles Quennell, authors of the educational series *Everyday Life In...* Poet, biographer, freelance critic. Taught English at Tokyo University in 1930. Edited the *Cornhill Magazine*, 1944–51. First volume of poems published 1920; later books include several works on Byron, *Baudelaire and the Symbolists* (1929), *Profane Virtues: Four Studies of the 18th Century* (1945), *John Ruskin: Portrait of a Prophet* (1949) and a collection of essays, *The Singular Preference* (1952).